Charles Wicks
July 1994

The New Israelis

ALSO BY YOSSI MELMAN

Every Spy a Prince: The Complete History of Israel's Intelligence Community (with Dan Raviv), 1990
Behind The Uprising: Israelis, Jordanians and Palestinians (with Dan Raviv), 1989
The Master Terrorist: The True Story Behind Abu Nidal, 1987
A Profile of a Terrorist Organization, 1984 (in Hebrew)
The CIA Report on the Israeli Intelligence Community, 1982 (in Hebrew)

1 800
322-0344

THE NEW ISRAELIS

An Intimate View of a Changing People

Yossi Melman

Birch Lane Press
Published by Carol Publishing Company

A Birch Lane Press Book
Published by Carol Publishing Group
Birch Lane Press is a registered trademark of Carol Communications, Inc.
Editorial Offices: 600 Madison Avenue, New York, N.Y. 10022
Sales and Distribution Offices: 120 Enterprise Avenue, Secaucus, N.J. 07094
In Canada: Canadian Manda Group, P.O. Box 920, Station U, Toronto,
    Canada M8Z 5P9
Queries regarding rights and permissions should be addressed to Carol Publishing Group,
600 Madison Avenue, New York, N.Y. 10022

Carol Publishing Group books are available at special discounts for bulk purchases, for
sales promotions, fund raising, or educational purposes. Special editions can be created to
specifications. For details, contact Special Sales Department, Carol Publishing Group, 120
Enterprise Avenue, Secaucus, N.J. 07094

Manufactured in the United States of America
10 9 8 7 6 5 4 3 2 1

Library of Congress Cataloging-in-Publication Data

Melman, Yossi
    The new Israelis : an intimate view of a changing people / by
Yossi Melman.
        p.   cm.
    "A Birch Lane Press book."
    ISBN 1–55972–129–4
    1. National characteristics, Israeli.   2. Israel—Civilization.
3. Israel—Politics and government.   4. Zionism.   5. Political
culture—Israel.   6. Religion and state—Israel.   I. Title.
DS102.95.M45   1992
956.95—dc20   92–23713
                                                        CIP

To My Parents

ANA AND YITZHAK MELMAN

Contents

AUTHOR'S NOTE   XI

PROLOGUE   The War Zone: Breaking Old Convictions   1

ONE   Loving Immigration and Hating Immigrants   13

TWO   Zionism: Dream and Reality   23

THREE   Nation Building   35

FOUR   Between War and Peace   53

FIVE   Changing the Guard   75

SIX   The Hidden Sephardi Revolution   97

SEVEN   In God We Trust   107

EIGHT   The Culture of Defense   131

NINE   The Rise of Political Extremism   149

TEN   "Our Arabs"   163

ELEVEN   The Arabs Over There   179

TWELVE   Death of a Dream   197

THIRTEEN   The Subaru Syndrome   207

Epilogue   223

Source Notes   235

Index   241

Author's Note

WHEN composing his *English Journey* in 1934, J. B. Priestley made great use of the bus. In accumulating my impressions and refining my perceptions of today's Israel, I used a different technique: I looked from my window, walked the streets, and sat in cafes. I studied in libraries and archives. While driving my four-wheel Suzuki throughout the land, I tried to meet as many Israelis as I could, from all possible walks of life: politicians, generals, artists, workers, and business people.

It was not my intention to write a comprehensive history or a travelogue, certainly not an "objective" study. What we have here is my Israel: a personal account of my thoughts and perceptions of Israeli society, supplemented by autobiographical detail. Inevitably, however, I realized I could not rely solely on my impressions and ignore the past. The Israelis are the sum total of their past, history, tradition, and heritage. Nevertheless, even what has come to be accepted as simple, value-free fact cannot escape reinterpretation and reevaluation.

I thank Mirjam Hadar, a writer herself, a scrupulous editor, and friend. I am also indebted to Gail Kinn, my editor at Birch Lane Press, for her useful suggestions and faith in the book.

The book is dedicated to my parents, Ana and Yitzhak Melman, for making, thirty-five years ago, the not so easy decision to emigrate to Israel.

Last but first comes Billie Melman, my fellow voyager, whose love, patience, and intellectual zest have inspired me through many years of our life together. Both of us are lucky to have each other and, above all, Yotam.

Ramat-Aviv
July 1992

The New Israelis

The War Zone: Breaking Old Convictions

O N June 23, 1992, three million Israeli voters turned their backs on the right-wing Likud, under whose rule they had been for fifteen years. By electing Labor's Yitzhak Rabin as their new prime minister, they expressed their desire for change, above all to achieve peace, tranquility, and stability. However, the seeds for these new hopes were sown out of despair, which came to a head during the Gulf War, eighteen months earlier.

On January 18, 1991, at exactly 2:01 A.M. a round of eight Soviet-made Scud missiles hit Tel Aviv and Haifa, the two largest cities in Israel. That night, a nation which has increasingly over the last two decades been torn by controversy, tension, division, and contradiction was plunged into the most urgent identity crisis of its brief and complicated history. The Scuds cast a blinding new light on the

Israeli psyche. Since its independence in 1948, there had never been a direct attack into the heart of Israel.

At the time, I was in my study on the ninth floor of a suburban Tel Aviv apartment building, preparing myself for an interview with a Chicago radio station. The interviewer wanted to know about the mood in Israel on the first day of the war against Iraq. I intended to answer that it seemed the war would pass Israel by without great effect. All day radio and television reports had been bringing news of allied air raids against Iraqi strategic targets. The Israelis were carried away by the news and were euphoric. I, too, began to think that Iraq would not substantiate its threat to launch chemical and conventional warheads against Israeli population centers if war broke out.

But just after 2:00 A.M. on Friday, we were awakened by sirens. My wife and I rushed to our seven-year-old son to carry him to the sealed room we had prepared earlier. In accordance with civil defense instructions, windows and door frames had been sealed with tape and plastic sheets to keep out poison gas. When I closed the door and put a wet towel under it, my son started crying. We all put on our black rubber gas masks, which, as instructed, we had kept within reach, stored, up until then, in their original ugly brown boxes.

Two or three minutes after we got to our sealed room, I heard two loud explosions and knew they had hit rather close. The walls shook and some of the windows cracked. During military service twenty years earlier, I had experienced gunfire, artillery exchange, and even air raids, but, until then, I had never experienced a missile attack. it was frightening, but even more than fear and anxiety, it filled us with a profound sense of helplessness. All we could do was sit and listen to the wail of sirens and to confused radio reports, wondering what was happening elsewhere in the country. I knew that in our sealed room with our gas masks on we would be pretty safe from chemical attack. But I also knew that a conventional attack could turn the apartment into a crumbling death trap.

More than an hour passed before the military reported that there had not been a gas attack. I spent the time reflecting on our bizarre situation. In several of my own articles I had warned that Iraq, led by

President Saddam Hussein, would not hesitate to use the chemical and conventional missile arsenals it had been steadily building up with the aid of Western countries. Yet I never believed that one night we would find ourselves similarly threatened in this way, just as the Kurds had been silenced in 1988.

The immediate impact of the Iraqi missiles was relatively minor. During the six weeks of the war Iraq launched forty-one missiles against Israel. Thirteen people died, most of them of heart attacks or suffocation or anxiety, but only one person as a result of a direct hit. There were a thousand injuries, of which only seventy required hospitalization. Eleven thousand homes were damaged, fortunately most of them with no more than broken windows. Yet these attacks created powerful shock waves that penetrated deep into the fragile fabric of Israeli society.

Before the war, there had been indications of a process of transformation within Israel, but they were almost imperceptible. Many of our customs, values, political beliefs, historical perspectives, and ways of thinking were on the verge of change. But the events of the war speeded up the process and crystallized the agents of change. Pillars of our old world either completely collapsed or were at least severely shaken.

As a writer, I had been reflecting on these trends and phenomena. To me, they signaled the emergence of what I would call the new Israeli. However, defining such a broad and complex notion was not easy. Living through the Gulf War and observing its impact provided me with a frame of reference that focused my earlier reflections.

The psychological hold of the Gulf War on the Israeli psyche is not unlike the loss of innocence and disillusionment of the American people in relation to their experience with the assassination of President John F. Kennedy. A whole fragile world seems to have been taken away that day. So, too, have Israelis—in a state of shock over the events—come to ask each other the fateful question: What were you doing when you first heard the sirens go off?

With the ground pulled out from beneath us, I could not help reflecting on the meaning of being a Jew. Like 80 percent of Israelis, I have always considered myself an atheist and have rarely attended synagogue service. But unlike many of those Israelis who were born after World War II, I am aware of the special, often confusing, problems we face concerning the question of our identity: Who, as Israelis, are we? We are born and nurtured in a free, democratic, and westernized society—but many of our institutions are intensely bureaucratic and reach into private life, not unlike many communist regimes. The state of Israel defines itself as a Jewish state, but what does this mean? Are we Israelis or are we Jews? Which identity takes precedence? What is our nationality—Israeli or Jewish? Does our Jewishness express itself in national terms, or rather, in religious ones? And what about the terms "the Jewish people" and "the Jewish state?" Do they exclude Arabs who live in Israel? Finally, what is our mainstream culture—European or Middle Eastern?

That terrible night, without knowing the answer to these questions, the threat of poison gas reminded me and all Jewish Israelis of our traumatic experience as a people, of our great vulnerability. It was difficult not to think of the gas chambers. And it was ironic that Germany was responsible for the advanced technology of Iraq's weapons—the chemical and poison gas.

Though there had recently been signs that Israel was beginning to release itself from the psychological stranglehold of the Holocaust—after decades of government exploitation of this tragic piece of history—this direct attack seemed to shatter the Israeli belief in the efficacy of struggling against the forces of history. The Iraqi Scuds brought home one additional truth, which many Israelis had tried to ignore, conceal, or sublimate during forty-three years of independence—that modernization and technological advances notwithstanding, Israel's existence was extremely fragile.

The founding of the Zionist movement had argued that victims of anti-Semitism would be able to lead a normal and safe life only in their own homeland. But the Iraqi attacks, which turned Israel's major towns into "hostages," raised serious questions about the continuing relevance of this Zionist notion. Is Israel really a safe place for Jews? That is, are the people of Tel Aviv more secure than New York's Jewish community?

The fact that Tel Aviv was one of the two Iraqi targets was not a coincidence. Erected on the sand dunes of the Mediterranean shoreline more than eighty years ago, Tel Aviv has become the symbol of Zionist and Israeli power. To the modern Israeli, Tel Aviv is the front-runner, an avant-garde city which sets the example for the behavior and lifestyle of the rest of the country. Tel Aviv today is in all ways a vital Mediterranean city: fast-paced, sharp, trendy, and cultured. Its mayor, the energetic, friendly, and talkative Shlomo Lahat, has described his vibrant city as the "city without a break."

On the first night of missile attacks, Tel Aviv was stopped short. Unofficial estimates say that 44 percent of all the one million citizens of greater Tel Aviv left their homes to escape the Scuds. Tel Avivians were, at once, confronted with the simple fact that, despite their pretensions and sense of belonging to another, safer culture, they were living in the Middle East and subject to its unstable reality.

In Ramat Aviv, the suburb in which I live among well-off middle-class professionals, most of the residents in our building abandoned their apartments after the first missile attacks. Most of them moved away to parts of the country that they believed would be beyond missile range. The normally full parking lot was almost empty. Inside the building, as elsewhere in the suburb, and indeed, everywhere in the city, an eerie silence reigned. Windows were locked and blinds were closed tight. Prosperous neighborhoods were as empty as slums. Jews, preferring to be called Israelis, but nevertheless Jews, were once again on the run. Unlike previous epochs of persecution and escape, this modern exodus took place in their own state.

I decided not to leave—not because I was not afraid. I know one reason I remained was my elderly parents, who live near my home, but I also didn't like the idea of becoming a refugee in my own country.

Mayor Lahat, who as a former general had commanded a tank division, called fleeing Tel Avivians "deserters." His remark sparked a bitter and heated public debate. There were many letters written, and radio and television shows carried a storm of responses. Those who had left accused their remaining fellow citizens of "endangering their children's safety" and of "carelessness"—while those who stayed on argued that those who left were "cowards" and "unpatrio-tic." When asked about his own son's decision to leave, the mayor responded, "Well, then, my son is a deserter too," and added with typical Israeli bravado, "I believe they should stay, even when the danger is great and perhaps mortal."

That such a debate had actually taken place in Israel is in itself extraordinary. Never, in the official history of Israel, has there been an open admission of a retreat from danger. But, in fact, during the war of 1948 several Jewish settlements were abandoned when they were faced with the invading Arab forces. The shame of such actions has always been deliberately wiped out of the national memory. With the Gulf War, the ethos changed; no longer was there coyness about retreat or desertion.

My own reflections upon this reveal the complications of life in such a country as Israel. It is true that individual human survival is of ultimate importance, but how does this survival affect an individual's obligation to society? Despite the apparent friction between these two ideas, there is no real contradiction between them, and both can coexist simultaneously. Israel, for most of its forty-four years, has been deservedly proud of its ability to walk a clean and honorable path, serving the personal needs of its individual citizens along with those of society. However, the particular history of the Jewish people and Israel has made the majority of Israelis aware that they are in a unique existential position as compared with most other nations. We are constantly faced with the tragic facts of our history as Jewish people. As a result, we grow up with a powerful sense of the necessity of standing by a position, of never giving up or retreating. In fact, Israeli military jargon has no word for retreat. Instead it is called "improving positions in the rear."

In a collection of essays called *There Is No Other Place,* published a decade ago, literary critic Gershon Shaked grappled with the questions that originated with the first Zionists: In what way is Israel unique? Can there be an alternative Jewish national existence outside of Israel?

If the founding fathers of the Zionist movement had merely aspired to find territorial safety and physical security for their followers, they would not have needed to seek a national home—certainly not in this part of the world. The wandering Jew would have been safer from danger had he kept his bags with him, ready to continue his journey at a moment's notice. The state of Israel was established to be a sovereign Jewish nation with the ability to defend itself. Zionism was meant to offer a solution to the problems of the Jewish people as a whole and, ironically, not to those of the individual Jew.

Another irony surfaced as Prime Minister Yitzhak Shamir, at the insistence of the United States, led the country to a historic decision: for the first time in its existence Israel would tolerate an attack without responding. Given the extreme, sometimes militant rhetoric of the right-wing cabinet, who would have expected Israel to agree to hold its fire? Many Israelis found this position difficult to understand, yet somehow most of them acclimated.

We also had to get used to the idea that, for the first time during a war, American troops were stationed on Israeli soil. Over the years successive Israeli governments of the left and of the right had maintained that Israel was capable of defending itself without any immediate external assistance. During all its previous military conflicts Israel did enjoy morale boosts, political support, and, of course, military equipment from the United States, but all of this was a long way from any deployment of foreign troops. "We do not want American soldiers to spill their blood in our defense" has been the Israeli line of thinking.

Indeed, all previous wars had been fought by Israelis who strongly believed that they were defending their homes and families. This war brought change. It is difficult to compare the Gulf War to the others in which Israel was at the center of hostilities. Yet the bottom line was that this was quite a real war.

After the first missiles hit, the Israeli public panicked. Many Israelis felt that the government was abandoning them without providing the promised active defense. When this sense of despair reached the government in Jerusalem, Israeli leaders decided to call in American troops. The next morning twenty Galaxy airplanes, the largest American air force transporters, landed at Ben Gurion airport outside Tel Aviv—the same airport where my family and I had arrived as penniless immigrants thirty-five years earlier. Within hours, four American-made Patriot batteries were stationed in the

suburbs of Tel Aviv and Haifa. From the windows of our apartment
we watched the hectic activity at one of these sites and, in the night,
heard the sharp whistle of missiles breaking the supersonic barrier as
they attempted to intercept the incoming Scuds.

Post–Gulf War studies in Israel and the United States have shown
that there was more damage in those areas protected by Patriot
batteries than in those neighborhoods that were exposed to Scud
attacks without any defense. A study by the Israeli Ministry of
Defense revealed that thirteen Scuds launched at Tel Aviv before the
deployment of the Patriots in Israel resulted in 115 human injuries
and caused damage to twenty-seven hundred apartments. The Patriots were fired at eleven Scuds that were aimed at greater Tel Aviv,
which led to 168 injuries and nearly eight thousand damaged
apartments.

There was a very logical explanation for this: the Patriot missiles
were not capable of completely annihilating the Iraqi Scuds. Thus,
not only did the collision cause the Scuds and the Patriots both to
disintegrate in mid-air spreading a rain of debris, but some missiles
exploded in mid-air without impact on a Scud, also showering
fragments over the land.

Israeli leaders and generals were aware of these facts but did not
share them with the Israeli public. A few years earlier Israel was
offered, for purchase, Patriot batteries, but found them unsuitable
for its defense plans. Instead the government decided to build a better
missile of its own. However, as the war broke out, this missile was
not operational. Now Israel's leaders realized that most of the
country was suffering from a serious loss of confidence and needed
to cling to something that gave them a sense of protection. Israelis
became dependent on the American missiles and American troops.
Israeli leaders encouraged the people to believe that the American
missiles could perform miracles. They chose to withhold the truth,
fearing that the public confidence and order might break under the
strain of protracted anxiety.

It was a cynical decision to sacrifice truth for the relative and
temporary public tranquility. By achieving their short-term goal, the
leadership helped to undermine one of the most sacred conventions
of old Zionism and modern Israel: the Jewish state must be able to

defend itself regardless of the circumstances. Many Israelis, moreover, were confused by the reappraisal the missile attack seemed to
demand of their more recent historical memory. Israelis are brought
up—they are almost conditioned like Pavlovian dogs—to believe that
their country is a very active, usually hyperenergetic state with lots
of initiative and quick reflexes. This has been the experience of all
previous wars. Whether Israel was attacked by its Arab neighbors or
was attacking them, it would take the initiative sooner rather than
later, conducting the battle according to their strategy of spreading
the war into enemy territory. Israel's concept of security used to be
based on deterrence—to build sufficient military strength to prevent
the enemy from attacking the state. However, during the Gulf War
Israeli traditional military theory was useless. A combination of
political, strategic, military, psychological and operational reasons
forced the Israeli cabinet to adopt a policy of total restraint, and they
were attacked internally.

While its policy of restraint regained for Israel the sympathy of
world opinion, it also brought about, especially among Arabs and
Washington's decision-makers, an unprecedented low regard, bordering on contempt. Israeli leaders told me that after the war, when they
met their European counterparts, they were asked: "How could you
sustain the attack?" I myself heard from American officials similar
comments: "We were astonished to see your reaction during the war.
It was so untypical of you the Israelis." Undoubtedly, this decision
will, in the foreseeable future, have significant military and political
ramifications for Israel's self-perception as well as for the way it will
be viewed, respected, and evaluated by others.

On the first Friday of the war, after the first attack, when my
family and others emerged from our sealed rooms at 6:00 A.M., we
were puzzled and troubled by the return to the normal world. It was
a wonderful morning. The weather was perfect—blue sky and
cloudless—like an Indian summer. The sharp contrast between the
calm morning and the preceding night's storm, through which all
Israelis—young and old, rich and poor, Israeli-Arabs and Israeli-
Jews—had passed, could not be ignored. On that morning and in the
days to come Israelis were forced to accept a new reality.

Israel today is already a different society from the one the world

knew twenty or even ten years ago. There might still be doubts about
whether Israel under Rabin's leadership is ready to take a different
political course in dealing with some of its troubling issues—the
Palestinian question foremost. It may take some time before the
Israeli people recognize how much their country has changed.
Perhaps some old convictions will endure, but the Iraqi attacks have
brought to light the crisis that has been building in Israel over the last
decade and now requires an urgent, perceptible resolution.

The new Israelis are walking a tightrope between modernism-
secularism and traditional religious expression. They are a strange
combination of liberalism mixed with a fierce narrowmindedness.
The desire to become a westernized society exists side by side with
middle-eastern ethnicity. Sexual permissiveness is confronted with
puritanism. Idealism, the desire for social justice, and a welfare state
are gradually being replaced by materialism and consumerism. Old
political pragmatism, characterized by policies of compromise, is
being challenged by extremism. The effort to maintain a democratic
and free society becomes increasingly difficult as the strong security
measures required by the continued occupation and the governance
of the West Bank and the Gaza Strip restrict personal freedom.

Israel is a highly politicized society. Everything from industry to
labor, health, education, art, and sport is dominated and controlled
by politicians. To be nominated for public office or to become an
executive or a business professional, one needs the right political
connections. Yet Israelis loath their political system. They want to
change it but lack the determination to make it better. They are tired
of wars but are afraid to make concessions for peace. They wholeheartedly pray for peace but support right-wing parties that refuse to
put an end to the military occupation of Arab territories.

The new Israelis are impatient and hedonistic. They can easily
identify with the middle-class love of quick satisfaction, short-cuts,
and immediate results and with the desire for easy, almost magical
solutions to political, economic, and social burdens. They are not
ready to make personal sacrifices on the national altar and are now
questioning the sacrifices Israelis have made in the past. In most
respects the new Israelis are different not just from the Zionist

founding fathers and their followers (with their pioneering, sacrific-
ing, and ascetic spirit), but also from later, less idealistic generations.
Still, this new branch of thinking is not wholly unrecognizable. In
Israel today, the past—both as recorded history and as symbol—is
ineluctably interwoven with the present. An attempt to understand
the new Israelis without an understanding of their past is like trying
to make a medical diagnosis without knowing a patient's underlying
conditions or medical history. It is, therefore, to the past that we turn
first.

ONE

Loving Immigration and Hating Immigrants

RUDYARD KIPLING, in a famous verse, said that East and West would never meet. But they do meet, and the State of Israel offers living proof. Approximately half of Israeli Jews are of oriental extraction: they are the Sephardim, which in Hebrew means Spaniards. Though most Sephardim came to Israel directly from North Africa, the Middle East, and the Balkans, their families had wandered to these parts when they were expelled from Spain in 1492. The other half are the Ashkenazim, of occidental origin: they come mainly from Western and Eastern Europe. *Ashkenaz* was the medieval Jewish name for Germany.

This human patchwork is the best evidence that Israel is a true immigrant society; of the four million Israeli Jews living in the country, over sixty percent are immigrants. There is hardly a country in the world that is not represented in Israel's population: India, the United States, China, Morocco, Russia, Ethiopia, Canada, Iraq,

South Africa, Yemen, Peru, and France. All of the various ethnic groups in Israel, like snails, carry their "homes" on their backs, bringing with them their own cultural, religious, and political traditions. The Zionist founding fathers believed that all Jews could live together in this tiny country. And it is this particular immigrant ethos, by consequence, which has dominated the country and its Zionist ideology.

The special status given to immigration in Israel is even reflected in the language of modern Hebrew. While English uses the words *immigration* and *emigration*, the Israelis coined two terms: *aliyah*, which means "going up" (to Zion) and *yerida*, which means "going down" (from Zion). These twin terms have their own political and historical associations. Aliyah, especially, has a mystical connotation which is close in meaning to such religious terms as "pilgrimage" and "ascension."

As early as the mid-thirties, before Israel gained its independence, the Zionist founding fathers, led by David Ben Gurion, later the first prime minister, had already developed their concept of Zionist power: immigration, or aliyah, was viewed as a major tool toward boosting the nation's strength, including that of its army. This was a simple equation: a small nation surrounded by enemies will not survive without the defense of a strong army. And the larger the population, of course, the larger the army. Ben Gurion noted in his diary that aliyah was the most crucial factor in the nation's security. Immigration, he believed, would secure the existence of the state. Then, however, came the Holocaust. The destruction, during the Second World War, by the German Nazis of half of the Jewish people shattered the Zionist dream.

It took a matter of weeks, in the summer of 1942, for the news of the Nazi campaign to reach the West; and it came from several sources. A conscientious German industrialist by the name of Eduard Schulte and Polish underground fighters conveyed the information to Jewish organizations in neutral Switzerland.

Until the end of 1942, everybody, from President Franklin D. Roosevelt to David Ben Gurion in Tel Aviv, either ignored the information about the massacre of Jews or refused to believe it. Even when the full extent of the Nazi horrors became clear to the Allies, they still didn't lift a finger to put an end to the atrocities. The British, who ruled Palestine, were afraid of Arab reaction and continued enforcing a policy which severely limited Jewish immigration, while the United States and most other free nations refused entry visas to Jews on the run. During 1943 and 1944 there were an increasing number of pleas from Jewish leaders in Britain and the United States, and even directly from the death camps, begging the Allies to bombard the camps or at least the railroads that carried Jews to their deaths. The Allied military commanders argued that the distances were too great for their bombers to reach the gas chambers. Later, when the death camps on Polish soil were within reachable distance, the party line refusal was based upon "limited military resources." This is one of the saddest and most maddening chapters in the history of the Second World War.

When the war was over, the West had to face its sins—its passivity in the face of such horror. The pangs of conscience suffered by Western leaders, and especially the American public, were one of the great catalysts in the establishment of Israel.

But it was not only the rest of the world who had reason to be ashamed. Ben Gurion and his colleagues, too, are to be blamed for having done too little; after all, they also had the information. As the Nazi trains punctually reached their deadly destination, and European Jewry was perishing in Nazi ovens, the mood of the discussions in Palestine was calm, business as usual. Inconceivable as this may be, minutes of the meetings of the Zionist leadership are filled with trivial passages and insignificant discussions about the crimes that were taking place in Europe. It is true that the Jewish community of Palestine lived under British rule and had no army of its own, but it also seems clear that the Zionist leaders had no sense of urgency about what was happening.

It is difficult to explain this skepticism and detachment toward the news and the failure to move heaven and earth to try to stop the liquidation of their fellow Jews. Radicals among the Jewish Orthodox—those who oppose the idea of Zionism and object to the very existence of the state of Israel—have arrived at an answer which is unrivaled in its harshness and cruelty. They accuse Zionism itself of having collaborated with Nazism. They argue that the liquidation of the Jews helped to speed up the establishment of the state of Israel. Of course, these arguments are deceitful and completely without foundation.

Still, there is one explanation that might shed light on Ben Gurion's behavior: the Zionist notion of the rejection of the diaspora. The Zionists were determined to create a new kind of man in Eretz Israel—the land of Israel, the Jewish name for Palestine. The Israeli Jew, unlike his diaspora counterpart, was to be strong, fearless, and prepared at all times to defend himself. He was to be "normal." This obsession with normality was an early characteristic of Zionist thinking. The so-called "passive" or "submissive" behavior of the diaspora Jews during the war only reinforced the long-despised image among Jews themselves of the diaspora Jew as a helpless being. In the eyes of Ben Gurion and the Zionist leadership, the diaspora Jews "went as lambs to the slaughter."

Torn by doubt after the Holocaust and feeling that they had not done enough, Ben Gurion and the Zionist leadership suffered terrible collective guilt and used the memory of the Holocaust to bind them morally to a commitment to diaspora Jews. They vowed that another such destruction of the Jews would never happen; they would protect Jews wherever they might be.

In its Declaration of Independence, in 1948, Israel was called the homeland of all Jews; the declaration stipulates that every Jewish person has the right to live in unity with his fellow citizens in their sovereign state. The country was established to offer Jews a refuge from persecution and its aim was to be a Gathering of Exiles— bringing together all Jews in their ancient land. The legal device that undergirds the mass absorption of Jews is the Law of Return. This law states that every Jew is entitled to immigrate and to receive immediate Israeli citizenship upon arrival, and without any process of naturalization.

However, Ben Gurion and Israel's leadership found themselves in a bizarre position at the inception of the state. Zionism originated in Europe, and its leaders were European Jews focused mainly on bringing their own communities to Eretz Israel. Their dreams of a Jewish state were structured on their own lives in Europe. As a result,

Zionism. After all, Zionism was striving to create a new people. One of its most popular symbols was its nickname for the native Israeli, sabra, which is Hebrew for the prickly pear that grows on a certain kind of cactus found widely throughout Israel. The fruit is rough on the outside but soft and sweet on the inside. The term refers to anyone born in Eretz Israel and functions as an elitist tag to distinguish "natives" from immigrants. Israeli literature and poetry of pre- and early statehood had long been mobilized to ennoble this image of the sabra.

This stereotype reached the summit of kitsch after the War of Independence in 1948, when the sabra was depicted as the ideal, nearly mythical young Israeli: blue-eyed and beautiful, with an abundance of healthy hair. The sabra loved the sea ("He was born from the sea," wrote Moshe Shamir, one of the generation's popular authors), was a member of the youth movement, and volunteered to serve in elite army units as a fearless, iron-willed soldier. He loved life yet was prepared to sacrifice it for the sake of a higher good: defending the fatherland. The sabra was ready to kill his Arab enemy but did not hate him. He fired and then cried. Of course, the young immigrant boy was the diametrical opposite of the sabra. He was, in the words of Leah Goldberg, one of Israel's foremost women poets of the time, "so ugly and scrawny that it was hard to love him." Some of the descriptions of immigrants that appeared in the Israeli press were hard to distinguish from the all too familiar anti-Semitic propaganda served by the rest of the world. In contrast to the sabra's idealism, the young immigrant showed "egotism, parasitism, and a lack of morality."

All new immigrants, whether they were European or Oriental, were viewed as aliens and aroused antagonism among the Israelis. They dressed differently, spoke foreign languages, and practiced different customs. Most Sephardis bitterly reminisce about their first humiliating years; this is not so for their Ashkenazi brethren. Perhaps the Ashkenazi repressed their unhappiness, not wanting to remember this or any early experience connected with their survival of the Holocaust. The power to forget might have proven a greater necessity for them.

they could only envision Israel as a kind of extension of the old familiar world. Israel, for them, would be designed to serve the European Jews coming out of the ghettos, Jews wounded by anti-Semitism and persecution. Oriental Jewry was never factored into their thinking. But after the Second World War, the only sizable human reservoir that Ben Gurion could turn to and trust to come to the new state was the Sephardis.

To further complicate the process of immigration, getting the Sephardis out of their native countries was difficult and usually involved breaking local laws. Israel was prepared to hazard this and spared neither effort nor money to that end; the Israeli secret service, the Mossad, was often mobilized. Time and again, when Jews were prevented from leaving their countries, Israel obtained their freedom with money, bribes, and, occasionally, weapons. The Mossad and other secret agencies conducted covert campaigns to protect Jews throughout the world and to help them immigrate to Israel. In 1948–1949, fifty thousand Jews were airlifted from Yemen after local officials were bribed. That set a historical precedent for other, similar projects, and the technique continues to be used, as it was most recently in the exodus of the Falashas, the black Jews of Ethiopia.

In Iraq, between 1948 and 1951, bribery was dressed up as "travel agency commissions," but the money was actually pocketed by the country's two prime ministers. In exchange, 130,000 Jews were allowed to leave the country. Hassan II, king of Morocco, and his top advisers permitted 150,000 Jews to emigrate to Israel between 1954 and 1962 in return for bribes, arms, and security know-how delivered by Israel, along with money raised by Jewish charities.

As a consequence, in the early years, Israel became a virtual tower of Babel. The aim was to absorb as many people as possible from all corners of the world, and it was upright; it was ardently pursued, but the challenge was overwhelming. It took little time to expose the gap between the dream of bringing all these different people to a new small country and the reality of such an undertaking. After their initial absorption, many immigrants cursed the day of their arrival and made desperate attempts to leave and settle elsewhere.

The first steps of an *oleh*, a new immigrant, brought him to an absorption center called "The Gates of Aliyah." In reality, the authorities considered these the locked gates of a detention camp. Reading the files in the Israel State Archives one gets the impression that the newcomers were perceived as potential criminals rather than brothers and sisters. The hardships endured by the immigrants were so formidable that one member of the government, who was in charge of absorption, admitted sadly that it seemed Israel wanted immigration but not immigrants.

My family and I had suffered from some of this resistance toward immigrants in Israel when, in March 1957, we arrived poor from Poland. The bureaucrats who received the five of us at the absorption center performed their work leisurely, as though they had all the time in the world. As a six-year-old, I thought it was odd that they smiled only when talking to each other and never at us. Every so often, the man who was dealing with us would get up from his desk and disappear for a long time. Upon returning to his seat and to the papers which were spread out all over his desk, he would not make the slightest attempt to explain or apologize. This continued for ten hours as my parents sat, luggage at their feet, not daring to utter a word. Even though they were accustomed to being treated differently, they were too scared of antagonizing the bureaucrat. Only years later, when my parents had adjusted themselves to Israeli life, were they able to look back on their initial experience without anger and recognize their fellow Israelis' antagonism toward the majority of its population as a paradox of the Israeli mentality.

There were many darker sides to the massive immigration waves of the early 1950s; contemporary records tell their disturbing stories. Eyewitness accounts describe the absorption camps as dreary places "in which an evil smell of decay had solidified in the air." Until people were given a roof above their heads—sometimes this was no more than a tent—they were forced to cope out in the open for some days. The Israeli winter was cold and rainy; the food was unspeakable. Dinner consisted of five green olives, a slice of bread, and cheese. Dozens of languages could be heard at one time; people couldn't understand each other and few could understand the unbending bureaucrats who spoke Hebrew and who, instead of helping them, showed indifference or, worse, malice. The new

immigrants often came to blows and scuffles about anything r to survival: a bed, tent, blanket, or food. The law of the j prevailed.

After staying in the center for weeks, the immigrants were g permanent housing. Conditions there were even more dismal. N immigrants lived in tents and shabby huts in camps which w called ma'abara, a word rooted in Hebrew for "transit." To this d the word has such awful connotations that it is used to describe a terrible place.

The ma'abara were usually located outside the big towns and very remote places. They offered neither showers nor running watel sanitary conditions were abominable. There were no roads, only miserable paths. Many people died as a result of the lack of medicine, physicians, and nurses. An inspector of the Department of Absorption, who visited one of the new camps-turned-shantytowns, reported that he himself witnessed "immigrants who are refusing to touch their soup because there are worms squirming between the vegetables." The state documents show that it was hard to find work and most new immigrants remained unemployed. They spent their time playing cards or hanging around the camps. Another official wrote: "We are destroying and harming these people. There's nothing we can do but weep quietly."

Ostensibly, everyone underwent an equally harsh reception: European Jews, most of them Holocaust survivors, and Oriental Jews. Everyone who passed through the "Gates of Aliyah" was subjected to a short medical examination and then asked to undress completely in order to be disinfected with DDT. That was a humiliating experience, particularly for the Ashkenazis who had survived the Holocaust.

This lack of sensitivity to the traumas of the immigrants was expressed particularly hatefully by Israeli children. They called the European survivors of the Holocaust "soaps." This cruel and macabre allusion to the Nazi's use of human fat to produce soap became synonymous with "outsider"—someone who doesn't belong to the gang, someone who is weak and different.

Oddly enough, in Israel there is a universally negative attitude toward immigrants that is actually linked with the original aims of

But the Sephardis, in fact, were really in a more troublesome position than the European immigrants. The Israeli establishment, having consisted mainly of European Jews, was more predisposed to the Ashkenazi immigrants; all of the major political, financial, military, and cultural institutions were entirely run by Ashkenazis. They shared the same culture, had similar values, and, most important, they spoke Yiddish. Many of the Ashkenazi immigrants already had relatives in Israel who helped them financially and, of critical importance, introduced and directed them through the Israeli bureaucracy.

Sephardis, for the most part, had no such connections to smooth their passage into a new life. So different was their folklore and culture from the Western European culture that Israel had adopted that the Sephardis suffered discrimination from all sides: both from Israelis and Ashkenazi immigrants. Government officials were instructed, for example, to make things easier for us, the Polish immigrants. Sephardis tended to stay in the absorption center longer. Many among the Sephardis, coming as they did from oral cultures, were illiterate, and they had more than the usual problems in social adjustment. Worst of all, they arrived without leaders, like sheep without a shepherd.

Zionism is largely a movement of people without choice. With the exception of a handful of idealistic pioneers who set out with a strong conviction about the rightness of their journey, by far most Israeli immigrants were forced by circumstances to leave their countries of origin. Holocaust survivors who had lost their relatives and homes had nowhere to go. Israel seemed the most hospitable to many of them. For centuries, Sephardic Jews—Yemenite, Iraqi, Moroccan, Egyptian and Libyan—have lived more or less peacefully, as a minority, with their Arab neighbors. But from the moment the Jewish-Arab tensions in 1948 expanded and caused political interests from other Arab countries to the conflict, their peaceful coexistence was shattered. Now surrounding Arab neighbors of Israel began to pressure their own Jewish citizens, interfering with their basic human rights. Those Jews who in their prayers had always yearned for Zion now had both the opportunity and the incentive to leave and make their dreams come true. However, Jews elsewhere, who were better off, were not persuaded by Zionism. Those who suffered no imminent danger did not want to consider immigration: neither the Jews of the United States, nor those of South America and Western Europe.

From the first arrival of the immigrants some of Israel's most trenchant social, political, and cultural problems were instituted.

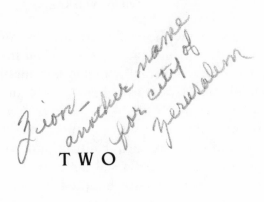

Zion — another name for city of Jerusalem

TWO

Zionism: Dream and Reality

THE TERM *Zionism* was first used publicly and with a political connotation at a meeting in Vienna on January 23, 1892. But the notion of Zion was not new: it was as ancient as the Babylonian exile. The book of Psalms spells it out clearly: "By the rivers of Babylon there we sat down, we wept when we remembered Zion." The Zion—or *tsion,* in Hebrew—to which this verse refers is actually another name for the city of Jerusalem.

Jerusalem was the name of the Jebusite stronghold captured by King David three thousand years ago. The Jebusites were one of the Canaanite tribes defeated by the invading Hebrews, or Israelites, who moved from Egypt after being set free from slavery and who settled in the land known today as Israel. These Hebrews, who had belonged to nomadic tribes of Semitic origins, the Romans would later dub Jews.

Zion proper is the southern part of a hill on the top of which the Jewish Temple was first built (approximately 970 BC) by David's son,

23

Solomon. The name Zion subsequently was given to the entire hill, to all of Jerusalem, and even to the nation. Indeed, it even came to stand for the same spirituality that spread monotheism, the belief in one, metaphysical God, throughout the surrounding pagan world. It is the Bible that up to this very day has been disseminating ideas which originated in Judaism.

However, despite its rich contribution to civilization, Jewish history has basically been a sad, and often tragic, story. After the Babylonian exile twenty-six hundred years ago, the Israelites returned to their land, regained their independence, and rebuilt in Jerusalem their destroyed temple—only to lose all of it again in the first century, this time to the Roman Empire. Roman outrage with the Israelites' recalcitrance was such that they even tried to wipe out the symbolic connections between the people and the land. Jerusalem was given the Roman name of Ilia Capitolina, and Judea became Palestine, named after the Philistines, tribes from the period of King David who originated in the Greek islands and reached the Mediterranean coasts of Canaan. The destruction of the Second Temple, in A.D. 70, sent the Jews into a second exile. This exile lasted longer, for nearly two thousand years. The majority of the Israelites were dispersed all over the world; only a handful continued living in the land of Israel.

It might have been logical to expect that the exile would lead to the disappearance of the Jewish people as such. Other nations and cultures in the Middle East no less splendid than the Jews' had thrived and yet had vanished from the earth. Who, today, has met a Sumerian, Akkadian, Assyrian, Philistine, or Babylonian?

Nevertheless, Jewish history has refused to fit into a mold and has defied theories that prescribe the rise and fall of civilizations. German philosopher Oswald Spengler, for instance, postulated that it was the nature of civilizations to be born and to die, and English historian Arnold Toynbee believed civilizations developed into progressively higher forms. Neither is the case with the Jews.

This great mystery can be partly explained by the strict religious observances and isolation of the early Jews. Both served as empowerment, enabling them to preserve their language, traditions, and heritage through the centuries.

are not Palestinean of today?

A distinct religion and isolation had, however, a negative aspect. It brought the Jews, who already carried the burden of being the presumed murderers of Christ, the hatred of their neighbors. Initially the roots of anti-Semitism were religious, but over the ages it branched out into various economic, social, racial, and political spheres. It bred disaster and calamity, caused backwardness and regression. The Jews of the eastern European diaspora lived in *shtetls*—little, almost exclusively Jewish towns—and enclaves, known as ghettos. In Europe Jews were different than their neighbors. They had strange names. They dressed peculiarly in long dark coats and robes and kept their heads covered. The Jews spoke in a foreign tongue, Yiddish, a mongrel language with elements of ancient Hebrew, Polish, and Old German. During their two thousand year diaspora, Jews did not speak Hebrew, they only prayed in it. Hebrew was the sacred language, the Holy Language of the Bible. One might pray, hope, and dream in Hebrew—but secular daily talk was conducted in Yiddish.

Jews, especially in Eastern Europe, were people without a definite occupation or profession, living from hand to mouth: *Luftmenschen,* the Yiddish for "air people," or people who lived from and of the air. Nevertheless, certain trades, like innkeeping, shopkeeping, and moneylending, were identified with the Jews.

Modern Zionism was meant to release Jews from their segregated communities, their isolation and backwardness, and to restore their pride. But as the national liberation movement of and for the Jewish people, it intended also to gain them freedom and statehood in their ancient homeland. The Zionists' burning desire was for normality: to make the Jewish people a nation like any other.

Historians like to define junctions of time and place to which they can point as the beginning of a historic turn of events. But they are also fully aware that most major historic occurrences are not static, one-dimensional events but rather a combination of forces that represent a process. The Boston Tea Party is perceived as such a landmark of the American Revolution. The French Revolution is associated, above all, with the storming of the Bastille. It is hard to point to the place and date of birth of the Zionist Revolution. It was not conceived in one place at a particular moment but developed over

Pogrom is "to destroy"

time and in several places. Yet one may say that certain events in
Russia, antisemitic riots known as pogroms, generated the Zionist
Revolution. Pogrom is derived from the Russian verb *pogromi,* "to
destroy." The word was used to describe the massacres of Jews and
the destruction of Jewish property which spread, during the 1880s,
like wildfire throughout the Russian Empire. From the ashes of the
pogroms arose the political movement of Zionism. Many of Zionism's great leaders had themselves experienced pogroms that left
their souls and psyches profoundly scarred. Many years later, in their
memoirs, they would tell of how they hid under tables and beds or
inside wardrobes when the rioters went on the rampage unhindered
or indulged in an orgy of killings. As a result, the old Jewish longing
for Zion underwent a dramatic metamorphosis and resurfaced as a
modern political idea. From survivors Jews became active dreamers
and planners.

The man who, more than anyone else, set about transforming the
dream into a reality was born in 1860 in Budapest, the second capital
of the Austro-Hungarian Empire. His name was Theodor (Binyamin
Zeev) Herzl. He became the undisputed leader of the Zionist
movement, its hero. Stefan Zweig, the renowned Austrian writer,
called him "king of the Jews"—the latter-day Moses who would lead
his people to the promised land. Herzl took the Jews' national
yearning out of the ghetto and placed it firmly in the arena of
international politics. Under his leadership Jewish nationalism was
transformed into a political force.

Herzl was born into a typical bourgeois Jewish family. Though the
children still received some Jewish education, the atmosphere at
home, as elsewhere in similar families, was one of assimilation.
Despite Herzl's Hungarian origins, he was educated in the German
language. In his diary he wrote that if ever he were given the chance
to be someone else, he would choose to be a German nobleman.
Upon receiving his doctorate in law in 1884, Herzl abandoned his
intention of becoming a practicing lawyer in Vienna in order to
dedicate himself fully to writing. Herzl was not at this time a
particularly serious thinker or penetrating commentator, but his
witty, acerbic style gained him a sympathetic readership and finally,

too, a steady job when he joined Vienna's most highly respected newspaper, the *Neue Freie Presse*. Its editors were young assimilated Jews like Herzl who believed that human progress and political liberalism would defeat the dark forces of anti-Semitism. He also wrote a number of plays, especially comedies, which like most other contemporary productions were trivial and not very funny.

The watershed in Herzl's life came with his assignment to Paris, in 1891, as his newspaper's correspondent. The early 1890s were characterized by a resurgence of anti-Semitism, both in France and in other Western European countries. The particular event which shocked him tremendously was the Dreyfus Affair.

Alfred Dreyfus was an officer in the French army and of Jewish parentage. Despite his completely assimilated upbringing and his loyalty to the army, he was arrested in October 1894 on the charge of selling military secrets to Germany, France's sworn enemy. Dreyfus was innocent, but in the subsequent military trial he was found guilty, and in January 1895 he was publicly degraded. Herzl, in his capacity as journalist, was present at the humiliating ceremony where Dreyfus was stripped of his captain's rank, and he heard the incited crowd yell: *"A mort! A mort les Juifs!"* Death! Death to the Jews.

Emerging from the trial in a soul-searching mood, Herzl reached the conclusion that the Jewish problem would not find its solution through assimilation and integration but only when the Jews had their own territory and state. Herzl went from existing as a rootless Jew who sought to merge with (what he believed was) the borderless culture of Western Europe to a full-blooded Jewish nationalist.

Upon his return to Vienna, Herzl threw himself wholly into writing an appeal to the Jewish masses. The result was *Der Judenstat,* a short essay printed in 1896. The central argument was that not only did the Jews need a state of their own, but the world, too. The full title of the essay, in English translation, reads: *The Jewish State: An Attempt at a Modern Solution of the Jewish Question.* The concept was that the Jews would rally for an independent state of their own, and a charter would be published to confirm this decision. Jewish communities all over the world would organize themselves to conduct negotiations with the foreign powers and to manage Jewish immigration from the diaspora to the new territory. The financial backing would come from wealthy Jews.

When the essay first came out, it provoked a mixed reaction, ranging from enthusiasm to anger and scorn. Gradually Herzl's program began to gain momentum. He tirelessly wrote letters and traveled all around Europe to meet other Jewish activists for the advancement of the Jewish state. His efforts were crowned, after a year and a half of hectic activity, when it was decided to convene a special conference: the first Zionist Congress.

Two hundred and fifty delegates from twenty-four countries from eastern and western Europe met on August 29, 1897, in the concert hall of the Basel Casino, in Switzerland. Some delegates had been chosen as representatives by their communities, others had been invited, and still others came on their own initiative. There were penniless students and wealthy businessmen, intellectuals, and workers. Orthodox Jews met confirmed atheists; political reactionaries mingled with revolutionaries.

The event lasted three days. Herzl's idea of establishing a Jewish state in Palestine was adopted. The delegates also decided to set up a Zionist Federation to win support for the notion of a Jewish state in Palestine. Of course, Herzl was elected the first president of the Zionist Federation.

Herzl's declared aim at the first congress was to initiate a plan that would serve as the basis for the future, "normal" state. The wish to become "a nation like other nations" amounted to an obsession among the Zionist founding fathers. The old shtetl Jews, in the eyes of the first Zionists, were physically weak, pale, and dressed in cumbersome black clothes. In their imagination, the Zionists got the Jewish masses out of this restrictive garb and put them in short, light sports clothes, ready for a run, gymnastics, boxing, or weight lifting. Their dream was of a "muscular Jewry." In order to make this dream come true they set up sports organizations and clubs carrying the wishful names of "Hakoach" (strength or power) or "Maccabee," in memory of the ancient Israelite heroes who had dared to defy the Greek occupiers more than two millennia before.

Moreover, the early Zionists stipulated that a nation could be called normal only when it had its own criminal underworld. They looked ahead with romantic passion to the sweet moment when modern Jewish society in the Land of Israel would have its own "Hebrew prostitutes and thieves." In this regard, the reality in today's Israel would undoubtedly exceed the fantasies of the early forefathers. The fourteen Israeli jails house six thousand criminals, some of whom are the most brutal kind and could take high honors among New York's organized crime families. The Israeli prison population has doubled over the last decade. Prostitution is illegal, but there are whores in every city, and there is no single innovation in the sex industry that does not reach Israel.

During the Zionist Congress of 1897, and shortly after it, Herzl was elated. In his diary he recorded that if he were asked to describe the Congress in one phrase—though perhaps not publicly—he would say that "in Basel I established the Jewish state."

There is a great contradiction, however, between the early vision of the Jewish state and what it has become. In 1902 Herzl wrote a detailed description of his envisaged "Altneuland"—the old new land. The book's Hebrew title was *Tel-Aviv*, which means the Hill of Spring, mentioned in the Bible, in the book of Ezekiel. The hill signifies the layers of an old land in which ancient cities are buried. The spring symbolizes hope for a new land with a better future.

The Jewish state, in Herzl's imagination, would be secular, liberal, and free of clericalism: religion and state would be strictly separate. The reality of modern Israel, though, is quite different. Perhaps more than any other Western society, Israel has religious, clerical parties and groups whose power affects the daily running of the country. In Herzl's dream, religious practice is determined by the Reform congregation. In Israel the religious establishment is ruled with an iron fist by the Orthodox, who stubbornly refuse to delegate power to other congregations, least of all to the Reform. The climax of religious achievement, for Herzl, would be the inauguration of the new temple. Of course, this temple would not be situated on the Temple Mount in Jerusalem, occupied as it already is by Islamic mosques. However, in today's Israel there are some radical and fanatical Jewish groups that strive to blow up these mosques in order to make room for the third Jewish temple.

"The Jewish state," Herzl wrote, "would be known for its tolerance and interdenominational harmony." In this spirit, he described a Passover banquet where representatives of all the nation's religious groups join in the celebrations. In Israel today, unfortunately, there is continual religious tension and nothing resembling harmony among its Jews, Christians, and Muslims. In October 1990 Israeli police and Palestinian youth met in a bloody battle over the question of who would control the Temple Mount. In one of the worst outbreaks of religious violence in modern Israel, nineteen Palestinian worshippers, while finishing their Friday prayers, were killed, and more than one hundred people were injured. These events, triggered by mutual misunderstandings and resulting in continual mutual mistrust, were another tragic reminder of the lack of tolerance in today's Israel.

Herzl also believed that the majority of the Jewish people would emigrate to the state and settle there, but in reality most Jews prefer to live outside the Jewish state. The United States, for instance, with five and one-half million, has a larger Jewish population than Israel. New York—with three million Jews—is the city with the largest Jewish population, not Tel Aviv or Jerusalem. In Herzl's Alteneuland there is no mention of the Hebrew language: everyday language was to be Yiddish, with German for the elite. For most Zionists, however, Yiddish was too strongly associated with the ghetto, which they wanted to forget. Therefore, Hebrew became the language of Zionism; its revival has been the most prominent success of early Zionist aspirations.

The Hebrew renaissance is an achievement that parallels the rise of Jewish nationalism. For nearly eighteen hundred years, Hebrew was an unspoken language, used only for prayers and hermetically closed to changing realities. Classical Greek and Latin, too, have been in existence for over two thousand years. But unlike Hebrew, these are languages which are no longer spoken; they are only learned at schools, universities, and seminaries. Hebrew in the nineteenth century was also a dead language, but less than one hundred years later it has become the chosen language among Jews.

Today, four million Israeli Jews and hundreds of thousands of Jews worldwide talk, read, write, love, and dream in Hebrew, and are the living evidence of the enduring success of this renaissance. Without the common bond of one language among Israel's early settlers, the national revival of Zionism and the state of Israel would not have been possible.

There are at least two more differences between Herzl's vision and Israeli reality. These discrepancies are connected with Israel's relationship to its Arab neighbors and with its security problems.

Herzl did not really consider the question of how the local Arabs would feel about the immigrating and colonizing Jews. In fact, in his original scheme it seems that Herzl barely concerned himself with the half million Arabs who actually lived in Palestine. In his novel he avoids the problem by hoping for mutual tolerance between Arabs and Jews. With this kind of thinking, Herzl laid the spiritual cornerstone for the approach of Zionists toward their Arab neighbors in the Middle East. Like an ostrich with its head in the sand, Israel has continuously ignored its surrounding reality. In Israel there is actually a widely held belief or hope that somehow, miraculously, the Palestinian problem will go away. Most Israelis, when asked about their sweetest dream, will answer that they would like to see Israel lifted out of the Middle Eastern chaos and Mediterranean heat and transplanted onto a cool, pastoral European landscape. Given the continued hostilities with their Arab neighbors, many Israelis would doubtless trade their borders with Syria, Jordan, Lebanon, and Egypt for borders with Switzerland or Italy. In Herzl's utopia, after all, Israel was to have been a western Jewish state that would serve as a bridge for the advancement of western interests. Zionists and Israelis have been and continue to be naive, if not irresponsible, in pretending their Arab neighbors do not exist.

As a result of his disregard for the conflicts between Arabs and Israelis, Herzl never applied himself to questions about the future state's security. Throughout all eighty pages of his utopian novel barely two lines are dedicated to a very cursory view of the matter: the Jewish state would maintain neutrality and have need for only a small permanent army. Israel, of course, is exactly the opposite. It is not neutral. The country is decisively pro-Western and keeps a large army of conscripts, permanent soldiers, and reservists. Modern Israel has in fact become the Sparta of the Middle East, the strongest regional military power. If someone had told Herzl a hundred years ago that his Jewish state would become one of the most modern warfare technologies, he would surely have laughed in his informant's face.

In his attempts to obtain international approval for his project, Herzl rushed between capitals to meet with various leading figures. He left no stone unturned and wrote persistently to prime ministers, presidents, kings, princes, writers, and artists. He wrote to Otto von Bismarck, the nationalist chancellor who in 1870 unified Germany; to Vittorio-Emmanuele, the king of Italy; and to the pope. After following the German emperor's entourage all over Europe, Herzl finally succeeded in meeting Wilhelm II in Jerusalem on November 2, 1898. Herzl took it for granted that the emperor would intervene, on behalf of the Zionist movement, with the Turkish sultan and support his idea for Jewish autonomy under German protection in Palestine. But the emperor was not interested.

In 1901, Herzl succeeded in meeting with the Turkish sultan, Abdul Hamid, thanks to bribes provided by the limited funds of the Zionist Federation, which were distributed generously among corrupt courtiers. Herzl had a deal to offer: in return for the sultan's charter giving the Jews the right to their own state, Herzl and the Zionist movement would marshal the economic support of rich Jews to develop the decaying empire.

Similar diplomatic tactics have been used repeatedly by the Israeli government today when trying to persuade the current leaders of third world countries to restore their diplomatic links with Israel. Nigeria for example, the largest African nation, admitted openly in August 1991 that underlying its decision to renew diplomatic relations with Israel was the old image of the rich Jew. Its leaders stated clearly, as though they had read Herzl's diary, "we hope that Israel and Jews with their influence on international financial institutions will help us to attract more investment." Israel promised to intervene on Nigeria's behalf in Washington and, moreover, to stimulate Jewish investment in its deteriorating economy. And indeed it did. Today there are nearly a thousand Israeli businesspeople in Nigeria.

Herzl, however, returned with nothing more than the diamond tie pin that the sultan had presented to him. Turkey had set such extreme financial conditions and strict political restrictions that Herzl had no choice but to withdraw his offer.

Although Herzl's pleas were eventually rejected by all the great leaders of his time, his basic concept still persists in modern Israel. Herzl's major legacy is the notion that the only way to build and develop the Jewish state is by rallying the support of one or more world powers. This reliance on foreign aid has become a leitmotif in Zionist and Israeli history.

The Jews' right to an independent homeland was first granted by Britain in 1917 and recognized by the League of Nations, the organization that predated the United Nations. Subsequently, in 1947, the United Nations recognized this right. In all but the first war Israel fought—for independence in 1948—Herzl's notion of foreign support was borne in mind. From the 1956 Sinai Campaign to the 1991 Gulf War, Israel's military battles were heavily determined by the wish to get the approval and diplomatic support of a foreign power. Before entering these wars Israeli leaders have always gone to considerable trouble to secure the consent of a foreign and friendly power—France and Britain in 1956, and the United States ever since—before firing a shot. Except for the Gulf War, Israel had never asked that foreign troops be stationed on its soil, but it indeed requested and enjoyed diplomatic, economic, and moral support throughout its history.

Herzl died on July 3, 1904, in Austria, probably of syphilis, with a grating sense of failure. He was only forty-four years old. In the last seven years of his life he was beset with troubles—personal, family, financial, and, above all, political. His mental and physical health had been taxed too much.

But despite Herzl's disillusion and the many divergences between the dream and the reality, the truth of the matter is that he envisioned with unprecedented clarity the establishment of the state of Israel. "If you will it, it shall be no fairy tale," he wrote in the introduction to

Altneuland, and indeed, within fifty years, many of the things he envisaged had materialized. His ideas became the raw material from which those who followed in his path continued to mold, build, and shape the Zionist nation.

ometimes overt anti-Semitism of their non-Jewish comrades. These
young Jewish socialists decided to combine their ideals of social
justice—equal distribution of wealth—with the national movement
for the revival of Jewish statehood. Influenced by the ideas of utopian
socialism and Russian radicalism, some of them suggested that the
land of the future Jewish state should be owned by the people and
that large industrial and agricultural communes should be established. Other young socialists drew on the Bible and believed that
Zionist socialism could be inspired by the Hebrew prophets, who
had fought against social injustice and corruption and for the
elevation of spiritual and moral principles.

The bulk of these socialist ideas arrived in Palestine with the
Zionist pioneers. Even before Herzl saw the Zionist light, Jewish
nationalist societies were already mushrooming all over the Russian
empire. While most Jews were thinking of emigration to America or
Western Europe, these societies believed that a move to those places
would only potentially solve the problems of the individual. In
Germany, America, France, or England, where formal emancipation
had been introduced, the individual Jew who had already enjoyed
some rights and freedoms was also likely to be met with anti-
Semitism and hostility. Hence the societies argued that the remedy
against Jewish hardship would have to take the shape of a collective
solution, not tailored to the problems of a single person or family,
but to those of the Jews in general. Palestine, or Zion as they called
it, was that remedy. Accordingly, these societies were known as
Hovevey Tsion, the "Lovers of Zion." Most of these tiny organizations had been initiated by young and courageous students, but their
membership included Jews from all walks of life: the Orthodox and
the secular, rich and poor, the uneducated and the enlightened.

On June 30, 1882, a group of thirteen young men and one young
woman began their journey to Israel via the sea, from Odessa. On a
small and shaky boat they crossed the Black Sea and arrived at
Istanbul, the capital of the Ottoman-Turkish empire; from there they
crossed the Mediterranean to the port of Yafo (Jaffa) in Palestine-
Eretz Israel.

These first immigrants opened the chapter of modern colonization
in Palestine. In Hebrew this is called Aliyah Rishona, First Aliyah or

THREE

Nation Building

WHILE Herzl had been the dreamer, the prophet of political Zionism and Israel, Ben Gurion was its builder. He was small and sturdy, his movements were sharp and fast. For many Israelis and foreigners alike, Ben Gurion embodied the spirit of the new state.

Born in 1886 as David Gruen, he learned about Zionism in his father's home in Plonsk, Poland, when it became a center for the local chapter of the Zionist movement. The turning point in young Ben Gurion's life, when he was eleven years old, came with the visit of Herzl to the little shtetl, where he bought his messianic vision of a Jewish homeland. Ben Gurion fell permanently in love with Zionism and, when he was twenty, changed his name to a Hebrew one. Later, that love would extend to socialism as well. Socialism was to become the major tool in the building of the Zionist nation. During the discussions of the first Zionist Congress in 1897 in Basel, Switzerland, very little mention had been made of socialism. Yet, within two decades, the socialist-Zionist group became the strongest bloc movement, and Ben Gurion its unrivaled champion. Most of the leaders of socialist Zionism were disillusioned with the latent and

35

immigration, and it has functioned ever since as the point of reference for counting the successive waves of Jewish immigrants.

The new immigrants were called *halutsim*, Hebrew for "pioneers." Zionists worshiped and admired these pioneers. They came to be seen as the rock on which the Jewish state was built. In a well-oiled propaganda campaign, the Zionist and Israeli history books made the pioneers heroes of mythic stature. Streets and entire settlements were named after the Halutsim. Poets and writers celebrated them, and, in schools and kindergartens, children were reared on their example.

I was taught at school what a barren and empty country the first pioneers found upon their arrival. We all believed every word we were told. Today I realize that this was more like an indoctrination into Zionism than a faithful account of the historical facts. The Jewish immigrants did not set foot on vacant land; an Arab population had lived there for many centuries.

In the beginning of the 1880s, Palestine had a population of over a half million. Of these, ninety-five percent were Arabs and five percent Jews. Most Arabs lived in small villages and made their earnings from working the land. They were tenants on the land which they cultivated for Arab landowners.

When the first group of Jewish settlers arrived, the Arabs treated them with equanimity, taking them for another lot of strange, eccentric European tourists. It was, ironically enough, the encounter between the new pioneers and their "brothers"—a small group of Orthodox Jews who had been living in the land for many centuries—that gave rise to friction and hostility and triggered mutual suspicions.

It is not difficult to imagine the feelings of the first pioneers who arrived in 1882 in an exultant, hopeful mood, only to be met with the harsh reality of Palestine. On the one side there were the Arabs, perceived by the pioneers as "Oriental" and stereotyped by them as backward, intolerant, and dishonest; the noisiness and strangeness of the Yafo market and its pungent smells; and the bargaining and petty trading practices which relied on flexible and confusing notion of time. "Tomorrow" could mean the next day or the next week. "Yes" was given a similarly vague meaning, which could be translated as anything from "perhaps" to "no." On the other side there were the old, local religious Jews. They reminded the pioneers too much of the repressive life from which they had just made their escape. To the idealistic pioneers, the local Jews were uncomfortably like their families in the ghettos of Eastern Europe.

The pioneers had come to Palestine in order to build a new society, hoping to provide a new social structure for the Jewish people. Their objective was to build their society based upon the geometric structure of a pyramid. The socioeconomic makeup of the diaspora communities consisted of a broad base of tradespeople, money-lenders, peddlers, middlemen, and people who lived on charity or, even worse, penniless beggars. The pioneers viewed these people at the base of the pyramid as parasitic and "unproductive." Only at the narrow top of the Jewish pyramid could one find the more "produc-tive" professionals—industrialists and even farmers. The pioneers in Eretz Israel and their Zionists supporters back home had firmly decided to change the structure of the Jewish pyramid. They came to Israel to cultivate the land and live off the fruits of labor. Seeing themselves as a social avant-garde, the pioneers wished to set an example that would motivate the Jewish masses to follow them. They aspired to be the exact opposite of the old, local Jews and what they stood for.

It took the first group of pioneers little time to learn about the harsh conditions of life in their new land. Many of the Jewish settlers spread over the country in search of work. In lots of cases they worked as unskilled laborers, near Yafo, at an agricultural school that had recently been set up by the French Philanthropic Alliance. Soon they realized the difficulty of making a living this way. The farm work was difficult, especially in the summer when the sun beat down on them mercilessly. Most of the settlers had the soft and tender hands of students and were unable to cope with menial work. They quarreled with their Arabs neighbors and even more so with other Jews. As the newcomers were not religious, many members of the old Jewish community viewed them as an embarrassing nuisance. The pioneers advocated the break with the monogamous patriarchal family, and they preached social justice in the spirit of the socialism that they had absorbed in their Russian hometowns.

The first group of Russian emigrés lasted for about two and a half years before they completely disbanded. Some of them returned to their homes and families, and others joined newer groups of pioneers. In school Israeli children learn about the pioneers, the First Aliyah, about their courage, unquestioning enthusiasm, and their readiness to make sacrifices and to suffer. Very rarely, though, is it mentioned that the majority of the immigrants, in the first and subsequent waves of immigration, were not able to cope and dropped out. Most preferred to leave Palestine and return home or to move on elsewhere, mostly to America. Nevertheless, more pioneers continued to arrive, enabling the Zionist movement to build a few more farms.

The demise of Zionist colonization founded on philanthropy and, apparently, lacking in broad support and an intellectual basis confirmed the worst fears of one particular writer, Ahad Ha'am. Born in Russia as Asher Ginzberg, he was assigned in 1891 and 1893 to write an eye-witness account on the settlers' conditions. He called his reports "Truth from Eretz Israel" and signed them with the pseudonym, "Ahad Ha'am," Hebrew for "one of the people."

Ahad Ha'am was shocked by the "laziness, carelessness, deception, waste, and lack of dignity that were eating at the very roots of the settlements." Ahad Ha'am wrote that the Jewish masses were in no rush to emigrate and that, even if they were, Eretz Israel was not ready to absorb them. He recommended that Zionism should take a completely different trajectory: Jews should channel their energies and resources into spiritual and intellectual achievements rather than materialistic ones. Instead of starting colonies and farms, Zionists should build schools, universities, and institutes for higher education.

His argument sparked off a heated debate among Zionist and Jewish leaders: What shape and direction was the newly-born movement for Jewish national revival to take? Should they settle for a limited cultural autonomy, as advocated by Ahad Ha'am, or pursue the broader goal of full independence through pragmatic colonization, as advocated by the Lovers of Zion?

This is an old, persistent argument between diaspora Jews and Israeli leaders. In early 1974 the positions of the "autonomists" and

"pragmatists" would reverberate in a debate between U.S. Secretary
of State Henry Kissinger and Israel's military attaché in Washington,
General Yoel Ben Porat. As a Jewish refugee and Harvard professor,
Kissinger perceived himself as a representative of the Jewish-intellec-
tual heritage. Kissinger saw in the Israeli general the embodiment of
what, he thought, the Zionist movement brought to Jewish culture.
"And what is Israel's contribution to civilization?" he asked.
"Farmers and soldiers? What have you done to our old values?"
General Ben Porat was shocked. The traumatic experience of Israel's
bloody battles with Syria and Egypt, during the 1973 Yom Kippur
War, was still very vivid in his memory. Like most Israelis, Porat
believed that the last war only proved the indispensability of soldiers
and farmers to the very survival of Israel and, indirectly, of the
Jewish people. Yet it occurred to him that his conversation with
Kissinger was also an unintended reflection of the age-old argument
between Ahad Ha'am's school of thought and mainstream Zionism.

In May 1991, Yehudi Menuhin, one of the most gifted violinists of
this century, expressed his concern with the Israeli disregard for
Jewish genius during a celebration in his honor at the Knesset,
Israel's parliament. Menuhin said that Israel's political intransigence
and unwillingness to make concessions to the Palestinians would
further suppress the old values of Judaism. The morality and values
of Judaism have helped to give birth to thinkers like Karl Marx,
Sigmund Freud, and Albert Einstein, as well as to top chess players,
brilliant musicians, and Nobel Prize laureates.

Ahad Ha'am had foreseen these dangerous developments a century ago, when he first expressed his fear that the Zionist movement
might be deviating from its desired course. But his argument was lost
to the "pragmatists" of the mainstream Zionist movement. Whenever it seemed that the colonizing project was about to collapse,
Jewish philanthropists were found to inject new financial blood into
the settlements' veins. Land was bought from Arab landowners, and,
within twenty years of the First Aliyah, twenty Jewish farms and
rural communities had been built.

Today, on the threshold of the second millennium, several of these
colonies have already marked their hundredth anniversary. Most of
the old colonies offer typical Israeli success stories. Many of them

have flourished to become Tel Aviv's satellite towns, with populations of thirty thousand or more. They still retain a few of their old
characteristics, such as fields on their outskirts that are farmed by
the few who still continue to cling to the land. But these settlements
are no longer rural communities. They boast of shopping malls,
office buildings, industrial parks, and even art centers and institutes
of science and technology. High-rise condos have been erected, and
only small enclaves of private, one-family houses remind visitors of
the town's origins. But even these houses have undergone a major
face-lift since the old days; from modest farm dwellings and
cottages, they have developed into luxurious villas and even huge
mansions.

Nowadays, the colonies are largely inhabited by prosperous
middle-class Israelis. Many of them are second-generation Oriental-
Sephardis, the sons and daughters of immigrants who achieved the
new Israeli dream. They have jobs. They make money. Their children
get a decent education. They buy clothes in fashionable shops. They
live in the old colonies-turned-towns for neither historic nor
nostalgic reasons but for financial considerations alone.

Of course, affordable housing was not the original aim of Ben
Gurion and his colleagues when they first set foot on the land in
1906, during the second large wave of immigration—known in
Zionist history as the Second Aliyah. Most of these immigrants were
young and single and in search of a new, secular religion. They chose
socialism.

The group of pioneers with whom Ben Gurion arrived detested
Yafo so intensely that they left the town that same afternoon for a
nearby Jewish colony. Like many others, Ben Gurion had difficulty
finding employment and journeyed from one settlement to the next.
Finally he reached the Galilee and found a job as a farmer. There his
earlier romantic notions about manual labor and the cultivation of
the land were tested during his struggle to survive. But soon Ben
Gurion became known for his writing, his passionate speeches, and
his political activities.

One of the first and major symbolic statements he and his
contemporaries made upon their arrival in Palestine was to change
their names into Hebrew sounding ones. This renaming functions

almost as a rebirth, since many of their forefathers had been forced to change their names when they migrated to Central and Eastern Europe. In the seventeenth and eighteenth centuries most Eastern European Jews were coerced by ignorant local officials into adopting new family names. Some of the people were named after their place of origin, others after precious stones, flowers, or occupations. Still others were humiliated into accepting unpleasant and derogatory names like Schmaltz (grease) or Eselkopf (donkey's head). In many cases Jewish family names were derived from overly simplistic descriptions and marks of identification as observed by the condescending immigration clerks: Gross (big), Klein (little), Schwartz (black), and Weiss (white). Now their offspring were reversing historical injustice by becoming masters of their own names. In an attempt to leap over two thousand years of repressive history, these new pioneers saw themselves as the immediate descendants of biblical figures. Taking their cues from paintings of biblical scenes and people, the pioneers put on sandals and wore long gowns, and collarless shirts. This costume was actually more reminiscent of the clothes worn by the Russian revolutionaries than by the ancient Jews. The immigrants adopted romantic notions of heroism and spoke of the forgotten wars of the Maccabees to serve as symbols of Jewish revitalization. Their yearnings were atavistic, mythical, and irrational. The new names they chose were heavily symbolic: On, which means vigor, for instance; Oz, courage—Ben Gurion means "son of a lion." Others preferred a more literal translation of their previous name. Thus Stein became Avni (Stone), Silverstein became Kaspi (Silverstone), and Rosen became Shoshani (Rose).

But aside from the romantic aspects of their pioneering, they were also dogmatic and zealous socialists. On May 1, International Labor Day, the Jewish settlements hoisted red flags, and socialist meetings were concluded with the "Internationale," the anthem of the international labor movement. On the surface they seemed perfect socialists. But Ben Gurion and his followers added to their socialism also a special brand of Jewish messianism. More than any other leader, he understood that political Zionism would not do without practical backing. In this view of things, the people conquer their homeland through their deeds, by establishing facts.

From the 1920s, the emphasis in Zionism gradually shifted from Herzl's reliance on international diplomacy to Ben Gurion's pragmatism. Thus, more settlements and colonies were built with stimulated immigration and created economic institutions. The first priority was aliyah—bringing as many Jews as possible to the land in order to turn a negligible minority into at least a sizable presence. The Zionists also needed land where they could develop an agrarian society and transform the Jewish people from a nation of traders to one of producers. Since most of the land belonged to Arab landowners, the only way to secure it was by buying parcels from them. The Zionists of the Second Aliyah, who were engaging in what elsewhere would have been called land purchases, called it "redemption of the land." This is still viewed as one of the most crucial and noble of their deeds.

In order to understand the refusal of successive Israeli governments since 1967 to retreat from and return the occupied territories of the West Bank, Gaza Strip, and Golan Heights, one has to understand something about Zionist mythology. Of course, the mythical attachment to the land was not invented by the Zionists. Every nationalist movement has had a sacred notion about land. In Zionism, the land is to be conquered, to be held and not abandoned. The land is the representation of national life and existence.

The history that is taught in Israeli schools speaks of how the agriculturally barren soil was "redeemed." From its insect-infested swamps, many a pioneer caught malaria and died a romantically untimely death. In order to dry up the swamps, seeds of eucalyptus trees were imported from Australia, because their deep-running, thick roots were known to absorb water. In history books, the pioneers are depicted as superhuman. What they usually don't teach in Israeli schools is the ugly side of land acquisition. In many cases the Zionists had to persuade corrupt landowners to sell off their property. Often the so-called "redeemers" of the land were no better than property pimps and greedy charlatans. They cheated not only the Arabs from whom they purchased the land but also the buyers, their Jewish brethren. Like shady speculators in the phoney land boom in Florida in 1925, dealers sold either land that wasn't theirs or overpriced, useless marshland.

Israeli governments that have been colonizing the occupied territories have used similar methods: bribery, deceit, and intimidation of the Arab owners. The end, now as then, in the eyes of most Zionists, sanctified the means.

No less important than aliyah and settlement was the concept of organization in Ben Gurion's pragmatic Zionism. Borrowing from the Russian Bolsheviks, Ben Gurion and his comrades strove for the centralization and organization of every aspect of Jewish life in Palestine. For Ben Gurion and his followers, it was Russian political culture in general, and Bolshevik culture, that shaped their world view and their political attitudes.

Ben Gurion and his supporters wanted to rally the whole Israeli society under the flag and to mobilize it for building a nation from scratch—all of this while engaged in a national struggle with the Arabs. In the process they set up organizations that penetrated the interior of the entire Jewish society. These organizations were the foundation for bureaucratic intervention in the private lives of Israeli citizens. It is these aspects of the Ben-Gurionist brand of socialism that still get under the skin of most Israelis.

Because of these pervasive bureaucratic constraints and complexities, Israeli citizens are burdened with a long list of restrictive procedures. Israelis cannot travel abroad, like any other member of a western democracy, by simply getting a passport, driving to the airport, and boarding a plane. The Israeli citizen first needs to pay travel tax, obtain official permission from his army unit, and fill out no less than six different forms. In Israel, it is hard to arrange one's business over the telephone. Even when requesting very simple information, such as schedules and verifications, civil servants and officials expect you to turn up in person. When phoning a government office, if you're lucky enough to get through (usually all lines are busy or the clerk in question has just left the office), you will be told to come in personally. The phrase for this no-win situation is telech-tavo (go-come).

The big difference between the United States and Israel, when it comes to dealing with the authorities, is that in the United States it doesn't matter whether you get in touch by telephone or in person. In Israel, a personal appearance may really make a difference. A clerk might be impressed by your argument, style, or body language and bend the rules for you.

The centralist system in which the state intervenes in the life of the individual was founded on the Soviet model. While the twentieth century brought the West a strong adherence to individual freedom and enterprise, Russia maintained a strict collectivist view in which the authorities were allowed to intrude into every sphere of public and private life. The founders of Israeli socialism grafted this collectivist approach onto Israel.

In 1920, probably the most important Zionist organization was set up by Ben Gurion's labor movement: the Histadrut, the general association of workers in Eretz Israel. In some ways the Histadrut was really a general association of trade unions. The idea rested on the history of European trade unionism: to organize labor and to create—as a verse in the "Internationale," says—an "army of workers." Through the establishment of the Histadrut, Ben Gurion and his colleagues wanted to protect the Jewish laborers, who were in competition with the Arab labor force and, as a result, had difficulties finding jobs. The Arab workers were also convenient to work with: they were cheaper, more obliging, and better skilled.

But the Histadrut was not just an ordinary federation of trade unions. Leaders of the Histadrut saw one of its tasks as the realization of Marxist socialism: the proletariat should be the owner of the means of production. Thus, the Histadrut opened and operated its own factories, business firms, shipping companies, a bank, an insurance company, medical care facilities, construction firms, old people's homes, newspapers, and even security services providing bodyguards. The Histadrut had its own kindergartens, schools, and colleges. Parents who sent their children to schools run by Histadrut and the labor movement were making a serious choice and were shaping their children's political future. At an early age Israeli children are indoctrinated and identified with a particular political party.

In the beginning the Histadrut had a valid purpose. In practical terms, it made a huge contribution to the development and economic growth of the Jewish community and, later, the state of Israel. It gave many people a solid sense of stability and social security. The

Histadrut was always there to provide for the needs of all its members from cradle to grave—and, in return, the members were faithful and obedient. But this was achieved at a high cost. With the Histadrut, political patronage gained a foothold: loyal members could count on jobs under a system which has come to be called *proteksia*. In Yiddish it means "protection," but in Hebrew *proteksia* has come to mean "favoritism." In Israel, those well connected to the authorities and their relatives enjoy many privileges. This practice has taken root in Israel's everyday culture. For example, if you are on the waiting list to be linked up to the telephone company, it could take up to two or even five years before you receive a line. Knowing the right person at the telephone company could significantly shorten the delay. The waiting list for open-heart surgery can be as long as one year. Of course, if the patient or a friend knows the surgeon, then the surgery may take place immediately.

This imposed collectivization by the Histadrut and Labor governments, whose symbiotic relationship made them into powerful, inseparable entities, paved the way for a tremendous politicization of Israeli society. Hardly any aspect of Israeli life is untouched by politics. Thus, even sport clubs are politically affiliated, Hapoel (Hebrew for "the worker") with Labor, and Maccabees (named after the Jewish dynasty that took up arms against the Greek occupier) and Beytar (named after one of Likud's heroes and the last Jewish fortress in the rebellion against the Romans) with Likud.

Soccer games can be violently political. Club managers still have strong links with their respective political sponsors. Even though the players have no particular partisanship—they play for the money—the match is still something of a political event. Each time I go to a soccer match—and I still support Hapoel Tel Aviv, for sentimental reasons—I am stunned by the political hatred on the terraces. When Hapoel players come into the field they receive a shower of curses including cries of "Reds" or "Commies," as if they were agents of the Histadrut or the Labor party. Though most of the Israeli public has only a vague historical awareness, when it comes to soccer matches, it seems as if no time has passed since the old political skirmishes between Ben Gurion and his right-wing Jewish opponents.

Throughout its existence, the Histadrut took political advantage wherever it could. Its members would be transported by organization buses to demonstrations and strikes. All party affiliates were obliged to buy their working clothes in Histadrut shops and were made to subscribe, whether they liked it or not, to the Histadrut daily newspaper *Davar*. Many Israeli workers contemptuously call the paper *Pravda*—the mouthpiece of the Soviet Communist party.

I myself experienced, a few years ago, how well this imposed system worked and how the long arm of the Histadrut could invade the privacy of its members. When I began work as the diplomatic correspondent of *Davar*, management forced me to open an account at a bank owned by the Histadrut, even though I was perfectly happy with my old bank. I was told that this was the only way I could be paid my salary. Similarly, I had to switch from my old insurance plan to the Histadrut medical care system. Because I did not want to forgo the health care of the other company, I was forced, for the five years I stayed at *Davar*, to pay double insurance fees. All these "arrangements" are legal and accepted practice and make it impossible for an individual to complain.

Today the Histadrut is still the largest single employer in Israel and the country's biggest economic empire. The paradox is that the same organization is wearing two hats simultaneously: one socialist and one capitalist. While representing the workers, it also employs them. One arm of the same body fights for pay raises while the other arm wants a pay freeze due to losses.

Because of this inherent contradiction, the Histadrut is currently about to collapse. Many of its plants have gone bankrupt. In the process of selling the assets, large-scale corruption has been revealed. Words like *equality* ring empty when a worker in a Histadrut-owned chocolate factory earns a meager $500 per month, while his or her boss makes ten times as much and enjoys a large expense account, company car, telephone, and free use of credit cards for personal purposes. The Histadrut has the worst of both worlds: it suffers from the diseases of a decaying socialism and wears the greedy face of capitalism.

It's no wonder that the Israelis hold the Histadrut in low regard. Right-wing Israelis have mistakenly concluded that Ben Gurion was seriously striving for a socialist society along Soviet Communist

principles. They thought that Ben Gurion's priority was socialism
whereas, in fact, he was more interested in Jewish nationalism. For
him, the adoption of various symbols of socialism was just a
superficiality. He saw the Histadrut and the Labor movement only as
instruments for achieving his true goals: mobilizing society, building
the nation, and consolidating his power base. A early as 1923, in a
speech to the party, Ben Gurion had said: "Our main and overriding
concern has always been the conquest of the land and its building
through mass immigration. All the rest is niceties and rhetoric."

These words might explain the terrible ecological and environmental problems facing Israel. The seacoast is so polluted that a walk
along the shore leaves the soles of your feet coated with a thick layer
of tar. The ecological state of the entire Mediterranean is very bad,
but the situation in Israel is particularly dismaying because of the
low environmental awareness of the government. Most rivers in
Israel, including parts of the River Jordan, where according to
Christian tradition Jesus and John the Baptist carried out baptisms,
have turned into sewers. For decades the Yarkon River has been the
dumping place for the industries and homes of Tel Aviv.

The drive to be "practical," to build anywhere at any price, grew
into a modern Israeli obsession. Israel's state emblem should be a
bulldozer diverting a river or crushing rocky soil to build a new
settlement. The new Israelis are quite prepared to destroy old houses,
even if that includes the historic house in which Herzl stayed on the
night of his visit to Jerusalem or that of Brener, a famous author in
the Second Aliyah. The same disregard is evident in the tearing down
of residences owned by Palestinians suspected of terrorist activities.
Just as some people can be called trigger-happy, one might call the
new Israelis bulldozer-happy.

Historically, one of the most effective tools in conditioning the
Jewish community to accept the prevailing notions of practical
Zionism has been the youth movement. Every political party in Israel
runs its own youth organization. The Israeli youth movement was
put together from a mixed bag of ideas from foreign sources: some of
the romanticism of the German Wandervogel—the organization that
later produced many a leader of the Hitler Jugend—a good dose of
Baden Powell's English and American scouts, with their practical

efficiency, and Russian influence. Yet, despite its unoriginality, the youth movement grew into one of Israel's trademarks.

The Jewish philosopher Martin Buber said, at the end of the First World War, just before he emigrated from Germany to Israel, that youth was the eternal good fortune of mankind. In a sense, Zionism was the rite of spring and youth of the Jewish people. Zionism worshipped youth and viewed it as a value in its own right: young people are free of the yoke of the past—whether in terms of family background or social status—and are the best investment in the future.

The shared objective of all of the worldwide Jewish youth organizations since the thirties has been to carry the message of Zionism to diaspora youth and persuade them to immigrate to Palestine. Indeed, they became the most useful vehicle for converting young Jews to Zionism. Besides this, however, every organization had and still has its own internal aims and interests: to educate their membership according to the respective views of the political parties with which they are affiliated.

The youth movement grouped children from eight to eighteen, according to age. Members received uniforms, badges, and a place where they would meet once or twice per week after school. I myself joined one of them, or rather, my parents sent me when I was eight to Hashomer Hatzair, the Young Watchman, an organization on the left of Israel's Labor movement. By the time we emigrated to Israel, in 1957, my parents had grown averse to communist or socialist ideology. Yet for practical reasons they agreed to send me to this left-wing group. It was the first organization to approach my parents, and it offered them a free summer camp for their son. My parents, then penniless immigrants, also hoped that my participation would help smooth my absorption into Israeli society.

Hashomer Hatzair originated in the Austro-Hungarian Empire and was founded by students from assimilated, middle-class families. Later the movement established a stronghold in Poland. Its foremost aim was to bring young pioneers to Eretz Israel, but its founders had been deeply influenced by Marxism and revolutionary Bolshevism, whose ideas they tried to integrate into Zionism. Had there been no such movement, many young Jewish socialists would certainly have joined the non-Zionist revolutionary parties of Eastern Europe. Hashomer Hatzair offered them the opportunity to combine both. The result was a unique brand of Marxist Zionism, but at the same time, they also sought cultural and spiritual fulfillment. Together with Marx and Lenin, their intellectual heroes were Freud and Nietzsche.

The early meetings of the Shomrim (the name Hashomer Hatzair used for its members) were dominated by leaders whose intense personalities inspired a cultish following. They were obeyed like admired rabbis or political dictators. The early Shomrim talked about "confession," "happiness through self-fulfillment," "redemption of the soul," "vestal fires" and "contemplation." In his memoirs, David Horowitz, a former governor of the Bank of Israel, opened a window onto these events. He described the tense atmosphere, not only from ideological and political points of view, but also sexual. The vast majority of group members were male. For every ten or more men there were two or three women. "Men and women lived in tents," writes Dan Horowitz, "or sometimes made their bed in the open air. The Shomrim often went to remote locales in Eretz Israel where the climate was harsh, the work, in agriculture or road building, exhausting, and food poor. After a hard day's work, the group would meet for discussion that went on deep into the night. Their isolation turned these groups into monastic entities, into religious orders with a charismatic leader and their own set of symbols. Their ritual was that of public confession, the kind of confession that recalls the attempts of mystics to face both God and the Devil simultaneously."

Some of this atmosphere was still there when I joined the movement, forty years after Horowitz left. The activities were held in the local chapter of Hashomer Hatzair in my neighborhood, Ramat Aviv; such chapters were found all over Israel. We, the Shomrim, had very detailed instructions about what to do and what not to do. Indeed, the organization's ten commandments were another aspect of its secular religiousness. According to these principles, the Shomrim were supposed to be proud, honorable, and morally upright. The course for self-fulfillment stipulated that we should not smoke and should maintain our sexual purity.

We had long discussions—conducted by our group leader, usually three years our senior—about the meaning of life, world literature, Freudian psychoanalysis, and politics. We were also given sexual education. Providing this information fulfilled part of Hashomer Hatzair's aim to be progressive, but the explanations were sterile and "scientific." It was forbidden to discuss the pleasurable aspects of sex and love.

Alongside all this spirituality and intellectualization, Hashomer Hatzair was also very down to earth. Like the German Wandervogel, Hashomer Hatzair strove to renew Israeli Zionist youth through a romantic return to nature and the soil. Our meetings were often quite impressive. Ceremonies were accompanied by marches, bonfires, and flags under torch light. Regular meetings consisted of folksinging, hikes, campfires, and folkdancing.

Hashomer's special forte was the big hikes it organized a few times each year. Carrying our backpacks, we explored the country and came to love it. The daily trek covered ten to fifteen miles, and during breaks we cooked our own meals. At night we'd sit around the campfire and passionately sing sentimental songs. To this day, such sessions around the campfire are called "Komsitz," a linguistic hybridization of the German phrase for "come and sit." Most of these songs were Russian, and the words had been translated into Hebrew. And when there was no translation or we couldn't pronounce the words, we just sang "la la la." Of course, these songs had been imported by immigrants, but they are one of the rare examples in Israel of something which was improved on and came to surpass its original source. I may be biased, but it seems that Israeli choirs are often better performers of Russian revolutionary songs than are their Russian counterparts.

In fact, Russian music became so ingrained in Israeli society that people without any connection to that culture, even Oriental Jews, know and love these songs. Contemporary Israelis enjoy singing together. A new industry of evenings of communal singing is flourishing in luxury hotels, community centers, and private homes all over the country. Men and women, all dressed up, perfumed and bedecked with jewelry, pay to sing to the accompaniment of accordion or piano, lost in nostalgia for their days in the youth movement. This new ritual constitutes the final rather weak link between Zionism, Israel, and its revolutionary past.

This association is disturbing to the latest influx of Jewish immigrants, the Russians, who have unhappy memories of such revolutionary zeal. Israelis, they insist, should not celebrate cultural expressions that were also shared by their persecutors back in their old homeland. Yet Israelis have continued singing. I know many who admit they can be moved to tears by this music—and I'm one of them. I am not a communist but, probably as a result of my years in the youth movement, I am practically in tears whenever I hear the "Internationale."

Part of Hashomer Hatzair's political indoctrination was directed to winning us over to Marxism. After being fed strong doses of ideological rhetoric against Israel's right-wing parties, we concluded every ceremony by flying the blue and white flag of Israel as well as the red socialist one. Meanwhile we would sing our two anthems: the Israeli "Hatikva" and the "Internationale."

In hindsight, one may say that Zionist socialism, including the Histadrut and the youth movement, were in many cases used as a tool for mass delusion. Socialism for Ben Gurion was never intended to deny capitalism, but was to be used only to the extent that it served the national Zionist cause.

Through its organizational and economic powers, Labor succeeded in being, for more than forty years, the dominant political party in the Jewish community and Israel. Their organization enabled them to turn the Jewish community, in 1948, into a modern and relatively stable state: obtaining independence, while in continual conflict with the Arab neighbors, and steering the Jewish state between the narrow banks of Middle Eastern war and peace.

FOUR

Between War and Peace

THOUGH the issue of war and peace has often been called the "Arab problem" by Zionists, in reality, most of them did not see the Arabs as a problem at all. This state of affairs began with Herzl, who barely devoted any time or thought to the Arabs of Palestine and the Middle East. Like generations of Zionist leaders to come, Herzl tended to assume Palestine was a vacant land. While touring the country in 1898, Herzl seemed to encounter no one but his fellow Jewish people.

Most Zionist leaders lived under the illusion that the Arab majority of Palestine would welcome the returning Jews. They thought that the Arabs would enjoy "the blooming of the desert" and the western-style progress promised by the Jewish immigration. The Zionists failed to acknowledge the fact that the Arabs had their own national aspirations. It is disappointing to realize that the Zionists, who had put such faith in the power of ideas to bring about human and historic change, ignored the parallel aspiration of the Arabs.

In 1881–1882, at the same time the Lovers of Zion were engaging in their first clandestine meetings, secret Arab societies in pursuit of their own national revival were being founded in Beirut, Cairo, Damascus, and Baghdad.

The heart of the matter, or, if you wish, the heart of the tragedy of the Arab-Israeli conflict, is the almost simultaneous appearance, on the map of history, of two nationalist movements. Both movements, inspired by the rise of nineteenth-century nationalism and located in the same territory, were destined to combat each other.

And, indeed, that was exactly what happened. Even when the Zionist project had already begun, the heads of the Arab community in Palestine failed to understand the permanence or determination of Zionism; they still entertained the hope that what they were witnessing was merely Jewish pilgrimage, or maybe tourism. Only after the Balfour Declaration in 1917, in which the British government recognized the right of Jews to a "homeland" in Palestine, did the Arab majority fully understand the meaning of Jewish emigration. Three years after the Balfour Declaration, the Palestinian community openly showed their opposition to the Jewish colonization of the land.

In May 1921, rioting broke out in the city of Yafo. The Arabs, frustrated by the continuous stream of Jewish immigration, channeled their anger into protest marches and demonstrations, which disintegrated into a week-long orgy of looting and killing Jews in urban centers and on farms. The Arab reaction came as a shock to both the British authorities and the Jewish community. Still, the Jews held fast to their illusions: rather than seeing the violence as a nationalist outcry, they called them "incidents," "disturbances," and even "pograms."

The 1921 riots were repeated in 1929 and 1936 in a more organized and threatening scale. Yet the Jewish reaction was the same: a total failure to face the facts.

This disregard continued with each successive Israeli government. The refusal to admit the genuine national aspirations and the right to self-determination of the Palestinians has led both Labor and Likud governments to act as if the PLO doesn't exist. In fact, both parties literally avoid spelling out the name of the Palestine Liberation Organization and refer to it as "the so-called PLO," or more crudely as "the terrorist gang." The official Israeli term is not even "terrorist"; instead, there is a special Hebrew word, *mechablim*, which means "persons who engage in subversive activities."

This practice of denial is rooted in a deliberate effort to debase the Arabs—to create the impression that the struggle is not between two nations but, rather, between us, a nation, and them, a bunch of animals. A constant effort has been made to employ linguistic, rhetorical devices in support of the national struggle—which explains why war and battles are talked about in abstract terms. The Israelis usually "clear" the ground of Arabs or "purify" it. In these barely disguised calls to rid Israel of its Palestinian population, the language used is reminiscent of the American campaign, during its frontier days, to wipe out its own Native Americans.

Violent Arab opposition in 1921, 1929, and 1936 to the Zionist project was an embarrassment to the British rulers. Like a referee in a ball game they found themselves locked between the two rival national movements. Unlike the Zionists, the British were able to admit to themselves the seriousness and the depth of the Arabs' resistance. As rulers of most of the Middle East they had to bear in mind other, wider interests, particularly the discovery of oil in the Arab world. As a result, the British changed their one-sided support for the Zionist cause to a more equally balanced policy. Such a shift purported to be a great disadvantage to both the Jewish community in Palestine and the Zionist movement.

Immediately, almost automatically, with every wave of Arab protest, the British responded by temporarily suspending Jewish immigration and, occasionally, by either limiting or completely banning Jewish land purchases. Eventually, the British authorities reached a decision that seemed sensible: when two sides quarrel over the same piece of land, let it be divided between them. In October 1936, a Royal Commission of Inquiry was appointed under Lord Robert Peel. After detailed hearings, the commission issued a plan to partition Palestine-Eretz Israel into an Arab and a Jewish state, with a "mandate enclave" which would continue to be governed by the British. The zone the British would retain, for the sake of imperialism and Christianity, included the holy places of Jerusalem, Bethlehem, and Nazareth.

It was the first time in the bloody conflict between Jews and Arabs that the notion of partition was raised as a possible solution. And today, fifty-seven years later, it still remains the only viable, concrete, and sensible way out of the vicious cycle of violence. But since it was a compromise, and as is often the fate of compromise, neither side took it. On the Palestinian side, rejection was almost universal among the Arabs, extremists, and radicals. In the Jewish community the response was more complex. The right wing rejected the proposal because they perceived something systematic in the behavior of the British: repetitive withdrawals from the original promise and commitment as expressed in the Balfour Declaration. But Ben Gurion's mainstream Zionism reluctantly accepted the partition, and having full control over the Histadrut and all vital political, economic, and paramilitary institutions, it forced the decision on the Jewish community.

Ben Gurion, at a fairly early stage, reached the conclusion that it would be impossible to come to an agreement with the Arabs. This is not because he did not want it, but because he saw that Arab nationalism wouldn't have it. And from that moment in 1936, Ben Gurion and the Labor movement joined—though they would never have admitted as much—the simplistic attitude of the Zionist right. A popular "joke" from that time remains so today: "How do you see the Arab problem? Through the eye of a gun."

In 1936, Ben Gurion started to prepare himself and the Jewish community for the greatest challenge—which he was sure would come soon and would be military in nature. It was then that he developed the concept of "Zionist power," which stipulated that only immigration, colonization, and a powerful military force would ensure the survival of the Jewish community and provide the necessary tools for achieving independence. From that moment, Ben

Gurion gave less thought to the impact of the Arab position than he had previously.

Unlike the right wing, Ben Gurion thought that friction with the British should be reduced to a minimum; that is, only those issues which were absolutely vital to Zionism and to building the nation— aliyah and land purchase. The purpose of minimizing the friction and cooperating with British was to make it possible to reap the fringe benefits. During the three years of Arab rioting that began in 1936, some British officers helped to organize Jewish commando units. These units took part, under British command, in attacks against Arab villages to push back the uprising and later provide the illegal Jewish force (the Labor-controlled Hagana, defense) with much-needed experience in night warfare. Israel's special forces of today evolved from this small British-sponsored units.

Indeed, without the Second World War and the Holocaust there might have been no Jewish state. Israel, arising from the ashes, became one of the first and most important results of the new postwar order. The Holocaust, a stain on the western world's Christian conscience, brought most nations and the two super-powers, the United States and the Soviet Union, to recognize the right of the Jewish people to a state of their own. The British were among forty-seven other countries in the United Nations who were in favor of partitioning Palestine into two states. But Palestinian leaders remained faithful to their all-or-nothing policy and rejected the partition proposal. Ben Gurion and his followers, for the second time in twelve years, decided to accept partition. With characteristic brinkmanship and daring to risk civil war, Ben Gurion tried to impose his authority and will over the small but threatening Jewish right; faithful to their own ideology of a Greater Israel, the right still rejected the United Nations solution. When the right protested, Ben Gurion did not hesitate to use his loyal military units to crush the opposition and enforce his will.

The United Nations vote was transmitted to Palestine in a live broadcast on November 29, 1947. Most of the Jewish citizens of Tel Aviv poured out into the streets to celebrate as the results of the historic vote were coming through. But for Ben Gurion, November 29, 1947 was a worrisome night. He knew chaos was rapidly approaching. At first the fighting militias of the two enemy communities tried to gain control of the main roads, junctions, and strategic positions.

The real battle, however, started about six months after the vote. On May 14, 1948, the last day of the British mandate, which had lasted approximately thirty years, Ben Gurion announced the birth of the state of Israel. On that very day, when he read Israel's Declaration of Independence, the Arab states, as Ben Gurion had expected, declared war on the newborn Jewish state and invaded Palestine.

Both Arabs and Zionists have constructed myths and legends about the 1948 war and its outcome. Most of the time these stories bear little relation to fact. Official Israeli historiography, for instance, compares the war with the biblical victory of the diminuitive David over Goliath. Arab historians, on the other hand, refer to it as "the calamity of 1948" and tend to blame the outcome on the entire world rather than on themselves.

The truth is that this was no ordinary military campaign. It was not a simple clash between armed forces exchanging blows until one army or the other won. The war took place on several political fronts, and the fighting was repeatedly interrupted and punctuated by ceasefires arranged by outsiders, mainly the United Nations. Officially, the war lasted eight months, from the Arab invasion of the fledgling state to the signing of armistice agreements by Israelis and Arabs. The real fighting lasted barely two months.

The Arab armies, with a combined population of some forty million behind them, had the obvious numerical advantage. They were also much better equipped than the Israelis. But Israeli forces, representing only six hundred thousand Jews in all, had the advantage of unity, cohesion, and will power as well as what could be called modern sophistication. Israeli commanders were more inventive and daring; they were much better at deploying their limited resources. Despite their political and ideological divisions, the Israelis were fortunate to have only one military command. The Arabs were divided into various national forces under the command of jealous and suspicious generals, who usually shared a common language, but who were far from having an agreed-upon strategy. Israel's strategists knew how to take advantage of this situation: they employed the old Roman tactic of "divide and rule."

King Abdullah of Jordan, who wished to control the sectors of Jerusalem having Muslim holy places, saw the Jews as a powerful force to combine with and share his goal: to weaken the rise of Palestinian nationalism. Abdullah met secretly with Zionist leaders and with them he formed an unholy alliance which climaxed in the war of 1948.

The Jordanian army was the strongest, best equipped, and most disciplined force among the Arab armies and militias that invaded Palestine in May 1948. However, while most of the Arab armies genuinely intended to help their Palestinian brethren fight against the Jews, King Abdullah had a different agenda: to take over the land designated to become the Palestinian state.

This is precisely the kind of information that is never discussed in Israeli schoolrooms. A realistic explanation of what happened during the war would destroy the myth; in reality it was not a war between David and Goliath. Indeed, King Abdullah, intending not to pose a serious threat to Israel, instructed his army to exercise self-restraint in the battles. In fact, he made his army keep the level of violence to a minimum.

Since the Israeli public never knew about these behind-the-scenes moves, which were being carried out in total secrecy, the outcome of the war was, for them, tantamount to a miracle. Six hundred thousand Israelis heroically stood up against the power of forty million Arabs and prevailed. As a result of all these factors, the war ended in a major victory for the Jewish forces. The invading armies were repelled, and the Arab nations were coerced into signing armistice agreements.

The most important of postwar myths concerns the Palestinian refugees—the real losers of the war. In the months between December 1947 and September 1949, nearly seven hundred thousand Palestinians lost their homes. The refugee problem was to become the most poisonous issue in the relations between Israel and its Arab neighbors, and it has been troubling the Middle East for five decades.

The basic viewpoint of the Arabs is that the Jews turned the Palestinians into homeless refugees by expelling them. This, they contend, was deliberate and carefully orchestrated. It is true that there have always been those in Israel—including top Labor movement figures—who believed that there should be a systematic expulsion of the Palestinian population. But their position was never officially accepted. This view is woefully aided by the presence today of Israeli political parties that openly call for the expulsion of Palestinians. Such parties have managed to gain seats in the Knesset (Israeli Parliament) and were even recently represented in the cabinet by a minister. For many years Arab propaganda has used this argument, which depicts Zionism as an expansionist movement, to deny Israel's right to exist. Israeli propaganda, on the other hand, has been claiming to this very day that the Palestinians left of their own free will after Arab leaders ordered them to temporarily abandon their homes and villages.

The intention of the Israeli propaganda is to preserve the image of Israel as an irrefutably just and moral society. As long as emotion and propaganda rule the day, and the archives remain locked, it is difficult to get to the roots of the problem of the Palestinian refugees. Only in recent years, now that some of the dust has settled, have a number of Israeli archives been opened to public scrutiny. It is now possible to reveal the historical truth behind this painful episode.

I believe that the problem of the Palestinian refugees is a direct outcome of the 1948 war but was not the planned result of either Arab or Jewish decision making. Answering the question of how this critical problem began involves a synthesis of the two contradictory accounts.

There were indeed cases where Arab leaders called for people to leave their villages and towns, with the promise that they would return home soon, after a speedy victory. But mostly the local Arabs left their homes on their own initiative because they were afraid of what was awaiting them under Jewish rule. It should be noted that during the 1948 war, almost the entire country was one large front, and almost every Jewish and Arab town or village was turned into a military stronghold. The Palestinians left their villages in the heat of battle, under pressure by the Israeli army. In big towns like Yafo and

Haifa, the first Palestinians to escape were the wealthy and well educated. Their departure had a profound psychological effect on those who remained behind, bereft of their ruling elite. And so the Palestinian exodus developed like an infectious disease, spreading from house to house, family to family, street to street.

But some Palestinians were indeed chased from their homes when their villages and towns were captured by the Israeli army. Israeli officers, either on their own initiative or occasionally on orders from higher up, turned local Palestinians out of their homes. Again, there was no clear and deliberate policy about such matters. In fact, sometimes, officers on the site made contradictory decisions; one officer might order the villagers to leave their homes, while another would proceed to help the villagers return to their homes. There were some instances of the use of psychological warfare: Israelis spread the rumor that if the Palestinians did not run, then they would be murdered and their wives and daughters raped.

Atrocities were committed, including massacres, murder, rape, and looting by Israeli soldiers. I myself heard such an account from Arik Nechamkin. At the time of our meeting, Nechamkin, a Labor member, was Israel's minister of agriculture. He was a typical farmer: tough, simple, open, and direct. In the 1948 war Nechamkin had served as the commander of a special unit and had witnessed, in a village of the Negev desert, the murder of a dozen Arab civilians who had been captured after their village was taken over by the Israeli army. Their hands were tied, they were shot in cold blood, and their bodies were thrown into the local well. Many of these small battles were fierce and brutal and did not gain the kind of attention that the more notorious massacres received.

Nowadays, everyone traveling on the highway from Tel Aviv to Jerusalem can view high-rise buildings that form a backdrop to a pleasant residential area. In 1948, the area was home to an Arab village called Deir Yassin. In April of that year, about a month before the invasion of the allied Arab forces, and at the apex of the fight between the Jewish and Palestinian militias, the village was entered by Israeli fighters. Hundreds of villagers, women and children among them, were murdered.

The massacre at Deir Yassin is perhaps the event that most

graphically describes the Israeli-Palestinian conflict, an event that epitomizes it at its most bitter. It is the darkest chapter of Zionist and Israeli history. The debate over the circumstances of the massacre, whether between Israeli and Arab historians or between Israeli Left and Right, is always charged. Not only are its consequences disputed, but even basic facts such as the number of people killed, or who gave the orders to kill and why, remain unresolved. To this day Arabs use the massacre at Deir Yassin to support their arguments for the existence of a secret Jewish policy to systematically force them to desert their land and destroy them. The Israelis counter that they had warned the inhabitants in advance to leave the village but that they had refused and died in the ensuing battle.

For many years Ben Gurion and the Israeli government were ashamed of what happened in Deir Yassin. However, in retrospect, even Ben Gurion and his people were not really sorry about the consequences of the massacre. The Deir Yassin killings became a watershed in the battle between Jews and Palestinians and was responsible for the subsequent "flight psychosis": the Palestinian exodus.

In 1947–1949 the Palestinians lost their country. Parts of it were captured by three different armies: the Gaza Strip by the Egyptians; the West Bank (according to the tacit understanding between King Abdullah and Ben Gurion) by the Jordanians; and the rest by Israel. Israel's success in the war, and the territories it gained and annexed as a result, gave it breathing space, self-confidence, and a sense of superiority.

From 1948 onward, the rules of the game in the Middle East changed. The Arabs refuse to take responsibility for the results that followed from their firm rejection of Israel's right to exist and of the Jews' right to self-determination. There developed a repetitive pattern in Arab-Israeli interaction: the Arabs always lagged behind events. To begin with, the Arabs rejected the compromises offered by international negotiators. The Israelis' response to these compromises was consent, albeit the consent was quite possibly tactical. Thus the Arabs missed the first opportunity. When they were finally ready to accept the initial proposal, it became the Israelis' turn to refuse. "Now it is too late," the Israelis would say, pointing out that the rules of the game had changed. In refusing, the Israelis declined to play along with the Arabs, and by rejecting any attempt to reverse the situation they opted to remain trapped in the same problem. The Israelis preferred to live in limbo, to remain suspended between peace and war.

Israeli propaganda maintained for years that it was the Arabs who did not want peace and who rejected Israel's proffered hand. However, declassified documents from Israeli and American national archives have recently revealed a more complex picture. During the first years after the War of Independence, secret meetings took place between Israeli and Arab leaders. Contrary to the prevailing notion that the two sides did not talk to each other, there was, in fact, no single Arab leader to whom the Israelis could not gain clandestine access. Israeli diplomats continued to meet and convey messages to King Abdullah of Jordan, Colonel Zaim of Syria, and to Palestinian leaders in exile. These Arab leaders expressed general interest and preliminary readiness to reach an accommodation with the Israelis. In return for signed public agreements, the Palestinians demanded concessions from Israel. King Abdullah wanted territorial adjustments to the borders between Israel and Jordan.

The Syrian leader, Colonel Zaim, offered to meet face-to-face with Ben Gurion in order to conclude a peace treaty. In return he demanded that Israel would agree to grant him sovereignty over half of the Sea of Galilee. Zaim's proposal is reflected in Ben Gurion's diary, from 16 April 1949: "The Syrians offered a separate peace treaty with Israel," he wrote, "a cooperation and a joint army, but they want border changes...." Ben Gurion declined. In 1949 Palestinian leaders hinted that they would settle for the return to their homes, now occupied by Israel, of only one hundred thousand refugees. The Arab position was supported by the United Nations and the American and British governments.

Then as today, Israel was split into two main camps: doves, or moderates, and hawks, or extremists. The doves thought that Israel must make certain compromises, if only to reduce friction with the Arab world. But Ben Gurion, with his hawkish position, had the upper hand in the internal Israeli debate.

Ben Gurion, as Israel's first prime minister, believed that the Arabs were asking too high a price. They had lost the war and yet were setting conditions and making demands. He did not want to cede territories. He thought Israel should under no circumstances give up its sovereignty over the Sea of Galilee since it was Israel's main source of water and a sine qua non in the arid Middle East. But more than anything, Ben Gurion did not want to hear of the return of Palestinian refugees. He was seriously worried that a return of even one refugee would set a precedent: more refugees would follow and demand also to return to their homes.

According to a study conducted at the West Bank's Bir Zeit University, 450 Arab villages and towns were taken over by Israeli forces during the 1948 war. Many villages were completely demolished. But many of them, too, still had houses in good condition. In the midst of the war Israeli soldiers looted Palestinian homes and businesses; the villages and towns became Israeli government property. Soon government officials were traveling extensively from one village to another to survey them. They changed Arab names to similarly sounding Hebrew ones, in a symbolic act of confiscation and appropriation. There were instances where the Arab name of a village was actually based on its ancient Biblical name, enabling the renamers to feel that all they were doing, in fact, was restoring property to its rightful owners.

The deserted and conquered villages were repopulated with Jewish immigrants. Today it is almost impossible to recognize these Arab villages. Israeli bulldozers left their marks and rebuilt them to look like typical Israeli urban neighborhoods or rural communities. Our neighborhood, Ramat Aviv, was erected on the ruins of a prosperous Arab village called Sheikh Munes and its orange groves. When my family moved there in 1958, building was already at an advanced stage, but among the new houses and the streets, you could still see parts of the orchards and the old village houses, which were by then inhabited mainly by Jewish immigrants. Over the years most of these buildings have been demolished. Where these spacious, architectually interesting residences once stood is now the modern campus of Tel Aviv University.

To Ben Gurion and Israel's ruling circles the logic was very clear: The Arabs had lost a war that they themselves had initiated;

therefore, they had to take responsibility for their deeds and their crimes. Their punishment was to yield their lost property: fields, homes, and the land that had originally been allocated to them. This seized property was given to Jewish immigrants—victims of anti-Semitism, persecution, and the Holocaust, who were now, after nearly two thousand years of exile and diaspora, returning to their ancient homeland.

The Arab minority in Israel that did not take flight and was not driven away during and after the war enjoyed, according to the Declaration of Independence, equal rights and freedom. Israel's Arabs were and still are eligible to vote and be elected to the Knesset. But in all of their villages and in their two towns (including Nazareth, Jesus' hometown) military administration was imposed, and their freedom of expression and movement was restricted. It was not the kind of brutal occupation later known by the Palestinians after the conquest of the West Bank and Gaza Strip in 1967. Yet the methods were quite similar. The military administration operated on a system of incentives and punishments based on a huge network of informers and collaborators. An Israeli Arab might qualify as a teacher only if he and his respective family agreed to cooperate with Israel's prying domestic security service.

Arab land was confiscated, and the Israeli authorities deliberately slowed down the pace of technological advance. The unconcealed intention was to maintain the Arab population as an agrarian, nonindustrialized society. Even when, in 1966, military rule was lifted, the Arab sector practically remained third-class citizens, preceded by the Sephardis, and then the Ashkenazis.

The conditions of the Palestinians across the border were even worse. The Arab countries kept them in refugee camps turned shantytowns and used their image in the propaganda war against Israel. The Arab governments of Syria, Egypt, and Lebanon made no efforts to improve the standards of living of their Palestinian brethren. Only Jordan treated them well.

The Palestinian organizations and Arab governments refused to come to terms with Israel's existence and time and again called for the annihilation of the "Zionist entity." Naively ignoring historical reality, they omitted Israel's name from their maps—printing instead politically derogatory names such as "The Tel Aviv Gang" or "The Zionist Fascists." The typical Arab caricature of an Israeli Jew portrayed a black-clad, long-nosed, sexually and financially greedy creature. This image was similar to the one featured in Nazi propaganda.

The Palestinians spearheaded military assaults against Israeli positions along its borders with Syria, Lebanon, Jordan, and Egypt. The four surrounding Arab countries organized local Palestinian infiltrators and guerrillas who were sent across the border to steal from farmers, plant mines, disrupt daily life, and attack army strongholds and patrols. Israel retaliated with all its military power on each such occasion. It held the respective Arab government responsible for every infiltration, every cow or chicken stolen, and hit back with harsh, often disproportionate punishments. Such retaliatory policy only added fuel to the Middle East conflagration and escalated the tension.

When, in 1962, a group of Israeli women soldiers on a trip in the Galilee mistakenly crossed the Lebanese border and were caught, Ben Gurion sent out an extremely threatening message: unless they were returned forthwith, Israel would open hostilities. This was, of course, the arrogant reaction of a government impressed by its own power and convinced, according to the saying, that "muscle power is the only language the Arabs understand."

In June 1963, Ben Gurion resigned in anger over disputes about domestic politics. At the time the issues seemed to involve life and death. Looking back on the episode now, it all seems quite trivial—certainly not so grave as to cause the premier to slam the door behind him.

Within two years of his resignation, Ben Gurion left the Labor party altogether and formed his own splinter group. He was then in his late seventies, and while he still had many followers, his political judgment was increasingly being questioned. Many Israelis felt that his recent behavior compromised the actions of his youth. Though the Labor party experienced some trauma in seeing itself fatherless, bereft of its "big daddy," it did manage to recover. Ben Gurion's position was given to Levi Eshkol, who belonged to a second generation of leaders, those who had lived all of their political life in the shadow of Ben Gurion.

Eshkol was a man of moderation, and he governed by policies of concession. He did not like arguments and discussions. He became the subject of many jokes. The one that probably best reflected his nature went as follows: When asked whether he would prefer tea or coffee, he would hesitate, think and think, and finally answer, "You know what? Make it half and half." He was a sweet-tempered man. He had a wonderful sense of humor, especially when he was speaking Yiddish. (Eshkol belonged to a rapidly declining generation of leaders who still spoke Yiddish.)

But the very traits that suited him in peaceful times—pragmatism, a conciliatory tone, and realpolitik—and made him a likable prime minister, worked against him at this critical juncture. Anyone with eyes in his head could see from 1963 onward that the countdown to war had begun. Yet when the war finally broke out in 1967, everyone was surprised. In response to the hit-and-run attacks and infiltrations by Palestinians, Israeli leaders began voicing unusually sharp threats against the Syrians. The Syrians, believing that Israel was not bluffing and really meant to go to war with them, turned to their patron, the Soviet Union. To deter the Israeli "aggressors," the Soviets alerted the Egyptians, who in turn marched their strong army in broad daylight into the demilitarized Sinai peninsula. Egypt had no real intention of declaring war on Israel—it meant only to frighten its enemy—but in moving their forces they had broken an agreement and left Israel no option but to mobilize its army. This tragic sequence of errors and misconceptions reminds one of Europe's descent into the First World War. As soon as Israel responded to the Egyptian move with mobilization, the Jordanians followed suit—in the name of Pan-Arabic solidarity and brotherhood.

And in this way, in May 1967, Arab armies found themselves joining fronts against Israel, and against their will. Each of the Arab armies and their political leadership were wrapped up in its own illusions. The Arabs imagined they were being given the opportunity to take their revenge and destroy Israel: their leaders were carried away by their own propaganda. The masses were called out into the streets shouting their nationalist slogan: "In blood and fire will we redeem you, Palestine." Leaders and commentators announced, via the radio and in newsreels, that occupied Palestine would be liberated and the Jews driven into the Mediterranean. The victorious Arabs would rape the women and seize the Israelis' possessions. In the absence of television, Israelis watched film newsreels showing fanatical Arab crowds screaming and shouting. They saw Arabs with their hands closed around their throats—a gesture whose symbolic meaning was not lost on the Israeli public.

Israel's sense of security and self-confidence was very fragile. Its very existence, during those three weeks leading up to the war, seemed to totter. The memory of Auschwitz returned. The Arabs were perceived as the new Nazis who were seeking to destroy the Jewish people, to finish off what the Germans had begun. Many Israelis saw themselves as a reincarnation of the ghetto Jews of Eastern Europe, surrounded by bloodthirsty enemies on the eve of a pogrom.

In early June, Eshkol eventually gave into public pressure and handed over the Ministry of Defense to General Moshe Dayan. In an attempt to raise the national morale and to boost a sense of national unity, Eshkol also introduced representatives of the right-wing opposition into his cabinet. Thus, after nineteen isolated years on the political periphery, Menachem Begin, the leader of the right-wing block, became a minister in the Israeli government. Eshkol and Labor helped to cleanse and legitimize their political archrivals. Thus a precedent was set. Using Eshkol's decision as a proof of their ability to govern, Begin and his party would, a decade later, persuade the Israeli public to allow them to run the country.

Three days after the formation of the national unity government, on the morning of June 5, 1967, Israel's armed forces went to war. The war ended six days later in a tremendous Israeli victory. From Egypt Israel captured the Gaza Strip and the Sinai peninsula, including the eastern bank of the Suez Canal. From Jordan it took the West Bank and East Jerusalem; from Syria, the Golan Heights. For this victory, Israel was greatly indebted to its premier and former defense minister Levi Eshkol. But the glory went to General Dayan.

Those six days in June brought about a complete alteration in

Israel's mood, from anxiety to euphoria. There was a great sense of relief. The victory was received by many Israelis as the working of Divine Providence, a sign that the Jewish state was protected by the Jewish God. From the highest rank to the lowest, Israel glorified its army.

But as the adoration of the army increased, so did the scorn the Israelis felt for the Arabs. The press depicted them as technologically primitive, culturally inferior, and miserable. Every possible joke was made about their uselessness. Some of the jokes about Eshkol that had been used before the war were now recycled to make fun of the Arabs' "stupid" generals and leaders. The movies (at that time, Israel did not have television) reran pictures of thousands of humiliated Arab POWs, sitting somewhere in the desert, next to burnt tanks and vehicles, barefoot, with their hands tied behind their heads.

To this national euphoria, with its compound of Israeli arrogance and condescension toward the Arabs, new dimensions were added: religious mysticism and messianic zealotry.

Eretz Israel had been captured, in its entirety, by Israel. What had been intended to become a Palestinian state in 1947, and what, after the 1948 war, had been divided among Israel, Jordan, and Egypt, now had fallen into Israel's hands. Israelis rushed to the villages and towns of the West Bank and Gaza Strip—driven by curiosity about the enemy and by the desire to explore a new place.

Only a few days after the war, more than two hundred thousand Israelis—nearly ten percent of the total population—flooded, like a raging river, to the Western Temple Wall in Jerusalem's Old City, which had been under Jordanian rule since 1948. They wanted to see the holy wall for themselves and touch its stones. So great were the masses of pilgrims that houses belonging to Palestinians were razed overnight in order to allow them access. From that day forth, Israelis began worshipping at the Wailing Wall in a way that has become increasingly kitsch and grotesque—particularly when bar mitzvah ceremonies are held on the adjacent square by affluent American Jews.

A month after the war, Eshkol's cabinet annexed East Jerusalem—despite international protest—and began, in defiance of international law, intensive construction in the Arab parts of the city.

Israel has never been unduly bothered by the fact that not one nation in the world, including its major ally the United States, recognized its annexation of Arab Jerusalem. More than any other place or issue, Jerusalem has become the sacred cow of Israel's politicians, as if it weren't, in the end, merely a city—a beautiful, fascinating, special, and historically interesting one, but still, just a city. The stones from which Jerusalem is built are, in the eyes of many Israelis, perhaps even more important than peace and human life.

The Palestinians in the occupied territories were in shock. They feared that the occupying forces would now inflict upon them what Arab leaders, before the war, had promised to do to the Jews. The Palestinians were viewed like animals in the zoo, to be visited and gazed at by Israeli tourists. Then curiosity was replaced by patronization and authoritarianism. After all, the territories were not alien to the Israelis. Nineteen years earlier, when the land was still under British rule, Jews visited these areas and even lived in them. They had learned about the places at school and knew their Biblical names. The West Bank of the Jordan River was to be referred to by its Hebrew origins—Judea and Samaria—from which the two ancient Israelite kingdoms emerged three thousand years ago. Soon Palestinians felt their whole lives were in the hands of the Israelis, who under the broad and ambiguous terms of the military administration could punish them, confiscate their land, and inflict injustice.

In the midst of the war and a few days after it was over, there had been sporadic incidents in which Palestinians were expelled. Israeli soldiers put them on buses or walked them to the destroyed bridges of the Jordan River and forced them to cross the shallow water to the Jordanian kingdom. As in 1948, it was neither a centrally planned scheme nor a well executed one. Nevertheless, more than a hundred thousand Palestinians were forcibly transferred and became refugees. They came mainly from Kalkiliya, a small and dreary town fifteen miles northeast of Tel Aviv, and from the suburbs of the ancient city of Jericho. Later some of the Palestinians were allowed to return and rebuild their homes.

The events of the weeks and months immediately following the war join the long list of missed opportunities for peace in the Arab-Israeli conflict. As soon as the war was over, Prime Minister Eshkol set up a team of experts and instructed them to determine the mood of the Palestinians in the territories. The team toured the West Bank and Gaza Strip and came to the conclusion that the Palestinians were still recovering from the shock of being newly exposed to the Israelis after a break of about nineteen years but that they were ready to consider some kind of agreement with Israel. The team proposed that Israel should initiate Palestinian autonomy in the territories—a Palestinian entity not far short of an independent state. They also suggested Israeli initiatives to rehabilitate the Palestinian refugee camps.

But Eshkol, as usual, could not make up his mind. Dayan was of the opinion that time was on Israel's side and that it was better to sit and do nothing. Dayan passed the buck to the Arab side and told officials that he would be awaiting their telephone call to talk peace. The solution offered by the Israeli government was "territorial compromise." Israel would withdraw from most of the territories, except Jerusalem, and retain only areas vital to its security in return for a full pledge of peace. However, the Arabs, hurt and humiliated by another defeat, refused to talk with Israel. Instead, they embarked on an arms race, supported by the Soviet Union. The equipment Israel had destroyed in the war was replaced with even more sophisticated weapons. At their August 1967 summit meeting in Khartoum, the capital of Sudan, the Arab states declared their famous three noes: no peace with Israel, no recognition of Israel, and no negotiations.

Officially, Israel's policy was that the territories, except annexed Jerusalem, were held as bond. Once a peace treaty was signed, Israel would withdraw and give back the land to the Arabs. As always, new dynamics emerged as a result of the political stagnation. The idea, an old-time favorite of mainstream Zionism, was to create a fait accompli that would quietly erode the official position. In the middle of the night, groups and individuals stealthily began to erect settlements, ostensibly against the government's policy. Jewish settlers moved into the Golan Heights, adventurers went looking for oil and other natural resources in the Sinai desert, and religious fanatics built settlements on the West Bank under false pretenses.

An example is the settlement in the Arab town of Hebron, the burial site of the Patriarchs. In April 1968, a group of Orthodox Israelis with clearly messianic tendencies rented some rooms in a local Arab-run hotel. They promised to return home after the Passover holiday, but they did not keep their promise: they took up residence in the hotel. Next, with the tacit assent of the Israeli government, they moved into the local police station; finally, they were given some land by the government. They thus succeeded in setting up a Jewish neighborhood next to Arab Hebron. Today this neighborhood is the second largest Jewish settlement on the West Bank and houses seven thousand Jews who have no intention of ever leaving the place, not even in return for peace. Recently, they have settled within the densely populated heart of Hebron.

Eshkol's government did not make serious attempts to remove the illegal settlers. Initially they and their activities were ignored. But not much time went by before the settlers actually began to receive financial aid from the government in the form of "humanitarian support." They received electricity and water, but soon enough roads were laid, houses were built, and kindergartens were opened. Within a few months, Jewish communities were sprouting in the occupied territories. Thus a credibility gap was opened. While the Labor government rejected the annexation of the territories and talked about trading most of the land for peace, in practice it lent a hand to the process of creeping annexation.

The Left and the liberal-minded opposed the euphoric nationalistic tendencies. Their objections were both moral and pragmatic. One of the most emphatic of those who swam against the current was the philosopher Yeshayahu Leibovitz. This octogenarian professor at the Hebrew University in Jerusalem cannot be easily branded a typical, secular left-winger. He actually wears the traditional skullcap and calls himself a religious man. It is precisely because of this that he opposed and still continues to oppose the Israeli presence in the territories. When Leibovitz witnessed the rush on the Wailing Wall soon after the '67 war, he did not hesitate to call it pagan idolatry: a phenomenon that flagrantly contradicted Jewish spirituality and its ethos. He referred to this phenomenon as "the Wailing Wall disco" and argued that eventually Israel would become a brutal occupying force. Leibovitz predicted that Israel would turn into a police state, in which security forces and the police would cooperate in oppressing the Palestinians. He suggested a voluntary withdrawal from the territories and freedom to the local inhabitants to determine their fate. There had been demonstrations and graffiti calling "for an end to the occupation," but in the reigning euphoric mood, Leibovitz's words, the writings on the wall, and the demonstrations were like the voices of solitary heretics. They were not taken seriously by the majority of Israelis.

Today, with hindsight, it is obvious that Leibovitz and the other minority voices were right. The sweet victory of 1967 turned sour. Since then Israel has become inextricable enmeshed. The issue of the territories has made Israel a divided society.

On the seventh day, the day following the Six-Day War, a national discussion erupted about how one should refer to the territories. For Leibovitz and his supporters it was occupied land. Officially, the Labor government called them "administered territories," but many people actually felt that the territories were liberated and that the land, the biblical land of the Patriarchs, had always belonged to the Jewish people. Until 1967, it was clear to all Israelis that they were living as citizens in the state of Israel. Nowadays, most Israelis, even those who object to the continued Israeli presence on the West Bank and in the Gaza Strip, use the term *Eretz Israel* so frequently that, if you remark that officially they still live in the state of Israel and that the name has not been changed, they would not know what you are talking about. Over the past quarter century, the territories, though never officially annexed, have become an inseparable part of Israeli culture, language, and consciousness. It is hard to believe that almost an entire nation could be struck blind. The madness of territory worship has attacked a whole nation. Israelis had found, once again, a golden calf and did not hesitate to start dancing around it.

Some Arab leaders—most recently Saddam Hussein—argue that one of the walls in the Knesset is adorned with a map that expresses the true aspirations of Israel. This map, they claim, is of greater Israel, whose borders include not just the occupied territories but areas spreading from the Euphrates River in Iraq to the Egyptian Nile. There is no such map, and the walls of the Knesset are bare, except for one large portrait of Herzl. But many Arabs believe there

exists a map that diagrams Israel's long-standing expansionist intentions. They are convinced that Israel's grip on the territories is part of
an old secret program of expansion. This conspiratorial argument is
connected to the repeated Arab insistence that Israel, during and
after the 1948 war, planned the expulsion of Palestinians from their
homes. The argument was unfounded then as it is now. As in 1948,
Israeli policies in 1967 were determined by the conjuncture and the
exploitation of opportunities as they occurred. This, rather than
sinister designs, is the real characteristic of Zionism throughout its
hundred years of existence.

What is interesting to note is that it was under the rule of the
socialist leadership, not the right-wing Likud, that Israel set off on
the track of territory worship. It might be argued that Eshkol and his
colleagues felt guilty about the decades in which, in their effort to
build up the state, they enforced secular Zionism as a form of
religion. The adoration of the territories served them as a nostalgic,
sentimental reminder of the true religious life at home, in the
diaspora, which they had tried for so long to suppress.

Israel has become a one-dimensional society. Beginning in June
1967, all the previously regular issues on the national agenda became
marginal and gave way to the one big issue of the territories. This
obsessive preoccupation with the territories has swallowed most of
the other topics that once concerned Israel. It is as if the country has
no other worries, such as its economy, social problems, health,
education, absorption of immigrants, and so on. In this respect, the
Six-Day War constituted a watershed. Israel's first nineteen years
form a chapter in its history that is totally different from the twenty-
five that followed.

Changing the Guard

MAY 17, 1977, at 11 P.M., Israeli television aired its election forecast declaring that the opposition Likud bloc was winning the elections and that Menachem Begin, its undisputed leader, would form the next government. That night, tears were shed in many Israeli households: tears of surprise at the conclusion of twenty-nine years of Labor hegemony. There were also tears of apprehension. People were not merely afraid of the unknown—they were truly frightened of what the Likud might have in store. Their real anxiety—the product of decades of relentless indoctrination—was that the election of Begin would mean war. That was how his Labor rivals had consistently depicted him: a warmonger. I remember the reactions of my family, seated in front of our television set, as the election results came through: the disbelieving silence, the first shock, followed immediately by anger, fear, and anxiety.

A few elderly statesmen of the Labor party refused that night to stick by the rules of the democratic game. They announced on television that the Israeli public should not accept the results—that these results did not indicate that the government should be replaced

but that the people had lost their senses. The Labor leadership, with typical arrogance, even as their power was crumbling before their eyes, could not let go of their belief that they were above the people and the state. Labor had always been sure that it *was* the state.

But Labor's greatest fear was that the Likud would now try to undermine Labor's economic empire: the factories, kibbutzim, banks, trade companies, construction firms—everything the party and its giant trade union, the Histadrut, had accumulated over more than fifty years. Behind the publicly expressed dismay, there were rumblings in the Labor party about plans to take the properties and wealth underground and hide them from the Likud's covetous eyes.

The panic and fear were understandable: both Likud and Begin were alien, and Israeli mainstream society had felt at ease under Labor rule. Even so, the Likud's ascent to power should not have come as such a complete surprise. It was a natural evolution over almost ten years.

When Levi Eshkol died in February 1969, Labor found itself entangled in one of the internal rows so characteristic of it during the sixties. It was difficult for the party to appoint a successor. Moshe Dayan was the candidate with the best chances to be chosen for the party leadership and consequently as premier, but the party's old guard did not want him. They feared his unpredictability; they felt uneasy in his company. They came from the Jewish shtetls of Eastern Europe while he was a sabra, born and raised in Eretz Israel. Eshkol himself had called Dayan, only half jokingly, "the highwayman." Dayan had no strong party commitments; he was his own man. The older party members suspected he would act on his own initiative, unmindful of the Bolshevik ethos that still predominantly guided them. As a compromise the choice fell to Golda Meir.

They couldn't have made a stranger decision. Meir, at the time, was an ailing and aging woman in her late sixties. She was suffering from cancer and undergoing radiation therapy. In the United States and in other western democracies, it is common practice to make public the medical record of a country's leader. In Israel, according to an older, conspiratorial, political tradition, the truth about such matters was well hidden. And so—as was the case with the private

lives of many other public figures of her generation—Golda Meir's disease was shrouded in secrecy. In order to achieve this, the premier was smuggled into the hospital for treatments in a little old car belonging to one of her aides.

Golda Meir had a long and interesting personal and political history, both dominated by her service in the Labor movement and markedly socialist inclinations. She rigidly maintained the movement's code of obedience and, accordingly, moved ahead in her career. She conducted secret negotiations with King Abdullah in 1947–1948 before the war. She was also Israel's first ambassador to the Soviet Union and served in several of Ben Gurion's cabinets in various capacities, including minister of foreign affairs. Though she was emotional enough to shed a tear on occasion, she also enjoyed the reputation of being tough and proud. King Abdullah went as far as to blame her for his decision to join the 1948 Arab war against Israel. He told his Israeli contact that, had it not been for Golda Meir and her headstrong attitude, the confrontation could have been avoided. The king was a happy man on the day, in 1949, when he was told that Golda Meir had been dispatched to represent Israel in Moscow. "Keep her there!" he remarked.

When the party decided, in 1969, to make Golda its leader, even though she had already left politics because of her age and poor health, the prevailing assumption was that it would be for only a short period of time, with Golda functioning as a sort of caretaker until Labor could unite around a commonly accepted candidate. Only shortly before Golda was called forth from political oblivion, she had scored no higher than three percent in a public opinion poll asking who the public wanted as the next prime minister. Despite this, the Israeli public loved and adored her. Six years had passed since Ben Gurion had resigned from the premiership, and now the orphaned Israelis could find comfort for the loss of their "Big Daddy" in a "Strong Mommy." The public seemed to melt in her presence. Even the awful troublemaker Dayan became a pussycat when Golda Meir was around. She was for most Israelis and diaspora Jews the archetypal Jewish mother. Broadway even staged a play about her, starring Ingrid Bergman. Golda fussed over her bodyguards, telling them to put on their raincoats when it started raining, and brought them into her home to feed them hot soup. She liked to sit in her kitchen discussing issues and events with her fellow ministers over a glass of tea and cake. These discussions came to be known as "Golda's kitchen talks," and they often took the place of more formal cabinet meetings.

Golda Meir was not an intellectual. To judge by her speeches, her vocabulary was limited: her sentences were plain and short, and the metaphors and images she used were predictable. In most of her public appearances she returned to the Jewish ghetto as her point of reference. In 1973, following her audience with the pope in the Vatican, she proudly recounted how, during the entire hour of their meeting, she had looked him straight in the eye while telling him of her childhood experience of the pogroms. To her this encounter served as poetic justice: a meeting between the deputy of the "pogromists" and herself, emissary of the Jewish victims. Once she even went so far as to suggest, with the arrogance that Labor typically displayed toward the Sephardis, that those who had not experienced the Eastern European ghetto could not be good Jews. Her impatience with the Oriental Jews showed again, on another occasion, when a group of young Sephardis, in an attempt to gain attention, called themselves—in American style—the "Black Panthers." "They're not nice," she said about the young people who were fighting for equal rights for Israel's Sephardis.

Golda approached the Arabs with a similar self-righteousness. "There is no Palestinian people," she stated in 1970. Her period in office, spanning the end of the 1960s and the early 1970s, was conspicuous for its complacency. Euphoria from the Six-Day War continued to reign.

In the summer of 1970, a new president, Anwar Sadat, was appointed in Egypt. He announced that he was prepared to make peace with Israel in return for the Sinai peninsula but that if this did not work he would not hesitate to go to war, even if it meant the sacrifice of "a million soldiers." Golda Meir lacked the sensitivity to understand that this was a new point of view: No more rhetoric about destroying Israel and chasing the Jews into the sea, but a real readiness to reach a settlement on the part of the leader of the most powerful of Israel's enemies. In Golda's reductive world view—where the Arabs, like the goyim (Gentiles), were nothing but Jew haters who wanted to harm them—there were no nuances, no shadings between black and white. Golda accepted the basic assumption of her minister of defense, Moshe Dayan, that "our situation has never been better."

Following this line, Golda, Dayan, and the entire Labor government rejected a number of peace initiatives from Arab leaders such as Jordan's King Hussein as well as from some international middlemen. They stuck with the status quo. What the Israeli leadership wanted was a full-blown peace for a partial withdrawal. King Hussein, in his secret meetings with Golda and Dayan, was demanding just the opposite: a total withdrawal for a partial peace. And so several more opportunities for peace were missed.

In this atmosphere, sanctioned by their leadership, all the Israelis wanted was "bread and circuses." After 1967 the Israeli empire resembled the ancient, crumbling Roman Empire. Bread there was in abundance through a steady increase in the standard of living— thanks to the generous support of the United States and cheap Arab labor imported from the territories. For games there were society parties.

It was during this period that Israelis started celebrating the New Year—not the Jewish calendrical Rosh Hoshanah but the New Year of Pope Gregory. Perhaps this happened because the Jewish calendar mostly commemorates gloomy events in Jewish history. Perhaps, too, it gave the Israelis a sense of belonging to the Western world. Paradoxically, the Jewish state is one of the rare places where the Christian New Year is still referred to by its original name of "Silvester Night," after a Christian saint. The most glittering parties in Tel Aviv of the early 1970s had as their theme "The Sadat Joke Parade." Almost an entire nation was having a laugh at Sadat's declarations. They were convinced he was bluffing. Soon he would show them that he was quite serious and meant business. Unfortunately, the Israelis only realized this after they had paid a heavy toll of thousands of dead and injured young men.

When Sadat finally understood that the Israelis were making light of his attempts to come to a peace settlement, he decided to engage in one of history's great acts of deception—ranking with the Japanese

attack on Pearl Harbor and the Nazi invasion of the USSR in the
Second World War. Together with Syrian president Hafaz Assad,
Sadat designed a simultaneous and coordinated attack against Israeli
lines and positions along the Suez Canal and in the Golan Heights.
The date they chose was October 6, 1973, coinciding with Yom
Kippur, the holiest day on the Jewish calendar. And indeed, the
Israelis, self-confidently, complacently, and arrogantly believing that
the Arabs were weak and backward, were taken by surprise.

In fact, during the first days of the war the attack proved worse
than a surprise: the country was in a state of shock, hysteria, and
panic. The swift advance of the Arab armies, cutting through Israeli
lines as if they were butter, completely shattered Dayan's confidence.
On the third day of the war he thought that the end of the state of
Israel had come. He spoke in apocalyptic terms of the "destruction
of the Third Temple"—the first by Babylonians; the second by
Romans; and now the third by Arabs. In 1973, after six years,
Dayan's mood and that of the entire country had changed radically.
In 1967, euphoria had set in—now there was defeatism and gloom.

The Israeli government's response was extreme: its nuclear
weapons system was put on alert for the first time. The decision to
build a nuclear reactor and to manufacture nuclear arms was a by-
product of the Holocaust. However, this decision, initiated by Ben
Gurion in the mid-1950s, was by far the most important development in the history of modern Israel and the Jewish people.

The discussion of Israel's nuclear affairs is taboo. Ben Gurion and
his close advisers decided to equip the country with its own nuclear
capacity and, ever since, only a handful of decision-makers, top
scientists, and generals have been in on the secret. The subject has
never been officially discussed in public. For many years, even
cabinet ministers were unaware of the huge construction that was
taking place between 1958 and 1963 in the heart of the Negev desert,
halfway between Beersheba and the salty waters of the Dead Sea.
Dimona, a bleak development town inhabited mainly by Sephardi
immigrants, was selected to be the atomic site because of its
remoteness.

The secret project had its beginnings on October 22, 1956, at a private villa in the Paris suburb of Sèvres. In its most spacious room men gathered from three countries. They included the French prime minister and his top staff, the British foreign minister, and Israel's prime minister, David Ben Gurion, with some of his top aides. They were secretly planning a war that would be known in Israel as the Sinai Campaign, and worldwide as the Suez Crisis. A week after the meeting, Israeli paratroopers and ground forces landed in the Egyptian Sinai Desert and started moving toward the Suez Canal. In accordance with the Sèvres plot, France and Britain then issued an ultimatum instructing Israel and Egypt to freeze their forces several miles from the canal. As prearranged, Israel accepted—but Egypt refused. The French and the British thereupon used the refusal as an excuse to drop paratroopers into the canal zone and take over the strategic waterway. The Israeli army, meanwhile, had completed the conquest of the Sinai Desert in only four days. It appeared that the Sèvres conference objective had been achieved: the many months of military and intelligence planning and diplomatic coordination had borne fruit.

The French and British aim was to retake control of the Suez Canal, which, a few months prior to the outbreak of the crisis, had been nationalized by Egypt. They were concerned about the new spirit of Arab nationalism generated by the Egyptian leadership; their Middle Eastern interests, especially oil, had led them to decide to initiate a war that was supposed to topple the regime in Cairo.

Israel's declared aims, as publicly outlined by Ben Gurion, were to destroy Egypt's army, a force that was preparing itself for a "second round" against the Jewish state in order to seek revenge and restore the honor it had lost in 1948. As a military operation the Sinai Campaign was a success. As a political maneuver, however, it was a failure. While still celebrating its army's triumph, Israel, within a matter of weeks and under American pressure, had to hand back the Sinai peninsula to Egypt. Severe damage, however, had been done to Israel's image as a progressive, peace-seeking nation. The operation was considered an old-style imperialist war, and the world concluded that Israel had taken part in an ill-judged imperialist plot.

The hidden truth, however, is that Ben Gurion joined the three-tiered Suez conspiracy as a result of his burning desire to gain nuclear capacity. And indeed, promptly a year later, in October 1957, the French government reciprocated by providing Israel with a large nuclear reactor, technical assistance, materials, and manpower. This eventually enabled Israel to produce nuclear bombs and to become the sixth nation—after the United States, Soviet Union, France, Britain, and China—to join the prestigious nuclear club. Ben Gurion's dream had come true. Nuclear weapons, he believed, would make Israel an unrivaled force in the Middle East and would function as the ultimate guarantee of the Jewish state's continued existence. By way of justifying their desire to become a nuclear power, Ben Gurion and his associates called upon the Holocaust. This modern Jewish tragedy was their explanation, pretext, and term of reference in continuing, despite the difficulties and international pressure, the nuclear project.

The history of Dimona and its place in Israel's collective conscience consists of a fragile fabric of myth and taboo. It touches on our most secret fears, anxieties, and paranoias while the national pledge of concealment, backed by military censorship, shrouds the nuclear subject in a thick padding of silence. In spite of this secrecy, Israeli leaders found a way to tell their own people, the Arabs, and the rest of the world—as if with a knowing wink—that Israel's existence was "somehow" ensured.

The 1973 war with Egypt brought the first challenge to Israel's nuclear policy. The Jewish state was ready to use the weapon it had secretly made and hidden in the Dimona reactor. It was intended only as a doomsday weapon, a last act of suicidal defense. In the nick of time, however, the leadership concluded that, despite the critical situation, Israel could best its enemies by means of conventional warfare.

Golda Meir and some of the generals showed remarkable calm during this crisis, especially when compared to Dayan, who had lost his self-control. Suddenly Golda's controversial rigidity and strong will was in her favor. If, before the war, her inflexibility prevented any political settlement, it was this selfsame characteristic that enabled Israel to stand up to the Arab attack once the war broke out.

With hindsight we can say that the Yom Kippur War ended in a draw. From the military point of view, Syria and Egypt made only very limited gains. The Arab states, however, made one important political gain: They broke the stalemate and brought the Arab-Israeli conflict out of the freezer. President Sadat had intended to get the political process rolling by means of a military move, and in this he succeeded.

Unfortunately, as is often the case, political solutions are usually reached only after war. After the 1973 war, and through the diplomatic involvement of the United States, led by its dynamic secretary of state, Henry Kissinger, interim agreements between Israel and Egypt and Syria were reached. Israel began its retreat from the Sinai peninsula and the Golan Heights.

For years Israel had argued that the only language the Arabs understood was the language of force. But so, too, did the Arabs believe that they could subdue Israel with muscle power and surprise attacks. Israel's agreement, following the 1973 war, to move out of territories it had previously refused to leave, showed that its headstrong leadership, too, was able to listen and compromise. On the other hand, Israel was now able to argue that the Arabs had seemed to be reconciling themselves to their existence.

There was another important factor. When President Sadat said that 90 percent of the conflict was of a psychological nature, he was right. The Arabs had shown the world and proved to themselves that they were not the backward fools the Israelis had been making them out to be. The war shattered the myth of Israel's invincibility and returned to the Arabs the honor and pride they had lost in 1948 and 1967—something which put them in position to sit down and negotiate with Israel.

In Israel, too, a profound change took place. The public saw the inability of Israeli intelligence to anticipate Egypt and Syria's intentions as a failure. The Israelis, accustomed to thinking of themselves as invincible, were traumatized by the war and its many victims.

In a small and tightly knit society such as Israel's, twenty-seven hundred dead is akin to about two hundred thousand in the United States. Some Israelis, especially the younger generation, developed a cynical attitude. The many cemeteries, spread nationwide to accommodate the bodies, came to be called "youth towns." But the majority of the shaken population demanded explanations from its leadership. The excuses and pretexts that Golda and Dayan supplied did not quiet the wave of protest that washed over Israel that winter. Parents of dead soldiers protested opposite Dayan's home with banners carrying the simple indictment "Murderer." Golda, and especially Dayan, were seen as the architects of this terrible showdown and were forced to resign by April 1974. "The awful knowledge that I might perhaps have prevented this war," wrote Golda Meir in her memoirs, "will stay with me until the day I die."

Four years later she was dead. The change in the Israeli public's attitude toward Golda and Dayan was dramatic and sudden. In 1967 they were worshipped and admired; six years later they were both despised and humiliated. Israel—unlike both democratic and totalitarian nations—does not traditionally erect monuments in honor of its leaders and military celebrities. The biblical commandment "Thou shalt not make thee any graven image" may have something to do with that. But as a nation of quickly changing moods, Israel excels either in the abandonment of or in turning its backs on its rejected hero-leaders while they are still alive. Golda and Dayan had lived the experience of the ancient Roman saying, "Sic transit gloria mundi"—"Thus passes away the glory of the world."

It was in October 1973 that Labor really lost its hold on Israeli politics, though another three and a half years would pass until the transition became official. In Israel—maybe more than in most western democracies—actual political punishment often comes after a delay of some years. In the elections of December 1973 the party still managed to win and put together the next government. The Likud's rise to power in 1977 was a late response to the 1973 debacle. In between 1973 and 1977, before Begin and his people finally received a majority vote, a few additional nails were hammered into Labor's coffin.

Replacing Golda Meir and Dayan in the spring of 1974 was an ostensibly new group of politicians headed by ex-General Yitzhak

Rabin. At fifty-one years of age, he was relatively young and good-looking when he was selected for the premiership. A young prime minister was a novelty in Israeli politics, which had grown used to old leaders. Rabin represented the generation of sons of the founding fathers. In his personal history, too, Rabin represents the legendary sabra par excellence. He has a heavy accent and articulates his sentences in a very measured way. He fought against the British in the elite forces of the mainstream Labor-oriented underground and was the youngest colonel in the 1948 war. In 1967 he earned great praise as the chief of staff of Israel's armed forces. As a secret CIA psychological profile points out, Rabin is extremely introverted and detests the double-talk required by diplomacy. He was, nevertheless, appointed Israel's ambassador in Washington for the four years after the 1967 war.

Under Rabin's leadership Labor did not succeed in getting the traumatized people back on their feet, and his rivalry with Defense Minister Shimon Peres undermined his authority. Inflation rose from one high point to the next, and the country was plunged into a profound economic crisis. More than most, Rabin's government suffered from the corruption of some of the senior members. The climax of these incidents was reached when it was publicly revealed that Rabin and his wife illegally held $20,000 in a bank account in Washington. In the eyes of the Israelis the Labor party became a symbol of corruption, a sectarian organization that cared for itself and its members only, while neglecting the interests of the nation as a whole. If in the past both the party and the public had viewed each other and themselves as one united body, many Israelis were now changing their minds. Labor rapidly lost its power base, and in May 1977—the night of the general elections—the party was removed from power and replaced with Begin's Likud.

Menachem Begin was a rare bird in Israel's political aviary—his manner was different, and among the country's politicians he stood out as rather alien. He was born in Poland in 1913. As a young boy Begin had been deeply influenced by radical, "Revisionist" Zionism preached by Vladimir-Zeev Jabotinsky, his political and ideological mentor.

Jabotinsky, born in the port of Odessa in 1880, was the child prodigy of the Russian Zionist movement. After the First World War, Ben Gurion and Jabotinsky worked together in the Zionist movement as political advisers, fundraisers, and all-purpose propagandists. In 1923 their paths began to diverge. Jabotinsky's hope that the British would make it possible to immediately establish an independent Jewish state and army was thwarted. He became alienated from Ben Gurion's mainstream Zionism and founded a revisionist opposing force in the Zionist movement. Thus his own political organization became known as the Revisionist movement. It did not perceive itself, however, as a radical departure from traditional Zionism. On the contrary, Jabotinsky and his Revisionists believed they were the torchbearers, the true heirs of Herzl and his old political Zionism. It was not Zionism that needed to be revised, Jabotinsky felt—only its current policies.

Jabotinsky adored Italian Fascism and its leader Benito Mussolini. Revisionism established a brand of harsh, merciless Zionism, without sentiment or compromise. It is this ruthless form of Zionism that was expressed by the words and deeds of Menachem Begin and, later, by Yitzhak Shamir. Members of Jabotinsky's Revisionist movement attempted in the 1930s to emulate the political style and culture of the European right. As liberalism and democracy, in their eyes, were weak, they opted for being Jewish Fascists. Like their role models, the people in Jabotinsky's movement wore brown shirts, organized parades and demonstrations, and worshiped their leader. Some even argued that, had Hitler not been anti-Semitic, they would have supported his national-socialism.

From 1923 on, Jabotinsky perceived the conflict with the Arabs as a "zero sum game," in which every gain of the enemy was a loss for the Jews. The only solution was to be strong and combative. He believed that the Jewish state would only emerge through blood and fire. Convinced that this was a historical necessity, he called, during the 1930s, for taking Eretz Israel and conquering it in a bloody struggle. It was also Jabotinsky's conviction that only an "iron wall," erected by fearless Zionism, would break the Arab's will and allow the Jewish state to prevail in a hostile region.

There were other differences in mentality and style between Ben Gurion and Jabotinsky. Jabotinsky was a daydreamer, a romantic, and an adventurist ready to take risks. Ben Gurion was more down to earth; he was practical, more politically sober, and responsible.

From the mid-1930s, disagreements between the Revisionists and the Socialists grew bitter and violent. Each group did its best to disrupt the other's meetings and political gatherings; these occasions frequently culminated in physical scuffles. Jabotinsky said that Ben Gurion and his socialist colleagues were adhering to conciliatory policies and he accused them of ceding both to the British and to the Arabs. Jabotinsky believed in Greater Israel: Jews were entitled to the entire biblical land of Israel, including the territory east of the River Jordan. This area had been granted as a British imperial gift to King Abdallah's Hashemite dynasty in return for their help in the war against the Turks. This is where the Emirate of Transjordan was established in 1923, known today as Jordan and ruled by King Hussein.

Ben Gurion and his supporters reluctantly accepted the separation of Transjordan from mainland Palestine. Jabotinsky and his followers in modern Israel, including Begin, Shamir, and many Likud members, still think that the Kingdom of Jordan historically belongs to Israel.

In April 1937, Jabotinsky launched a military wing of his Revisionist movement and called it "Etzel," a Hebrew acronym for National Military Organization. This organization was known later as simply "Irgun" (organization). It attacked British soldiers and military installations and organized the illegal immigration of European Jews to Palestine. At the same time the members employed terrorist techniques, including killing innocent Arabs who were passing through Jewish quarters and throwing bombs on Arab buses and into Arab markets.

After Jabotinsky's death in 1940 and with the outbreak of the Second World War, Irgun military activities were suspended. They resumed in 1944. Menachem Begin was appointed political heir and commander of the Revisionist movement. During the war in 1942 Begin was arrested in Vilno, Lithuania, by Soviet agents and put into jail on charges of initiating Zionist propaganda. When he was released, he was allowed to enlist in the exiled Polish army. This British-sponsored army, after retreating from its German-occupied

homeland, moved into Russia and into Palestine. Many of the Jews in
the Polish army took the opportunity to defect and remain in Eretz
Israel, but Begin refused to do this. His dignity as a Polish soldier
wouldn't allow this. Only when he had officially left the Polish army
did Begin feel able to take command of the Irgun.

Mutual animosity between the two branches of Zionism grew
even worse after Jabotinsky's death and especially after the establishment of Israel.

For years Ben Gurion's aversion to Revisionists ran so deep that he
refused to call Menachem Begin by his name, referring to him
instead during parliamentary debates as "the man who is sitting next
to..." During the first decade of the state, the Labor-ruled government boycotted Begin's people and kept them out of public office.
They prohibited them from becoming teachers and educators in
order to protect their children's minds from being "poisoned." They
would not promote Begin's people in military service. Ben Gurion
and his socialist colleagues refused to accept them into Shabak,
Israel's FBI. The Labor movement did not hesitate to use the domestic
secret service for political aims. Intelligence agents were instructed,
in the early 1950s, to infiltrate Israel's political parties, especially
Begin's Herut (the "freedom party"), founded as a successor to the
Revisionist movement. In the early 1970s Herut was incorporated
into the newly formed Likud bloc.

Begin was a product of his time, political environment, and
personal experience. He was a fervent hater of Communism and the
Germans. He had lost all of his family in the Holocaust. The mass
destruction of the Jewish people became for him a torch that would
light the way to all his political decisions. Begin saw the Holocaust as
a continuous, ever-present threat. In almost every speech he made, he
mentioned the Holocaust. It became his anchor. Moreover, he
enlisted the "Holocaust heritage" as a political tool in his struggle
against Ben Gurion's ruling Labor government. This struggle had
reached a climax early on, in 1952, when Begin organized a large
protest demonstration in Jerusalem. The protest ended with the
stoning of the Knesset building in reaction to the government's
decision to accept German compensation payments. The incident

helped Begin to establish the Holocaust heritage as an alternative value system to Ben Gurion's unemotional style of realpolitik.

Similarly, Begin and the Likud, once they had come to power in May 1977, launched the notion of Eretz Israel as an alternative to Labor's idea of the state. It could be said that the notion of Eretz Israel came to replace, for Begin and the Likud, that of the Holocaust as a political weapon.

The truth is that it was rather easy for the Likud to do this. After all, since the '67 war, "Eretz Israel" had already partially been planted in the hearts and minds of Israelis by the previous Labor government. So Begin had only to pick up things where Labor had left them.

In July 1977, two months after winning the election, Begin went to Alon Moreh, on the West Bank, the first in a series of melodramatic moves that would become his trademark. Alon Moreh, according to the Bible, was Abraham's first stop in Canaan after he left Mesopotamia. There he built an altar to God. To the religious and the nationalists, Alon Moreh was and still is the cradle of the Jewish nation. In 1975 the Israelis had established a settlement there on land that was confiscated from local Palestinians. On this day in 1977, Begin joined the enthusiastic settlers in their dances and promised "many more Alon Morehs."

This was one of Begin's first statements to the world media: a symbolic gesture and a signal that his heart and his support were with the settlers. The Arabs and the rest of the world interpreted the message to mean that the Likud would never give up the West Bank. However, far from the television spotlights, Begin was sending different signals, too. Using the old and well established backdoor channels between Israel's secret service, the Mossad, and the Arab world, Begin exchanged secret messages with Egypt's president, Anwar Sadat. The task of conducting the secret negotiations was, surprisingly, assigned to Moshe Dayan. Begin lifted the political freeze imposed on the eye-patched general by the Israeli public for his role in the 1973 war.

Dayan, who was undaunted by the prospect of being seen as a turncoat within his own Labor party, became Begin's foreign minister. It was a golden opportunity for Dayan: through the peace negotiations he might repair his public image, which had been damaged by his role in the near disaster of the Yom Kippur War. Begin's choice of Dayan did not help his image much in his own party or among the Israeli people. It cast a doubtful light on whether Begin felt he or his party could really run the country. Apparently, Israel's new prime minister felt pressured by the "warmonger" propaganda that had been used against him. Begin decided to prove that he was a man of peace. He entrusted this job to the experienced Dayan because Dayan was still respected by the Arabs. Begin believed that Dayan, the sabra, would better know how to deal with them. And so it was: Dayan became Begin's peace subcontractor.

Begin's provocative remark about Alon Moreh at the outset of his prime ministership didn't really bother the Egyptian president. What Sadat wanted to know from other world leaders was whether Begin was a leader of honor who could be trusted to deliver the goods of peace. Dealing previously with what he perceived as Rabin's weak leadership had allowed Sadat to reach an interim agreement with Israel but not a full-fledged peace treaty. The answer Sadat received from around the world was a qualified yes. Thus began Dayan's secret negotiations with Sadat's advisers in the useful offices of the Moroccan king, Hassan II. Together they drew the rough sketch of a peace agreement.

During interviews on prime-time American television in November 1977, Sadat expressed his readiness to "go to the end of the world, including Jerusalem," in his efforts to seek peace. Begin immediately reciprocated and invited Sadat to speak in the Knesset; the Egyptian president accepted the offer.

In less than one week, Israel, Egypt, and the whole world got ready for the first official visit of an Arab leader to Israel. There had been earlier visits by Arab leaders, such as King Hussein of Jordan, but they had always been secret. That Saturday evening, November 17, 1977, all of Israel was glued to their television screens. Many of us wiped away tears as the Egyptian airplane touched down at Ben Gurion Airport and Sadat appeared, dressed, as always, in an impeccably tailored suit, and shook hands with his hitherto Israeli enemies. Among them were not only cabinet ministers but also opposition leaders, including an aging Golda Meir. All of them heard Sadat, who was no less moved, explain that "I am not bluffing. I want peace." There was a sense that history was being made here, as the whole world watched.

In their speeches at the Knesset, Begin and Sadat pledged "no more war" and "no more bloodshed"—the peace process was set into motion. An important factor in this, too, was the invaluable support of United States president Jimmy Carter, who became personally and emotionally involved in the negotiations. Inspired by his strong religious sentiments about the Holy Land and his genuine desire to make the world a better and safer place, it was Baptist Carter, more than any other person, who made the peace accords possible. For as long as the situation seemed critical, he intervened. At a certain stage he even brought Sadat, Begin, and their advisers to the presidential resort of Camp David, Maryland, for something that became a strange cross between group therapy and kindergarten, with Carter acting as both therapist and childminder. He coaxed, threatened, flattered, and forced them into reaching an agreement.

The historical peace between Israel and Egypt—the first official peace treaty between the Jewish state and any Arab nation—was signed in a large, colorful tent on the White House lawn and sealed with a widely televised, three-way handshake between Sadat, Begin, and Carter. It was more than a symbolic gesture: The three leaders really had been the architects of peace.

Fortunately, despite their differences—Begin, the contentious, nitpicking lawyer, and Sadat, a man unconcerned with the small details—the men had some things in common: their taste for drama and sense of history, and their desire for a place in history. The eight-page Camp David accords were extremely detailed, but it soon became clear that Begin and Sadat each understood them in his own way. Sadat thought that through the accords he would obtain United States financial assistance—which indeed he received—to help him improve his country's collapsing economy. Moreover, he got back all of the Sinai peninsula, in which Israel had invested, since 1967, twenty billion dollars in development, including oil fields and Red Sea diving resorts. At the same time, Sadat believed that he was building the foundation for a future agreement between Israel and the Palestinians. Begin, on the other hand, actually thought that he had made peace, separately, with the strongest and largest Arab nation. Begin hoped that by returning Sinai, Sadat would abandon the Palestinians and give him support in dealing with the West Bank and Gaza Strip. He felt able to return Sinai because, in his view, it was not part of the biblical notion of Greater Israel. Both Begin's and Sadat's expectations were misguided.

In the end, the peace accords, despite their historic and practical significance—they have held up for thirteen years now—were the result of mutual misconceptions by Sadat and Begin. President Sadat once remarked that "Begin regretted the peace treaty three hours after he signed it." It seemed that Begin, though not exactly sorry, was afraid of the consequences with regard to the Palestinian issue. The PLO rejected a proposal that it join the peace accords. The PLO claimed that autonomy would not satisfy them as it did not meet their aspiration for a state of their own. Abba Eban, Israel's best-known and most widely appreciated diplomat, once said that the Arabs, and the Palestinians in particular, never missed the opportunity to miss an opportunity.

The 1979 peace accords mentioned negotiations about Palestinian autonomy in the occupied territories as an interim solution for up to five years. After that time the Israelis and the Palestinians were to decide on the permanent status of Palestinian autonomy. Though it was Begin who had drafted the autonomy plan, now he began to worry about his new image. If initially he had been looking for peace in order—among other things—to prove to his rivals that they had misjudged him, that he was a changed man, now he felt the need to show his supporters that he had remained the same Begin. Many of Begin's most ardent supporters had been shocked to see Begin, the Arab-hater, going "soft" on the Arabs. Worst of all was that their admired leader had agreed to dismantle a dozen Jewish settlements in Sinai and to sacrifice thousands of settlers on the altar of peace. Suddenly, Begin found himself in conflict with many of his friends and allies. People who had been on his side over the decades now saw him as a "traitor" sowing the seeds for the establishment of a future Palestinian state. A few of his most dedicated associates even resigned from the cabinet and the Likud bloc, in 1979, in order to set up the new Renaissance party, which carried the torch of "rejectionism." Emotionally, the stress was unbearable for Begin. He decided to change directions before it became too late: he decided to forestall the process leading to Palestinian autonomy.

The main instrument for delay, in dealing with the Palestinian issue, was the establishment of as many Jewish settlements as possible in the Israeli territories. Begin decided to stand by the pledge he had made two years earlier, before he began the peace process, at Alon Moreh. His government began littering the West Bank with dozens of new settlements. New neighborhoods were purposely planted right in the middle of the densest Arab populations. It's no wonder that the Palestinians and the world at large saw the Israeli government's settlement policies as consciously intended to sabotage the peace process.

Begin's and, later, Shamir's plan was to make Israel's grip on the territories irreversible. The Likud's success in this matter has been considerable: Now that a Labor government is back in power, it will be difficult, if not impossible, for that government to come to a peace agreement on the basis of a territorial compromise that returns most of the West Bank to the Arabs. The truth is that Begin and the Likud transformed the area into a virtual patchwork in which Palestinian villages either live side by side with the settlers or are surrounded by them.

The man who conducted Begin's Jewish colonization project was General Ariel Sharon. Sharon is one of a line of senior army officers who joined the Likud in the early seventies. The fact that military men were joining the party, even before the Likud came to power, showed that it was gaining a firm foothold throughout Israeli society. In fact, Sharon can be viewed as one of the pillars of the Likud when it was formed in 1973 as a bloc of right-wing parties and groups. His failure to become chief of staff of the army led Sharon, furious, to resign about three months before the Yom Kippur War and further provoked him to organize the right-wing alliance.

When the war broke out, Sharon was drafted like any other reservist and came to be seen by the common soldier as one of its heroes. They called him "Arik, King of Israel," in contrast to the opinion of other generals, who believed he showed ill judgment and committed tactical mistakes. Sharon's presence, wherever he chooses to appear, always causes a stir.

Sharon, a sabra, was born to a farming family, in a rural community not far from Tel Aviv. He fought in the 1948 war, was injured and recovered, and had a long career in Israel's armed forces. As the commander of Israel's first special forces unit and the country's first paratroopers brigade, he gained a rather controversial reputation as a brave fighter. He has been known to walk a tightrope between following his superiors' orders and interpreting them in his own idiosyncratic way; he has been involved in some of Israel's most brutal battles against the Arabs. In 1953 he supervised retaliation against Arab infiltrators into Israeli territory who had caused the deaths of dozens of immigrants in border settlements. In one particularly controversial case Sharon's unit retaliated against a Jordanian village called Kibiyah. Sharon and his subordinates were supposed to take charge of a certain number of houses, empty them of their inhabitants, and blow them up. But the evacuation was carried out improperly, and some of the inhabitants stood their ground. Forty-nine of them died as the explosives went off. The world was shocked. Ben Gurion, depressed and anxious, resorted to lies when he explained that it had been the action of unauthorized "Jewish settlers"—refusing to admit the responsibility of the army and, therefore, of himself as defense minister.

This kind of misrepresentation had, in fact, been a characteristic strategy of the state's founding fathers. It suited them better to have the dirty work of vengeance, of punishing and intimidating the Arabs, carried out by young and enthusiastic people like Sharon, while they preserved their clean-handed, morally correct image.

Army officials as well as Labor politicians developed a dual attitude to Sharon: they simultaneously respected and feared him. When he left the military, some Labor politicians wanted him to join their ranks. Their attitude was like the one ascribed to President Lyndon B. Johnson: better have the bastard inside the tent pissing out than the other way around. They wanted Sharon on their side, or else, they feared, he would cause them trouble. But the opposition to

Sharon in the Labor camp had the upper hand, and he has not accepted.

When Begin formed his cabinet in 1977, he appointed Sharon minister of agriculture. Sharon, who owns a large and prosperous farm in the south of Israel, sees himself essentially as a farmer. He makes a point of stressing that he has always remained a Labor man, but that Labor itself had changed and moved away from its own credo.

Sharon had hoped to become defense minister, but Begin, too, was ambivalent about him. On the one hand, he called Sharon "the greatest general of the Jewish people since the Maccabees," who heroically fought against the Greeks more than two thousand years ago. On the other hand, he feared Sharon and did not like some of his traits, especially his boundless ambition. One of Begin's trusted ministers once revealed that the prime minister had expressed concern that if Sharon were in charge of the army as a defense minister, he would soon surround the prime minister's office with tanks and assume absolute power. Begin hastily explained that he'd really been joking—but few were fooled.

Sharon approached the business of building settlements like a military attack. Between the years of 1977 to 1981 he established one hundred settlements in the West Bank and Gaza Strip. Many of these communities were very small, numbering no more than ten or twenty families, but he caused the Jewish population in these areas to increase from about ten thousand to fifty thousand.

The system Begin and, later, Shamir used was simple: backed by government incentives and subsidies, cheap housing could be provided. These affordable new houses in the territories were especially in demand among young couples who came from the poor neighborhoods that were established in the 1950s. It's no wonder that many people began to support the activities of Begin, Shamir, and Sharon. As far as these new settlers were concerned, they had come full circle. Labor had sent them to appallingly poor areas, and the Likud was getting them out, giving them a golden opportunity to acquire a place of their own.

SIX

The Hidden Sephardi Revolution

IN 1964, three years before the Six-Day War, a significant change in the history of Israel had already occurred—but it went almost unnoticed. For the first time in Israel's history, the number of Sephardi Jews surpassed the number of Ashkenazi Jews. It was only a decade later, when Likud came to power, that the significance of this demographic change was fully understood. It was the Sephardi vote that eventually changed the balance of power, toppling the Labor government and putting Begin's Likud into the seat of government. To gain a better understanding of the impact that demographic and ethnic developments have had on Israel today, we must move away from the big-city bustle of Tel Aviv and from the power politics of Jerusalem to the enchanted, mountainous landscape of Galilee.

In the woodlands near Safed, the central district town of the Galilee region, there is a concentration of shrines. These sites are said to be the tombs of prominent Jewish rabbis who lived during the

Middle Ages and earlier, when the majority of the Jewish people were in exile. Many Jews of Sephardi extraction view these shrines as holy places. The convergence of so many "holy" sites around Safed is not surprising since the town bears a close connection with the history and development of the Kabbalah.

The Hebrew word *kabbalah* literally means "reception" but is also interpreted as "tradition." The key Kabbalist text is attributed to a Jewish scholar of the second century A.D., who lived near Safed—one of the four holy Jewish cities. While mainstream Jewish theology focuses on rationality, Kabbalah examines the world beyond reality and reason. Kabbalah is a kind of Jewish mysticism with the primary goal of learning to approach God intimately—to "feel" Him, rather than to merely understand Him.

As a by-product of this mysticism, believers attribute magical powers to the graves near Safed and regard those who are buried there as *tsadiks*, or saints. The notion of the tsadik originated in the eighteenth century among the Ashkenazi Jews of Eastern Europe, but it reached Sephardi communities as well, especially those in Morocco. The tsadik is a righteous person known to have conducted a morally pure life, to have helped the poor and simple people; he is believed to have healing powers.

Many of the tombs, for instance that of Rabbi Jonathan Ben Uziel, function as pilgrimage sites for thousands of women who wish to be married or to conceive. In addition to reciting prayers, worshipers also leave behind a piece of material torn from their scarves or light a candle on the grave. Prayer at the grave of a tsadik, it is believed, will mediate between God and his faithful.

The pilgrimage often turns into a noisy, colorful family event. Loud music blares from portable radios and tape recorders, and the air is thick with the gray smoke of barbecues. Sanitary conditions on these pilgrimages-turned-festivals are very basic. Vendors and peddlers sell food, drinks, pictures of the tsadik, music cassettes, and a plethora of trinkets used to ward off the evil eye.

Archaeologist Meir Ben Dov explains that holy grave worship is a late phenomenon in Judaism. Interest in, and a yearning for, holy shrines and rituals for the dead first emerged in the Middle Ages. The old biblical tradition was averse to such practices. It is no coincidence that, in the Bible, Moses' grave is unknown. Thus it was, according to religious explanations, impossible to eternalize the site, to worship it, or make it into the destination of pilgrimages.

Originally, the cult of the dead was a pagan ritual. It was adopted by Christianity and Islam. Early Christianity took great care to build its churches in Palestine at places associated with Christ, the Apostles, and his disciples. Most famous of all is the Church of the Holy Sepulchre, built in the fourth century A.D. in Jerusalem—on the spot where, according to tradition, Jesus was entombed.

In the seventh century, the Muslims invaded Palestine following the appearance of their prophet Mohammed. While adding new tombs of their own, they also sanctified old Christian ones believed to contain Muslim saints. For a long time, Judaism condemned such practices, regarding them as one of the marks of a decaying and inferior culture. As part of the effort to prevent cults of the dead, mainstream Judaism pronounced cemeteries impure places. Anyone who visited them was required to undergo ritual purification.

But Jewish tradition gradually began to change and imitate the customs of Christians and Muslims. The Muslim influence is especially visible in the tombs of the Galilee, which display a strong similarity to the design of Arab graves. Some of the tombs even bear Arabic inscriptions.

Mystic cults and expressions of mysticism are becoming so widespread throughout Israel that they exist in almost every Sephardi community. In the winter of 1991, a rabbi in a town in southern Israel traveled to Morocco to the tombs of his ancestors, where he dug up the dry bones of four bodies. He put them into an ordinary suitcase that he then smuggled successfully through Moroccan and French customs. He was not motivated by the tradition-cum-obsession of reburying the mortal remains of Jews: the rabbi believed that the four dead men had been tsadiks and he simply wanted to enjoy their proximity. In Israel the suitcase was lost, and the rabbi's whole world momentarily caved in. Only after extreme searches was the lost property found. The bones were reburied in his town, and since then the four "holy" graves have become a popular place of pilgrimage.

The modern Israeli fascination with mysticism, and the belief in magic, finds its most extraordinary and flamboyant expression further south, in Netivot. Going there is not just a fifty-mile car drive (from Tel Aviv), but a journey through a time machine: from the modern, vital twentieth-century city to the sleepy, poor development town in the Negev desert. Most of the town's inhabitants are religious and of Moroccan-Sephardi origin. Unemployment in Netivot reached twenty percent in 1992, nearly double the national average. There is a high rate of illiteracy among the town's twenty thousand inhabitants, and the number of high school students who successfully conclude their college entrance exams is less than fifteen percent—one of the lowest in the whole country.

Unfortunately, a place like Netivot is attractive to charlatans and other dubious characters who exploit the local population. In the early 1980s, "Baba Baruch" Abu Hatzera, a shrewd religious entrepreneur, anointed himself a "saint" and erected in the center of Netivot a complex serving as a shrine for pilgrimages. Prior to that day, "Baba Baruch" had been sentenced during the 1970s to three years in jail for fraud. Upon his release, the enterprising offender and past politician became a "born again" Jew. Using his family name— his father had been a celebrated religious authority in Morocco known as "Baba Sali"—Abu Hatzera declared himself his father's heir. Claiming that his father's sainthood was reincarnated in his body and soul, he raised money and succeeded in building a huge enterprise.

The court of Baba Baruch is more similar to an oriental palace than a synagogue. Run by Baba Baruch and a handful of relatives and assistants, the center in Netivot has flourished, becoming a multi-million-dollar industry. They sell "holy" tap water for the sick, superstition-proof cameos, posters, tapes, and other memorabilia celebrating the cult of Baba Baruch.

Once a year, in January, tens of thousands of people attend a special celebration in honor of Baba Sali. A mixture of pop concert and Middle Eastern bazaar, the feast has also become an attraction to politicians who cannot resist the opportunity to mingle with so many potential voters. Baba Baruch, the self-proclaimed crowned prince, will not correct you if you address him as Rabbi, although he has never actually been ordained. Indeed, the celebration has been so financially successful that it has become a major source of income for the town.

Baba Baruch's success has inspired many others to announce their own "sainthood," adding to a flourishing new Israeli industry of witches, astrologers, healers, clairvoyants and fortune-tellers. Some insist that their power is rooted in the Kabbalah. These charlatans promise solutions to a variety of human ills, from infertility to terminal diseases. Their fees can add up to hundreds of dollars.

The phenomenon became so widespread that, in 1991, Israel's IRS opened an investigation into the unstated earnings of these charlatans and swindlers. The police, too, have been brought in on a number of different accounts. For instance, one practitioner, claiming that he was gifted with healing powers, exploited the naïveté and ignorance of one of his female "patients" by raping her. Another was prosecuted for indecent behavior and other sex offenses. Still another ordered some teenage high school girls to put their menstrual blood in the water bottles of two boys; only by doing this, he persuaded them, could they make the boys love them.

Educated Israelis and the media ridicule this phenomenon and tend to view it as evidence of the gullibility of the desperate. Because most of the people who seek out such advice are of Sephardi origins, a certain prejudice about so-called Sephardi primitiveness and backwardness has developed. Belief in the supernatural, however, is certainly not the exclusive domain of Israel's Sephardi population. There are tens, if not hundreds, of thousands of Ashkenazi Jews who also foster such superstitions. In the case of Israel's oriental (Sephardi) Jews, the relatively sudden preoccupation with mysticism is interesting in light of its social and historical context.

Since the early 1950s, when Sephardi Jews first emigrated to Israel from Yemen, Iraq, and Morocco, Labor-party-sponsored-Ashkenazi-patronage resulted in the Sephardi being relegated to second-class citizenship. The Sephardi community was underrepresented in politics, business, and the army. Sephardi Jews earn less money: there are fewer Sephardis in managerial jobs than Ashkenazis, and more Sephardis work in low-paying jobs as manual laborers in construction, factories, and farms. Their children are less educated, and not surprisingly, a higher percentage of the country's criminals have come from Sephardi communities. Oriental music was for a long time banned from Israeli radio and television because producers felt it was "inferior" and part of a "subculture." In 1951, Ben Gurion said that Israeli society would be fully integrated only when a Sephardi became the army chief of staff. The clock is still ticking.

Most of the Sephardi immigrants arrived in Israel without their leaders. Their intellectual, elite professionals and businessmen—especially in the case of the Moroccan Jews—had preferred to emigrate to the West. In Paris and Montreal you can find the nameplates of physicians, lawyers, and accountants bearing traditional Jewish-Moroccan names. In Israel, on the other hand, for many years after the Moroccan aliyah was completed, these names very rarely appeared in medical directories, law offices, or among the business communities. Only recently, since the Sephardi revolution, has there been a perceptible change. Though the number of Sephardi doctors, lawyers, engineers, and journalists is still relatively small in Israel, it is on the increase.

In addition to losing their leaders, there is also the matter of pure prejudice and racism. The Ashkenazi hosts have clearly always felt superior to the Sephardis. I remember my own family's patronizing attitude toward our Iraqi neighbors. On the surface, relations were good: we greeted each other on the common staircase and smiled politely. But behind their backs we constantly commented on their ignorance and, as it seemed to us, their vulgarity. At one point their daughter was hospitalized. For a few days she hovered between life and death, but eventually she recovered. When she returned home, her family organized a noisy party on the common lawn of our apartment building. The women put their fingers in their mouths and ululated as an expression of their joy. They slaughtered a lamb to celebrate the occasion. Its blood dripped all over the stairs and its remains littered the lawn. My family watched from the window, in horror, as if we were witnessing a witches' sabbath. We were mesmerized. Rather than treating the event respectfully as a part of foreign custom, my family saw it as confirmation of the belief that our neighbors—and all Jews of oriental extraction—really belonged to an inferior culture. Now, after thirty years of neighborly coexistence, we have finally come to know and respect each other. The position of the Sephardis in Israel painfully shows how no one is exempt from being a potential racist, including those who have recently been the objects of racist aggression.

This negative attitude toward Sephardis has become deeply ingrained in Israeli society. Sephardis have been stigmatized, and racist stereotypes, accompanied by crude, insulting generalizations, have prevailed. "National characteristics" have been attributed to them, such as the idea that all Moroccans are "criminals." In 1949, Ben Gurion himself said that the Moroccan immigrants were "savages." In fact, their prononiciation of Hebrew has been called "guttural and Arab-sounding."

The early Israeli establishment intended to change the Sephardis to fit what they viewed as the Israeli way of life. The sabra was the ideal citizen whom all Israelis should emulate. The government's belief has always been that foreign cultures can be absorbed through modernization. Whoever does not cope with the modern pace of living is branded a failure. Within this ideology, nobody stopped to consider the enormous difficulties of integration experienced by those of massively different cultures, who were expected to bridge gaps of centuries in a matter of months.

The prevailing approach has been somewhat Bolshevik in nature. As the Soviets began to industrialize in 1917, the Russian peasants were hurled into the twentieth century. Similarly, when the Sephardi immigrants arrived in Israel, they were stripped of their spiritual luggage, their heritage. Traditional clothes were replaced with dreary khaki, which was very popular at the time and served as a kind of unofficial national uniform. Upon their arrival many immigrants discovered that their valuable items, like old books and jewelry, were "lost." Somehow most of these items eventually found their way to souvenir shops or collectors' shelves. When immigration officials had difficulty pronouncing a name, it was immediately changed to an "easier" one. This was done in the same manner, ironically, as East European bureaucrats had done it to the wandering Jews two or three hundred years earlier. A concerted effort was made to obliterate the Sephardi past.

Most of the Sephardi immigrants come from a religiously observant background. The secular authorities, attempting to wean them from their religious practices, would not accommodate their basic religious needs. Children were sent to secular schools; Yemenite boys' earlocks were shorn off.

One particular episode remains unresolved and still infuriates today's Yemenite community. Approximately 350 Yemenite infants unaccountably disappeared in Israel between 1949 and 1950. The babies, who were presumably taken to clinics all over the country, did not return from their "treatment," and their parents were told that they had died. Their places of burial were never revealed. Some community leaders insist that these children were sold for adoption by Israeli Ashkenazis and foreign families.

Even when some consideration for religious expression was shown, it was done condescendingly. The Ashkenazi religious organizations provided Sephardi immigrant children with a religious education, but in a manner that was no less coercive than the secular. The immigrants were forced, once again, to abandon their traditional clothes and customs—this time in the name of God, not the state. The Sephardi religious tradition was most often replaced by the Eastern European Ashkenazi tradition. Hence, today, you may come across a peculiar anomaly: Orthodox Sephardis dressed in black clothes and hats who speak Yiddish just as if they had emerged from a Polish ghetto.

Both religious and secular politicians have treated the immigrants as fodder for their political interests. Political agitators from all parties have tried to win the immigrants' votes through false promises and bribes. During the 1950s and 1960s several elections were riddled with such fraud.

Since the early 1950s, Israel has witnessed the emergence of "two nations"—one Sephardi and the other Ashkenazi. Because of the Ashkenazi dominance there was never any serious effort made to integrate the two communities. In fact, Ashkenazis usually refrained from intermarriage: marrying a son or daughter to a Sephardi mate was considered a real misalliance. New towns were set up that were ethnically "pure." New city areas were created for Sephardis, with entirely separate neighborhoods for Ashkenazis. Sephardis were often dispatched to agricultural settlements in harsh terrain and less affluent regions of the country, the mountainous areas near

Jerusalem and the sweltering, arid Negev Desert. The more fertile land of the coastal strip was reserved for Ashkenazis.

Only a small number of the Ashkenazi elite at that time tried to alert the leadership to the fury and the desire for revenge that such a paternalistic attitude would one day unleash. In 1949, David Horowitz, a senior treasury official who gave such fascinating testimony of the early pioneering life in the youth movement, was one of them. As early as 1949, he was writing that the new immigrants "form a kind of second nation, a nation in revolt who sees us as a plutocracy. Moreover, a special attitude towards them has developed—one of superiority from our side. In certain ways they are taking the place of the Arabs. This is inflammable material—great material for Mr. Begin and his party...." Horowitz's words contained the seeds of Israel's future. Why then, one might ask, were so many Israelis surprised, in May 1977, when Menachem Begin was selected prime minister with the overwhelming support of the Sephardi sector? Why are many Israelis still shocked today when they witness traditional Sephardi gatherings at Baba Baruch's court in Netivat or the renewed Sephardi interest in mysticism? Why are they taken aback at the rage and protest directed at the Ashkenazi establishment? Forty-three years ago, David Horowitz envisioned the potential results of a Sephardi suppression—their behavior today is simply a delayed reaction.

In this respect, the last fifteen years of Likud governments have gone a long way toward rehabilitating Israeli Sephardis. The Likud has restored their lost pride and honor and offered them equal economic, social, and political opportunities. While Labor, in its twenty-nine years of power, had only three cabinet ministers of Sephardi origins, the Likud chose five leaders out of twenty to represent the Sephardi sector in its last government.

Today, it is possible to see the emergence of a new social category: the Sephardi middle class or the "Sephardi bourgeoisie," as the author Amos Oz phrased it. There are first- and second-generation Israelis who have come up in the world and live comfortable lives. On the fringes of my own neighborhood new streets are being built. The new apartments are outrageously expensive, sometimes over half a million dollars, but there are plenty of buyers. Many of the new residents come from the poorer areas of Greater Tel Aviv, known for their large Sephardi populations. The newcomers and their children dress according to the latest fashion: they wear expensive clothes and sneakers, like Reeboks or Nikes, and drive posh cars. In the winter they visit fashionable ski resorts, and in the summer they visit the northern Italian lakes.

In terms of his domestic policy, Begin promised to "give the people a good deal": he reduced taxes and enabled the lower classes, mainly of Sephardi origins, to improve their standard of living. The prices of VCRs and TV sets came down by thirty percent, and more goods became readily available. Just like Wall Street during the Reagan era, the tiny Tel Aviv stock exchange was flourishing. Israeli speculators—like their rich American colleagues, albeit on a smaller scale—were having the time of their lives.

Likud governments introduced a free market policy, lowering taxes, encouraging economic initiatives, and selling state assets to the private sector. With nearly fifty billion dollars of American aid over the last fifteen years, Likud could credit itself, through successful diplomacy, with a significant rise in Israel's standard of living. The main beneficiary of these changes has been Israel's Sephardis.

Nevertheless, the Sephardis' rise on the economic and social ladder has not managed to eradicate their nagging sense of cultural injustice. They are constantly burdened by the feeling that Ashkenazis consider them culturally and socially inferior. They wear upon their hearts the scars of their parents' or their own traumatic experiences. Today, Sephardis are returning to their folklore and cultural roots. They are no longer shy about their special foods, music, and heritage. An inseparable part of the Sephardi tradition has been the way in which even those who are not leading a particularly Orthodox life express their religious feeling in almost every aspect of their everyday existence. By virtue of this, the Sephardi community has contributed to the rise of religious expression in Israel today. This kind of worship is in direct contrast with Ashkenazi-style Judaism, where the difference between Orthodox and nonreligious activity is quite distinct.

SEVEN

In God We Trust

C UT!" ordered the rabbi, and the undertakers swiftly obeyed. On a lovely spring day in April 1991, one of the most bizarre rituals in the history of Judaism was being performed. The undertakers had just removed the penile foreskin from a corpse.

It had all begun a day earlier, when Alexander Basov, an architect from what used to be the Soviet Union, and a new immigrant in Israel, had traveled to Tel Aviv with great anticipation. Basov, like most of his fellow immigrants, could not find a job. In Nahariyah, the small and sleepy coastal town where he lived, the job market was almost nonexistent. So he went to Tel Aviv. There, after a long search, he got lucky and found a job. But as the happy, thirty-four-year-old immigrant was crossing one of Tel Aviv's busy streets, he was hit by a car and killed. His body was taken to Nahariyah to be buried at the local cemetery.

In Israel each cemetery has a closed annex known as its "purification house." According to Jewish tradition, the corpse is undressed, cleansed with water, and covered with a shroud before it is put to rest. Unlike Christians, Jews are buried in the ground without a coffin. It fulfills the verse in Genesis: "Dust thou art, and unto dust shalt thou return."

Aesthetic simplicity is one of Judaism's characteristics. But Israeli-Jewish burials are sadly unaesthetic. All too often the undertakers are dressed in shabby clothes, leaving the mourners with the unpleasant feeling that they have just participated in an undignified ceremony. The secular Israelis, however, have no choice. The religious establishment has control of all the cemeteries, and of all other religious services, for that matter.

While Alexander Bosov's body was awaiting the purification rite, the undertakers discovered that he had not been circumcised. Taken aback, they felt that they could not possibly give him a Jewish burial in this "condition." Thus, they decided to perform a circumcision—the ancient ritual which every Jewish male child has to undergo at the age of eight days. This rite symbolizes his entry to the faith and the nation in accordance with, and in remembrance of, the bond between Abraham and his lord.

This macabre anecdote serves as just one reminder of the power of the religious and Orthodox circles. Indeed, Israel is one of the few countries in the Western world which maintains no real separation between church—or rather synagogue—and state. The strong presence of religion might give the impression that Israel has become a country, like Iran, which is controlled and run by fundamentalists. Though it is tempting to draw this analogy, it is too simplistic a view of Israel. Israel's present-day reality, where state and religion are tied up in a Gordian knot, is complex and requires an understanding of what came before. Moreover, the problem does not merely involve issues of society and the secular state on the one hand and religion on the other. It actually reaches back to profound questions, regarding Israelis and Jewish identity, concepts and definitions of nationalism, redemption, and statehood.

It would be inadequate, too, to blame only the alliance formed by Begin and the Likud with the religious parties for the emergence of this reality. Though it is obvious that this alliance between right wing and clerical politicians has been well preserved and that it has functioned quite harmoniously since 1977, as in other matters, here, too, the Likud can rightfully point to a precedent: It was Labor that laid the foundations for the special relations between secular Zionism and religion.

Toward the end of the nineteenth century, when Zionism began to emerge, it was considered a heretical movement, not only by the rabbis of the Eastern European shtetls, but also in Western Europe and the United States. Though Zionism was formulated for Jews by Jews, the majority of the religious establishment saw it as sinful. First, the Orthodox opposed any secular, modernizing influence. Moreover, the rabbis viewed Zionism as an unwelcome challenge to their leadership and authority, which aimed to replace Judaism with a modern and secular form of religion. Worst of all, in the eyes of rabbis, Zionism viewed itself as the Messiah.

One of the most salient differences between Christianity and Judaism concerns the issue of the messiah: Christians believe that Jesus Christ was their savior, whereas the Jews are still waiting for their redeemer to come. According to Jewish belief, the redeemer will only arrive when Divine Providence finds the conditions ripe. Such a decision could and would only be made in heaven, not on Earth by mere mortals. The Messiah is said to arrive "at the end of days." Thus, Jews throughout their history have hoped for his coming but have never really expected him. Jews both wanted him and feared him. So the Jewish notion of the Messiah was more metaphysical than corporeal: his role was to bring hope into their daily misery, to add a utopian and spiritual dimension to their constricted life in the diaspora.

Yet Jewish history contains occasional incidents where abstract hope strayed into temporary illusions of reality. The combination of a longing for Zion and a palpable despair among the Jewish people seemed to produce a series of self-appointed messiahs. This is, in fact, the way the Jews view Jesus. In the first century the revolt against the Roman Empire was also motivated by messianic fervor. In 1665, Shabtai Zvi, son of a rich merchant from Turkey, had a divine vision that led him to proclaim himself the Messiah. He experienced episodes of exaltation, hyperactivity, and ecstasy, which alternated with sudden lapses into deep gloom. A modern psychiatrist might have diagnosed him a manic-depressive, but it's likely he was merely a deluded charlatan and con man. To his followers, however, he appeared to be a gifted man with extraordinary powers. He captured the imagination of many Eastern European Jews and promised that he would restore the glory of the Jewish nation and lead the Jews back to the land of their forefathers. They readily welcomed him as the Messiah and gave him their money and jewelry; he, of course, cheated and let them down badly. In 1666, Turkey's sultanate court had Shabtai Zvi and his entourage arrested. Faced with the choice of death or conversion to Islam, Shabtai Zvi chose Mohammed. He donned a turban and changed his name to Mehmet Effendi Aziz and lived out his life on a government pension.

The conversion of Shabtai Zvi to Islam and, thus, the collapse of his movement deeply shocked Jews worldwide. It led them to develop a suspicion of any future would-be, self-proclaimed messiahs. At the end of the nineteenth century, Zionism, for the Orthodox establishment, was a mere repetition of the Shabtai Zvi debacle. It is true that the Zionist leadership was motivated by a keen rationalism, shorn of any of the mystical elements typical of messianism. But by concluding that only human intervention would redeem the Jewish people, and that they must no longer wait for divine action, the Zionists actually secularized the notion of the Messiah. They hijacked him for their own political-secular purposes and emptied the Messiah of his religious content. For the rabbis, this Zionist concept which claimed to know what God wanted was unforgivable. It had to be condemned and rejected.

The intensity of Orthodox opposition to Zionism, however, lessened over time. It is, indeed, possible to identify three major developments in the attitude of the religious Orthodox toward secular Zionism. To a great extent, these three tendencies have become an integral part of the complicated relationship between religion and Zionism and the state of Israel.

The first of these attitudes was ideological in its essence: the rejection of Zionism because of Zionism's interference with the divine scheme of redemption. This philosophy, and its followers, see Zionism and the state of Israel as an evil force that corrupts traditional Judaism. Today, however, this school of thought has been relegated to one religious camp in Israel. What is left of these followers can be found in one small Jerusalem neighborhood. Israelis watch it with curiosity, and foreigners visit it as a tourist attraction. The enclave is called "Mea Shearim" ("Hundred Gates") and it is inhabited by the ultra-Orthodox Jews known as Neturei Karta (guardians of the wall). The word *wall* has a double meaning: it refers to the walls of the city of Jerusalem, and, metaphorically, it represents the wall these people form as torchbearers of traditional Judaism. Wearing the long black clothes of ghetto Jews, they consider Zionism and the state of Israel as serious deviations. Their attitude toward Israel is: none of your honey, none of your sting; we don't want your services, and we owe you nothing. They refuse to pay their taxes and don't allow Jerusalem's trash collectors to enter their territory. They burn the Israeli flag and never join in the national anthem. Instead, they support the Arab demand for the "annihilation of the Zionist entity." During the Middle East peace conference held in Madrid in October 1991, their representatives joined the Palestinian delegation.

The second attitude stands in sharp contrast to the first and has led to the development of a national religious branch of Zionism. It originated around a political group named Mizrahi, a Hebrew acronym for "spiritual center." Its members are religious Jews, but they also support the Zionist enterprise politically. In their opinion there is no contradiction between Zionism and religion. On the contrary, the Mizrahi believe that Zionism is a realization of the process of redemption. The majority of Mizrahi members argued that the "great redemption" should of course be left to the Messiah, but Zionism was contributing to the realization of a redemption on a smaller scale. Through their everyday life in Eretz Israel, Jews fulfill themselves individually. A minority led by the Rabbis Kook, father and son, went even further. They wholeheartedly embraced Zionism from religious-ideological motives. They believed the Zionists, unwittingly, were the Hand of God, carrying out the divine mission of bringing the redemption nearer. By their emigration to Eretz Israel, their settlement and building of the land, their forming of an army to protect that land, they were inadvertently helping in God's work, which would culminate in the "great redemption." For the Kooks and their supporters it was not merely that the religious should stand by the side of the Zionists: their holy duty was to join the Zionist venture. To that end religious Zionists set up kibbutzim, rural communities, and became full-blown pioneers, just like Ben Gurion's socialists. They divested themselves of their shtetl and ghetto clothes and changed into the dress of their socialist comrades, except for the small crocheted skullcap—the sole external mark of their difference.

The third response to Zionism resulted in the formation of Agudat Israel, Hebrew for the Association of Israel, an umbrella organization that aimed to stop the spread of Zionism among Orthodox Jews. It represented, in fact, a synthesis and compromise between the two other religious attitudes toward Zionism. It rejected Zionism ideologically but actually favored its political and organizational achievements. Agudat Israel's ideological rejection went hand in hand with pragmatic resignation: if you can't beat them, and you don't want to join them, then at least accept them.

After the Holocaust and on the eve of Israel's independence, as secular Zionism grew stronger, a clear understanding was reached between Ben Gurion's Labor movement, the religious Zionists, and Agudat Israel. It was based on the notion of "status quo." The origins of this status quo are evident in a 1947 letter from Ben Gurion and a Mizrahi leader to Agudat Israel, in which they pledged that the conditions of the religious population would not deteriorate in the new state. Ben Gurion wanted to impress on the British and the Arabs that he had all of the Jewish people behind him, and he wanted to secure the support of all the religious parties for his Labor government. Thus, a political alliance was formed that lasted thirty years—until the 1977 election.

As soon as the state of Israel was born, Ben Gurion and the religious parties agreed to wider-ranging interpretations of the 1947 letter. The religious parties were given the freedom to act as sole mediators within the entire country in matters of state and religion. The most important of Ben Gurion's concessions to the religious parties was in the field of education. While Labor's own educational network was dismantled and replaced with one unified secular system, Mizrahi and Agudat Israel were also allowed to run their own independent educational systems.

From the first day of Independence, Saturday or Shabat was instituted as the official day of rest: public activities on that day, in

Jewish areas, more or less ground to a total halt. Only power stations, airports, and telephones were allowed to be run on minimum capacity, and there was no public transportation, which extremely limited the freedom of movement of any Israeli not in possession of a private car. Ben Gurion also agreed that cafes, cinemas, theaters—virtually all public entertainment—would close down on Shabat. It was agreed that only kosher food would be served in such public places as hotels, hospitals, and army bases.

The most controversial of Ben Gurion's concessions was to allow a limited number of students at Jewish seminaries—yeshivas in Hebrew, from the word for "sitting"—to be exempted from military service. Initially, there were no more than four hundred yeshiva students who made use of this privilege. Over the years, however, their numbers have skyrocketed. In approving the exemption, Ben Gurion and the Labor party created a rift between the two categories of Israeli high school graduates: those who must serve as conscripts for three years, and those who are exempted from national service.

There were also financial rewards for the religious parties. In 1966, for instance, the government ordered the governor of the central bank to license Agudat Israel to open its own bank.

All these special deals in favor of the religious gave Israel, in its first years, political breathing space and stability and ensured Labor's rule. But they also molded Israel into a peculiar sort of country, one that struggles, to this very day, with many contradictions and problems of identity.

Israel has no constitution. It has not yet defined its territorial borders and, thus, it has difficulties in identifying its citizens. The Declaration of Independence of May 1948 is the country's principal source of legal authority. Former judge of the Supreme Court, Zvi Berenson, who was one of the architects of the declaration, revealed that it was hastily composed, within forty-eight hours, and under difficult circumstances. "I was not able to get the necessary information and review the different constitutions and declarations of independence of other nations." Nevertheless, the quality of the declaration is very high and packed with reason and meaning.

The absence of a clear delineation of Israel's boundaries in the declaration was a conscious decision. While drafting the declaration, jurists had been pressing Ben Gurion to define the borders according to the United Nations 1947 partition plan. They argued that omitting them went against legal principles and that it would put Israel in an awkward position in relation to the rest of the world. Ben Gurion, however, rejected their argument for two reasons. He feared religious opposition because the religious were convinced that Israel's boundaries should coincide with those that God promised to Abraham. Secondly, Ben Gurion was also sure that the borders would change after the war with the Arabs, which he saw approaching. Indeed, since independence, Israel has expanded its borders several times. The conspicuous lack of mention has served to fuel Arab claims that Israel has entertained expansionist dreams right from the start.

The fact that there is no constitution is another example of Ben Gurion's deference to the religious parties. The religious argument has always been that if Israel really wants a constitution, then it should adopt the laws of the Bible and the legally complex, ancient codex of the Halacha—developed during two thousand years of exile by the great rabbis. Of course, Ben Gurion and his Labor associates, who had envisaged Israel as a secular democracy, could not consent to a religious constitution that would turn Israel into a theocracy. The solution—typical for Israel—was not to decide. Ever since independence there have been regular protests about the need for a proper constitution that would prevent infringement of civil and human rights. Jurists, however, disagree about whether or not a modern democracy needs a constitution to safeguard its citizens' liberties and rights. On the one hand, the American and French constitutions offer two excellent examples of the effectiveness of a constitution. On the other hand, it is not hard to see that a constitution does not automatically prevent tyranny—one need only look to South Africa or Syria for examples of countries having constitutions and widespread oppression. Indeed, Britain has no constitution, and is nevertheless considered a progressive country that abides by the law and maintains its citizens' rights.

The Israel declaration does state specifically that minorities in Israel will not be subject to discrimination and will enjoy full and equal rights: freedom of religious expression, education, and all the other liberties of civilized, modern democracies. Israel has no state religion, and Israeli law gives religious communities the right to maintain their traditions and apply their own laws of matrimony. So the Jews have rabinical courts, the Muslims have shariya courts, and the Christians have the right to set their own religious laws for their respective communities. But the declaration states explicitly that Israel is the Jewish state.

Judge Berenson is convinced that Israel's founding fathers had no intention whatsoever that the state would have a Jewish-religious character. His argument is that nowhere within the declaration does the adjective "religious" appear in conjunction with the expression "Jewish state." But for all intents and purposes Israel is a Zionist-Jewish state: the blue-and-white Israeli flag is decorated with the star of David and the traditional Jewish menorah, the official state emblem. More significantly, the Declaration of Independence asserts that "the State of Israel will be open to Jewish immigration." This right was bolstered in 1950 with the introduction of the Law of Return, which privileges diaspora Jews who wish to become Israelis. Since 1950, every Jew who chooses to become an Israeli can automatically become a passport-carrying citizen. To non-Jews, the Law of Return does not apply.

The Law of Return has made many Arabs and people in the West suspicious of Israel and its segregationist policy. In fact, save for this law, Israel's legal system has no other referring to Jews only. There are many loopholes, however, in the language of Israeli jurisprudence that effectively discriminate against the Arab-Israeli minority. Though a constant effort has been made to preserve a facade of legal justice and equality—to prevent discrimination on the basis of religion, race, or ethnic and national origin—real inequities continue.

The situation is compounded by the fact that on the Israeli ID card (carried by all citizens) the religion of the cardholder is entered under the heading of "nationality." Ben Gurion and his advisers, who were concerned that the Arab minority remaining within Israel's borders after 1948 would be disloyal, sought an easy and simple way of distinguishing between the Arabs and Jews. The religious community, on the other hand, resented the idea that the nationality of

Jewish Israelis would be registered as merely "Israeli"—they felt this would erode the Jewish character of the state. And thus it came to pass that Ben Gurion's strong desire to appease the religious community, combined with his security apprehensions, led to an identity registration that differentiated between Israeli Arabs and Israeli Jews.

All of this confusion leads to amusing anomalies and deplorable legal ambiguities. An Israeli can, for instance, be listed under two religions simultaneously: a son to a Muslim father (according to the Islamic, faith is determined by the father) and to a Jewish mother (in Judaism, religion passes through the mother) will belong to both religious communities. The unfortunate son of a Muslim mother and a Jewish father will not be recognized by either religion. It's no wonder that many Israelis confront serious identity problems. The unresolved tension between the secular majority and the religious minority raises profound questions that the Israeli leadership has declined to address.

What is Israel? If it is the state in which Israelis live, then why doesn't the system reflect this? Is it, then, a state of Jews—a state for the Jewish people? If this is so, then why do most Jews reside outside Israel and refuse to move here? And if we are Jews in a Jewish state, in what ways are we different from New York, London, or Moscow Jews? What about the non-Jews who live here? What is their nationality and status?

The question is: Who are the Israelis? Is there such a thing as an Israeli? Lastly, what does it mean to be a Jew? Is it a religion or a nationality? Maybe it is both at once. There are no clear-cut answers to these questions that haunt the state of Israel.

The most interesting and coherent attempt in the secular camp to settle these contradictions and problems was made by a group known as the Canaanites—a small but influential movement of mainly intellectuals, writers, and artists. Though the name originated in the Bible, the Canaanite ideology started surfacing in the early 1930s, when it became clear that Zionism was not going to disengage itself from Jewish past, tradition, and religion. The Canaanites perceived Zionism as a national revival movement but forcefully rejected the Jewish religion, which they saw as the root of all evil and corruption in Jewish society. The first ideologue of the movement was Adolph Gurevitz: a Russian Jew who studied and lectured history and Semitic languages at the Sorbonne in Paris, Gurevitz divided his time between Palestine and the United States. Gurevitz, who hebraized his name to Gur-Horon, gained a few young followers who spread his message. The most prominent among them was poet Jonathan Ratosh.

Ratosh, born in Poland in 1909 as Uriel Halperin, had emigrated to Israel at a young age with his parents. From early on, he was educated in the Hebrew language, which he used enthusiastically, to the exclusion of his mother tongue Polish and Yiddish. Many original Hebrew words can be credited to him. His creative talent, though, was poetry that had a considerable erotic and sensual intensity. His writing was only acknowledged when he was quite old, and even more so after his death in 1981. Most of his fame came from a conspicuously hedonistic lifestyle. Ratosh drank heavily, spent a lot of time womanizing in Tel Aviv's cafes, and despised the literary establishment, which rejected him. In 1942 Ratosh established the movement of young Hebrews. They mocked the Jewish religion, its rituals, and Yiddish. Though most of them came from Eastern Europe, they made a point of pronouncing their Hebrew in the guttural way that probably was more like that of their ancient ancestors. The young Hebrews had an insatiable yearning for mythic symbols, especially those representing strength, nature, and the bond between man and soil. Their sculptors and painters depicted motifs of farming, hunting, and ancient Canaanite gods and rites. Their writers and poets used lots of biblical imagery and developed rather sentimental, abstract visions of place and nativity and often idealized Mediterranean cultures. In their view, the sea, the beaches, and the fishermen figured prominently. They stressed harmony between humanity and nature. Unsurprisingly, they opposed what they viewed as the Israeli-Zionist obsession with building, colonizing, and taking possession of nature.

The movement was a small organization without financial resources, and yet it was feared by mainstream Zionists because of its growing influence on young Israelis. In an attempt to discredit the emerging movement the Zionists portrayed the movement as a bunch of licentious, hedonistic fools, carrying on orgies in the style of the ancient idol worshipers they admired. In mockery, their rivals dubbed them Canaanites. To the young Hebrews' dismay, the name stuck.

For Ratosh and his friends Zionism meant Judaism. They insisted on the difference between the diaspora-born "Jew" and the person who lived in Eretz Israel. What the Canaanites envisioned was not a Jewish but a Hebrew state that would herald a renaissance of the golden days of the ancient Hebrews. And as the ancient Hebrews were actually part of their surrounding Canaanite civilization, from whom they had conquered the land—so should the new Hebrew nation look to become an integral part of the Middle East, to strike its roots in the area, instead of maintaining what appeared to the Canaanites as artificial ties with alien European cultures. Israel was to embody the genuine trinity of the Hebrew language, Hebrew nation, and Hebrew land—the alternative to what they perceived as the mistaken combination of the Hebrew tongue, the Jewish people, and the Zionist destiny. According to the Canaanite ideology, their nation would have a clear identity, a territorial basis, and linguistic and cultural unity. In short, their intention was to found their nation on the modern principles of the nation-state, in which there is a correspondence between territory, citizenship, and ethnicity. But they failed. Despite their considerable and still enduring appeal, the Canaanites never really took root in Israeli society. The political mortar of the status quo, as preached by the coalition of Labor and the religious parties, put the brakes on any initiative to break the deadlock regarding matters of Israeli-Jewish identity.

Interestingly, though the status quo could be seen as just an obstacle and a serious nuisance, in reality, dozens of ways have been devised to circumvent the limitations imposed on secular Israelis by the religious. In fact, the alternatives to the status quo often seem themselves a part of the status quo. So instead of bus service on the Sabbath, only taxis and shared cabs were and still are allowed to transport passengers in and between towns along the established bus routes. And though most entertainment is suspended on the Sabbath, football games and other sports events are played. Tens of thousands of supporters who drive to the stadiums are accused of "desecrating" the Sabbath. Beaches are also open on the Sabbath to hundreds of thousands of bathers during the long summer season.

Though it is impossible to get a civil marriage in Israel, the secular courts (whose authority exceeds that of the religious courts) instruct the Interior Ministry (ruled by the religious parties) to recognize and register couples who had civil marriage ceremonies abroad. During the period up to 1967, open outbreaks of hostility between secular and religious public sectors were rare. Nevertheless, most cabinet crises of that period had their roots in religious issues. Mostly, it was the religious parties who were dissatisfied with the government's policies. Their primary concerns involved religious education, budgets for religious institutes, and, more than anything else, the question of "who is a Jew?"

In answering this question, the religious parties demanded that, as part of the Law of Return and ID registration, it should be stipulated that only those whose mother was Jewish or those who had been converted according to the Halacha law, qualified as Jews. Halacha—which is the Jewish legal codex—functioned as a code word for identifying those who were converted by an Orthodox rabbi. In Israel there has been only one religious establishment: the Orthodox rabbinate. These religious parties found it intolerable that the state of Israel would recognize conversions carried out by Conservative and Reform rabbis abroad. They demanded an amendment to the Israeli law but neither Labor, nor later Likud, gave into their religious pressure.

In the years leading up to 1967, a clear order of social stratification came into existence. As in an expertly staged play, each sector and group had a well-defined role. The Ashkenazi elite ruled the Sephardi majority, who obediently accepted second-class citizenship. The Israeli-Arabs constituted the third tier. This tacit arrangement was hardly questioned, except for a few insignificant dissident voices. In the religious camp the source of unrest was among the younger generation.

Young religious people were embarrassed about the religious role they had been allotted in the political setup with Labor. Most Agudat Israel Yeshiva students did not serve in the army, while Mizrahi youngsters did—usually for a shortened period and in functions related to religion, such as, undertakers, kosher food supervisors, and providers of prayer books.

In a male chauvinist society like Israel's, where army service is equated with social status, the religious folk were perceived as marginal and ridiculous. Secular kids called their religious peers names and treated them as inferiors. Some, especially radical young religious men, had been biding their time and waiting to strike back. Their moment arrived in June 1967, with the outbreak of the Six-Day War.

Most religious Israelis interpreted the swift victory as a divine miracle which reached its climax when the soldiers entered East Jerusalem and arrived at the Wailing Wall. The former humiliation of religious youth by the secular public was now replaced by a sense of elevation bordering on ecstasy. From that moment, Zionist-religious youth assumed a very different self-image. It was a process that gradually crystallized in 1974: religious youth emerged victorious after the traumatic Yom Kippur War and in the twilight of the last Labor government. Instead of religious officials, they would become the vanguard of West Bank colonizers.

The hard core and leading force of the religious and militant settlers of occupied Palestinian territory called itself Gush Emunim, or the Bloc of Faithful. An elitist group of zealots, Gush Emunim believe that only they are able to grasp the theological-historical significance of events in Israel. Gush Emunim's newly gained religious vigor and confidence is displayed in the kind of skullcaps they wear. The small, plain, almost invisible yarmulkes have been replaced with large, brightly colored ones. Most of Gush Emunim's leaders hail from a Jerusalem-based yeshiva called "The Rabbi's Center" presided over by Rabbi Yehuda Zvi Kook. Forty years earlier his father had developed the messianic dialectics according to which the socialist pioneers, albeit unwittingly, were helping toward the redemption of the Jewish people and in the historic unfolding of God's secret design.

For Gush Emunim, until 1977—as long as Labor was still in power—the government was the enemy from within. They took the law into their own hands and erected illegal settlements in opposition to government settlement policy. Gush Emunim clashed with

soldiers who were sent to evict them and organized violent demonstrations and blocked roads when United States Secretary of State
Henry Kissinger (whom they called "Jew Boy") was trying in
1974-1975 to achieve interim agreements with Egypt and Syria.

When Rabin's cabinet fell and Begin became premier, Gush
Emunim now had the added, considerable support of government.
The historic alliance between religious Zionism and the Labor
movement had been replaced with a new pact between the Likud and
Israel's religious parties. Gush Emunim has one of the strongest and
most versatile political lobbies in Israel. They know how to raise
funds, and they have also succeeded in presenting themselves to the
Israeli public as the successors to the old Zionists. As the pioneering
Zionists did before them, they, too, are colonizing the land.

But Gush Emunim's appetite eventually proved too large for
Begin's Likud to satisfy: they believed that Israel's military rule in the
occupied territories was not as brutal and aggressive as it should be.
Soon enough they used the same words, previously reserved for
Rabin, to describe Begin's regime: too soft on the Palestinians. And
when their demand to quash the Palestinian's national aspirations
went unanswered, they decided to change gears and radicalize their
action.

In spring 1980, after consulting their rabbis, twenty members from
Gush Emunim's hard-core center formed a terrorist organization.
The group injured three prominent Palestinian mayors and, in the
next four years, carried out a campaign of indiscriminate violence.
Three Palestinian students were murdered in cold blood at the
Islamic College in Hebron. Another plan to blow up school buses
carrying young children fortunately miscarried.

Inside this terrorist gang, another smaller gang was operating.
They planned to blow up the mosques on the Temple Mount in
Jerusalem. These mosques are situated on the site of the ancient
Second Jewish Temple, which was destroyed by the Romans. The
Jewish zealots planned to raze the mosques so as to make room for
the Third Temple. They were guided by the idea that the Messiah and
final redemption will only come when the Third Temple is ready. To
the Muslims, however, these two mosques are the holiest of all,
excepting those of Mecca and Medina, in Saudi Arabia, the cradle of

Islam. It is not difficult to imagine what would have happened had the Jewish extremists succeeded. If the mosques were blown up by Jews, the entire Islamic world—more than three hundred million believers spread over about forty nations—would doubtlessly call for a jihad, a holy war against Israel.

Such an apocalyptic prospect was too much, even for the military-minded Likud cabinet. Up until then, Likud had ignored the Jewish terrorists. In fact, initially they had denied their existence by hinting that the assassinations were provoked by Palestinian terrorists. In May 1984, twenty young and middle-aged religious zealots linked to Gush Emunim were arrested. Most of them were given light sentences. Only three, who were found guilty of murder, were sentenced to life imprisonment. Since then, all of them have been released.

Still, the idea of building a Third Temple has not perished. In the Muslim quarter of the Old City of Jerusalem are the premises of the Ateret Kohanim Yeshiva. These Yeshiva students specialize in the study of the First and Second Temples. It boasts models of these two complexes and copies of the ritual implements: the altars, the king's throne, even the high priests' robes according to their detailed descriptions in the Bible. In a state of messianic fervor some of these students once tried surreptitiously to get to the Mount Temple to make ritual sacrifices. Neither the students nor their tutors publicly advocate demolishing the mosques; however, they do believe that somehow it will happen. A visit to the yeshiva makes it clear that as far as these people are concerned the construction of the Third Temple is only a matter of time.

In contrast to this radicalizing trend, which has moved the Zionist religious sector from pragmatism to militancy, a similar process has taken place among the Orthodox. From a passive acceptance of Zionism and the state during the Labor era, the Orthodox have moved to a greater involvement in state affairs. They began receiving financial benefits once the Likud came to power in 1977. My own family's business, a factory that manufactures public kitchens, has also felt the effects. Most of the orders used to come from the army, hospitals, hotels, and industry, but in 1977 my father started being approached by Orthodox yeshivas.

Consecutive Likud governments have channeled hundreds of millions of dollars to the Orthodox. Their sudden prosperity enables them to enlarge enrollments—more yeshivas and more students, means more kitchens and the like. It also accounts for an increasing number of young men dodging military service. In the heyday of Labor, yeshiva students added up to a few thousand. Under the Likud government, their number is now into the tens of thousands.

"The new Orthodox," argues author Haim Be'er, who lives in an Orthodox neighborhood and whose novels describe their present-day life, "treat Israel as a bank machine." Whenever they need money—and their need for it is pretty much insatiable—they act like the average consumer; they go to the machine, press some buttons and get the cash. Instead of inserting plastic cards, they insert the politics of intimidation. As they hold the balance of power—the Likud cannot do without them—the Orthodox parties use only the simplest of languages: Give us this, don't give us that, or we will not vote for you.

The new Orthodox and their relation to the state is a one-way street. President John F. Kennedy once said: "Ask not what your country can do for you; ask what you can do for your country." The Orthodox seem to ignore the second part of the statement and concentrate on what the state—as they see it—owes them.

The shift in attitude of the Orthodox, which includes active involvement in the cabinet mixed with unstoppable greed, was helped along by the emergence of Shas. This is a relatively new Orthodox party which mainly represents the Sephardi population. The party came into existence in the 1983 election with the hope of fighting discrimination against Sephardis. The party, ironically, was founded by an Ashkenazi rabbi who had a bitter row with his colleagues. Most of its political and spiritual leaders are Moroccan-born rabbis, who were educated at Orthodox Ashkenazi yeshivas. They adopted the ways of their educators but lived with a steady sense of deprivation.

Its nominal leader was a younger rabbi by the name of Yitzhak Peretz who left the party in 1991. When Shas joined the Likud government in 1988, Peretz was appointed cabinet minister of the interior and, later, to the Ministry of Absorption. With its phenomenal success—thirty percent of the total religious representation in the Knesset—Shas did to the religious parties what Likud had done to Labor. Running on the sectarian-ethnic ticket, it exploited the hard feelings of Oriental Jews.

Unlike the other religious parties, especially Agudat Israel which always relied on a more or less homogeneous electorate, Shas has a wider-ranging appeal. Their critical mass, in fact, is the Sephardi population at large, not just the Orthodox among them. Many Sephardis who would not be considered religious in the Ashkenazi sense, define themselves nevertheless as observant and traditional. They identify with at least some aspects of the religion and observe some of its practices. With one cabinet minister, six Knesset members, and several senior government officials, Shas is well on its way to becoming a large grass-roots political organization. Most of its efforts are invested in consolidating the independent educational network the party has built over the last eight years. This means that three educational systems, out of four in Israel, are run by the religious parties.

The leaders of Shas, unlike the somewhat remote and austere Agudat Israel rabbis, are populists. They use slang and do not hesitate to mingle with their supporters. Since watching television is essentially forbidden in their way of life, the old Orthodox leadership refused to appear on television. Shas's leaders, on the other hand, quickly grasped the importance of the media and are frequently interviewed on television. They treat the television as a vital instrument in their efforts to bring back secular Israelis to their religious roots.

In this sense, Shas is the most missionary party in the country and has turned the rite of repentance into a mass industry. The party annually gathers thousands of their sympathizers in large sports arenas. More than anything, these events resemble live rock concerts. Between the popular religious music, the audience gets heavy doses of indoctrinating sermons from frenzied rabbis, similar in style to the American television evangelists. Shas's "soul-hunters" employ all the technological tools and techniques of modern marketing: commercials, advertisements, and audio and video tapes. They are expert at spotting and exploiting the weaknesses resulting from Israel's identity crisis. They criticize what they call the emptiness, corruption, and decadence of secular Israeli life and promise to fill this void with meaning. There is no data on the exact number of the born-again Israelis, but judging from the media attention they receive, it seems that they are booming in the 1990s. There have been many stories about celebrities and ordinary Israelis who have seen the light and joined Shas.

Shas's success brought them the envy and the wrath of their religious rivals and dragged the religious parties into a bitter struggle for political supremacy. It seems that these parties hate each other more than they hate their secular opponents. A comic peak in this religious rivalry was reached in the 1988 election campaign. In one of their television broadcasts Shas rabbis appeared in long gold-embroidered robes and turbans to parole sins, exorcise the evil eye and undo oaths, excommunications, and curses. It turned out that Agudat Israel had persuaded voters to pledge allegiance to their cause and threatened that whoever would break his vow would be cursed and punished along with his entire family.

The television appearance of Shas's rabbis amused Israel's secular audience, who saw it as another exaggerated chapter in the party's political soap opera. But this episode also threw a light on the darker and more primitive side of religious politics in Israel: the cynical exploitation of the backwardness and of the mystical leanings of part of the electorate.

Shas's first political leader, Rabbi Peretz, especially excels in making wild statements against the secular way of life. When twenty children on a school trip were killed in a collision between their vehicle and a train, Rabbi Peretz announced that this was God's punishment for the lack of spirituality among Israelis. On another occasion he attacked Israeli education and especially the universities that teach the works of Charles Darwin. He advocated the eradication of evolution and noncreationist science because they teach that "man came from the apes." Rabbi Peretz expressed his hope that, one day, Israel would teach its students that the world and the human race were created by God alone. But what really shocked Israelis was his unprecedented, vicious attack against kibbutzim. In June 1991

Rabbi Peretz tried to prevent kibbutzim from absorbing Ethiopian Jews. He argued that the kibbutzim not only did not have any Jewish culture but that they also actively encouraged the faithful to drop their religion. He revealed how his sister had been brought up in a kibbutz and hence, unlike him, had stopped being religious and became a dancer and painter. "You in the kibbutzim are guilty of the ruin of my sister!" he shouted dramatically in a live television interview.

Alongside the rhetoric, the religious politicians do not hesitate to show their muscle by endless efforts to introduce religious legislation that aims to undermine modern life, progress, and basic civil rights. They are looking for further limitations on abortion, on archaeological excavations, on the rights of physicians to transplant organs and dissect corpses. They have succeeded in stopping El Al, Israel's national airline, from flying on Saturdays. Other attempts, so far unsuccessful, aim to end the production, marketing, and sale of pork all year round and of bread during the week of Passover. "Now the religious want to be in your kitchens," Shulamit Aloni, leader of the Movement for Citizens' Rights and Peace, warned secular Israelis; "soon they will want to be everywhere: on your streets, your beaches, in your schools, and in your bedrooms."

While Aloni, who is one of Israel's most outspoken politicians, is alarmed by what she described as "the encroaching influence of the religious," historian Emanuel Sivan sees it from a different angle. For him, Shas's religious zeal and Gush Emunim's nationalism are just Israel's contribution to religious fundamentalism and fanaticism, which also exist in other societies. "Christian, Islamic, and Jewish fundamentalism share," he explains, "the yearning for a theocratic regime and a grave opposition to any expression of so-called Western materialism and corruption."

Corruption, however, is not limited to the secular. The police and public prosecutor have investigated allegations of misuse and illegal transfers of public money by Shas's cabinet ministers and Knesset members. It also turned out that some Shas leaders, who came from poor backgrounds, have become rather well off quite rapidly. They live in luxury apartments, drive flashy cars, and are seen in posh hotels and expensive restaurants. "The behavior of the religious politicians and their activities," explains Ora Namir, a minister in Rabin's new cabinet, "are teaching the public to hate religion."

Secular contempt of the Orthodox has been further strengthened by their double standards and what seems to be their hypocritical attitude toward modern life. On the one hand, they despise modernism and view it as their enemy—on the other, they like to enjoy its technological advances. As a result, the Orthodox have found convenient ways around the very traditions they claim to hold high. Tradition, for instance, forbids them to engage in many activities on the holy Sabbath because the Bible prohibits work and the making of fire. These ancient prohibitions were extended, in the twentieth century, to the operation of any electric appliance. Instead, the Orthodox invent tricks that enable them to circumvent the prohibition of lighting a fire on the Sabbath. A special Shabbat lamp was created which is lit before the onset of the Shabbat and operates throughout the entire night and day. There is a special telephone which allows the observant to receive and make calls. A ruling by Israel's Chief Rabbi in winter 1992 has made it possible for the Orthodox to use the telephone in an emergency, on the condition that there be no direct physical contact with the phone while dialing. It is suggested that a pencil might come in handy for this purpose.

In the past Judaism had erudite, inspired rabbis. The most famous of all was Rabbi Moses Ben Maimon who lived in Spain in the eleventh century. He interpreted the Bible and the accumulated tradition in a way that was relevant to his era. For centuries, however, Orthodox Judaism has not produced authoritative rabbis of his caliber, who could take responsibility for updating and modernizing the tradition. Instead, the rabbis today occupy themselves with tactical decisions of marginal importance which seem vain and even ridiculous.

For all these reasons the early 1990s have witnessed an increased tension between the secular majority and the religious minority. In the past, secular Israelis watched religious activities apathetically. Here and there, organizations like the Canaanites were set up to confront "religious coercion," but they did not leave any really significant impact. Recently, however, this attitude has been changing: more and more secular Israelis are ready to fight for their views and their way of life. Families of the deceased demand that non-Jewish dates should appear on graves, alongside those of the Jewish calendar. Despite the strong opposition of the Orthodox establishment, Reform and Conservative congregations and synagogues have been opened. The request of one of these Reform congregations that it have a cemetery of its own has found great public support. Left-wing parties and even sections of the Labor party have been demanding a separation between state and religion, which would make possible civil weddings, divorces, and funerals.

This new mood has been stimulating secular Israelis to switch from a passive to an active response. Jerusalem has become the major battlefield in this struggle. In one part of the city, Orthodox platoons smash billboards showing half-naked fashion models and throw stones at cars driving on the Sabbath. Elsewhere groups of young secular protesters fight against what they describe as "the siege of secular Jerusalem by the invading forces of Jerusalem fundamentalists." The groups use unconventional publicity stunts and occasionally resort to street violence. In their efforts to lift the "siege," the secular warriors conduct raids on Orthodox areas and cover walls with antireligious graffiti. Their unorthodox warfare also includes the opening of cinemas, theaters, and restaurants on Friday nights and operating public bus services on Saturdays. Secular activities came to a brutal climax when, in the spring of 1991, a pig's head was placed in the doorway of a synagogue. It was clear that whoever committed this act was over the top. No one claimed responsibility.

In fact, the Orthodox frequently argue that the behavior of secular Israelis reminds them of anti-Semitism. Nowhere, it seems, are Orthodox Jews more feared and hated than in the Jewish state itself. "When I see those Orthodox folk I can understand the anti-Semite" is a fairly common expression among secular Israelis. They have taken to calling the Orthodox "black Jews" or simply "the blacks," on account of their predominantly black clothes. A leftist weekly dubbed them "The Black Power." The Orthodox are viewed as parasites who drain the secular society's vital juices.

The religious parties, however, are in fact less powerful and more vulnerable than they are perceived to be. Since the first elections in 1949, the religious parties have not succeeded in increasing the number of their Knesset members in any significant way—despite the fact that Israel's Jewish population has grown seven times larger. The number of their Knesset seats has always been between fifteen and eighteen, out of 120.

Moreover, it is possible to counterbalance those who returned to their religious roots against those who take off their skullcaps, change their traditional dress, and adopt a contemporary secular way of living. The attempt to subvert the status quo by introducing new religious legislation, more often than not, has failed.

The religious, too, complain sorely that the status quo has been eroded—but to their disadvantage. They see how ever more cinemas, restaurants, and bars open on Saturdays, intruding on their holy Sabbath, even in Jerusalem, their holy city.

Especially hurtful to the religious community is a recent phenomenon known as "The Yom Kippur Bicycle Syndrome." On this, the holiest day in the Jewish calendar, all road traffic in the country stops. Instead of cars, the roads used to be filled with people, secular and religious families alike, on their way to the synagogue. There was a very special, almost holy atmosphere. But the mood has changed, and the number of synagogue attendees has shrunk. And though cars are not used, the roads are now full of bikes. This trend started with children who couldn't resist the temptation of empty roads. Now it involves whole families who take the opportunity to go on bike trips. The beaches are crowded with bathers, who until recently would have been embarrassed to spoil the holy atmosphere. Yom Kippur is on the verge of becoming a day of national recreation.

Against this background, religious protest actions can be seen in a different light. Rather than aggression and expansionism, they can also be understood as the desperate reaction of a people who feel they are losing ground in the cultural battle.

The emerging mood of religious-secular relations is one of increased friction and growing, mutual isolation. On the one hand, it seems that both sectors are becoming more militant every day and willing to take risks in confronting each other. On the other hand, each sector is sinking ever deeper into itself and concentrating on its own secluded communities. Their children attend separate schools and usually marry within their own communities. There are no serious attempts to exchange useful ideas between the two sectors, to explore better possibilities for peaceful coexistence and mutual reconciliation.

While middle-class secular Israelis are in constant pursuit of a more materialistic life in their suburban neighborhoods, the religious of Shas, Agudat Israel, and Gush Emunim are retreating into their own quarters, settlements, and oblivion. This is the phenomenon Emanuel Sivan calls "a culture of enclaves."

EIGHT

The Culture of Defense

IN THE EARLY 1970s, the American artist George Segal sculpted a large plaster figure of a father clutching a knife while his son crouches at his feet. The source for Segal's idea is obviously biblical; it is Abraham's sacrifice of his son, Isaac. According to the story, God tests Abraham's faithfulness by ordering him to take his son to a hill in Jerusalem to sacrifice him.

Segal's sculpture has been hidden in the basement of the Tel Aviv Museum for about twenty years now. It is rarely on public display because the museum's curators and their political bosses at Tel Aviv City Hall have viewed it as Segal's critique of Israeli reality: a state which sacrifices its sons to war. The sculpture draws a parallel between the patriarch's willingness to kill his son in order to please God and the readiness of Israeli parents to see their children die in return for a Jewish state of their own.

Israel has paid a very high price for its survival: the bodies and the souls of its young generation. According to official figures issued in May 1992 by the Ministry of Defense, 17,500 Israelis have lost their lives and more than 56,000 have been injured in the country's seven wars and other military confrontations.

Modern Israel is one of the most mobilized societies in the world. The country's security still occupies the crucial position in the national consciousness. This mobilization has been achieved by a carefully designed educational program that begins in kindergarten.

The state's overriding goal has been to draw a broad consensus by convincing its citizens of the righteousness of its ways and to minimize doubt. As long as people are motivated and have faith in the cause, it is possible to maintain a high level of commitment. A society—it was reasoned—whose members experience and express doubts about the government's objectives will be less cohesive and hence more vulnerable, especially when surrounded by enemies, under continuous threat.

The Israeli public has been given a one-dimensional version of their own history—beginning with the Jewish colonization of Eretz Israel—but especially regarding the events of the War of Independence and thereafter. Like mainstream American historiography, which has painstakingly avoided the embarrassing truth about the massacring of Native Americans, Israel's history too has been painted in black and white. Israeli myth has its own good guys and bad guys. Taking its cue from the western movie—where, according to the hackneyed formula, the good guy wins by natural justice—the Israeli spin on their own history tells of an unfailingly righteous nation that has always only desired peace. This same legend speaks of how Israel has looked untiringly to open windows of opportunity. But the Arabs, the bad guys, closed the windows and went to war.

One evening in May 1992, when I took my eight-year-old son to the Remembrance Day ceremony at his community grammar school, I was reminded again how the need to inculcate this way of thinking affects Israeli schools. The system does not encourage individualism and independent thinking; rather it stimulates group thinking and conformity and operates like a factory assembly line, turning out a standard product—our children.

There is virtually no Israeli school—elementary or secondary—that has not suffered some bereavement. The Remembrance Corner at my son's school consists of a simple stone on which are engraved the names of those ex-pupils who have fallen in Israel's wars.

On the Day of Remembrance, in every village and town and in Israel's many cemeteries, people gather together to commemorate. The Day of Remembrance always precedes Independence Day by twenty-four hours. The decision to celebrate independence on the day immediately following remembrance, carries a clear message to the public: these fallen soldiers have made Israel's independence possible. Or, in the words of the celebrated poet, Nathan Alterman, "They are the silver platter on which the state was given to you."

Remembrance Day begins with the sounding of sirens—the same that are used in times of war, including the recent Gulf crisis, when they warned of incoming Scud missiles. When on Remembrance Day the sirens go off, all Israel comes to a standstill for two minutes. The national flag is lowered to half-mast and the remembrance torch is lit, usually by a bereaved parent. The ceremonies are concluded after about a half hour with the joint singing of the national anthem.

All national cemeteries and monuments, as George Mosse observed, have at least something in common: "As honor is accorded to the fallen soldiers, military cemeteries become increasingly important as a site for national identification." Thus, many of the war monuments erected in Europe did not only eternalize the dead, but obscured the atrocities of war in order to bestow on death a superior value and a historical national purpose. When the victims are represented as saints, it is easier to come to terms with their deaths. The majority of these monuments are studies in funerary kitsch: they show the dead soldiers as sword-wielding knights or in glorious neoclassical nudity to bring home the male chauvinist message. War, as depicted in such cemeteries, stands for human and nationalistic values of valor, supreme sacrifice, and the soldiers' collective brotherhood.

Israel's greatest myth of heroism is that of Masada, which is an impressive fourteen-hundred-foot-high rock, still found on the edge of the Judaean desert overlooking the Dead Sea. The place, more than nineteen hundred years ago, was turned into a fortress by a marginal group of Jewish extremists and zealots. From there, they fought a desperate and futile rebellion against the legions of the Roman Empire. The generally accepted version of events is that once the Jewish defenders realized they no longer could repel the Roman siege, they decided to commit mass suicide rather than to be humiliated as prisoners. However, there are historians who argue that this was not a case of mass suicide but, rather, a massacre of the Jews by the Romans. Nine hundred and sixty Jewish fighters, including their women, children, and elders, died in A.D. 72. For centuries the drama of Masada was deliberately erased from Jewish memory. Mainstream Judaism does not accept suicide: those who die in this way are buried outside the fence of the cemetery.

Only when the Zionist colonization project got under way did Jewish writers, historians, and politicians adopt the saga of Masada. This mythmaking reached a peak when, in 1927, Ya'acov Lamdan, a Zionist poet, wrote, "Never again will Masada fall." This line became the guiding words for future generations of Zionists, and Masada became the symbol of the renewed heroism of the Jewish people in their struggle for independence.

School children are taught to admire the heroism of Masada. All the youth movements visit the site and make the steep, hot ascent in order to breathe the air of Jewish bravery. New army recruits are brought to the austere rock for their army allegiance ceremony and to study the strategic details of the Masada siege.

Masada worship made a quantum leap forward after the discovery of human bones near the site during the 1960s. Under the auspices of the Labor government, Israel's orthodox rabbis jumped on the opportunity to indulge in their much beloved reburial ritual. The dry bones were interred in a state ceremony in appreciation of these suicidal defenders. Needless to say, this veneration of the site does not preclude a healthy exploitation of the myth for commerce and tourism. Together with Yad Vashem, the Holocaust memorial in Jerusalem, Masada has been made into a tourist imperative by the Ministry of Tourism. Once the Likud came to power in 1977 Masada's popular appeal was used even more intensely: its story serves the Likud's ideology and policies particularly well. Its message has increasingly become that since all the world is against the Jewish people, there is no room for compromise in Israel's struggle for survival. Israelis, in short, have been conditioned to believe that in some cases it is preferable to choose freedom in death over bondage in life.

This kind of glorification and sanctification of the dead reaches another acme in the Galilee area in the monument dedicated to Yosef Trumpeldor, the most celebrated hero in Zionist mythology and martyrology.

Born in Russia, Trumpeldor served in the czarist army and lost one arm in the war with Japan in 1905. After his recovery he became a Zionist, emigrated to Palestine, and befriended Jabotinsky, whom he helped to organize a Jewish legion in the British army. After the First World War, Trumpeldor led a group of pioneers who settled in a small colony in upper Galilee and cultivated the land. In 1919 an argument broke out with the local Arabs, who suspected Trumpeldor and his friends of supporting French and British officers. The Arabs stormed the Jewish farm and killed eight of its people. One of them was Trumpeldor, whose death gave birth to a tenacious myth. Songs were composed to laud the farmer who "with his single arm pulled the plough at daytime and held the rifle at night." A lion with its mouth forever opened in a stony roar commemorates Trumpeldor and his friends on the spot where they died. In their mythmaking zeal, the early Zionists attributed last words to their hero to boost Zionist and Israeli patriotism. Generations of Israeli children learn that Trumpeldor, as he lay dying from Arab bullets, spoke the improbable words, "It is good to die for our country." This line is now engraved on the stone lion.

It is not surprising, therefore, that patriotism is fed to children with their mother's milk. Israeli towns "adopt" army units and celebrate their "birthdays" on the town squares. Designed to strengthen the link between the rear and the front lines, these kinds of exhibitions are rarely seen elsewhere in the democratic world. Their target public is the local children. While their young counterparts elsewhere love to visit amusement parks, Israeli children are encouraged to visit army or weapons exhibitions.

The city of Tel Aviv has adopted as its own the armored corps. Every year in the fall, on the "day" of the armored corps, tanks and troop carriers are driven onto Tel Aviv's central square to impress the lation with their power. Tens of thousands of children accompanied by their parents visit the site and climb all over the tools of destruction and chat with crew members. To many Israelis, this relationship seems very natural—as if children were born to worship the military. It's no wonder that five or ten years later, when their time comes, boys are keen to join the air force, tanks, paratroopers, and all the other units who conduct their marketing on the town square.

For its first three decades, Israel's education was primarily designed to indoctrinate and encourage the country's youth into volunteering for the elite and commando units. These special forces make a big point of emphasizing their unique abilities. Their soldiers receive special decorations, medals, wings, and different uniforms. School children, from early on, are fed on heroic stories, and they learn to worship these elite units.

Just as American high school students dream of being enrolled in an Ivy League university, their Israeli peers yearn for the prestigious and elite units of its armed forces. Those who have not served in a combat unit are condescendingly called "Jobniks." Already in the 1950s the incentive slogan of the Israeli air force was "The good go flying."

I remember very well how intent I was, as a schoolboy, on getting myself into one of these elite units. They symbolized to me, a new immigrant, my eventual acceptance into the highest category of good, patriotic Israelis. My initial training period was especially tough—to ruthlessly change the boy into a man. Reward came in the form of short furloughs, when we went out among civilians to inflate our chests like peacocks and show off our wings (decorative pins), which meant that we were fighters.

It is in these units that one can also find the roots of Israeli machismo. The boy-soldiers are conditioned to endure suffering. Expressions of emotion are to be suppressed, and military orders are delivered in a staccato rhythm. I remember spending nights without getting any sleep. Whoever made the mistake of dropping his gun was immediately punished by having to stand up for hours, with his heavy weapon high above his head, until his arms failed. Those who took their training too lightly were branded as "dead" and were made to spend the entire night digging a hole—their "grave." It is often difficult to draw the line between this "military training" and outright sadism. The belief that harassment toughens the soldiers and makes real men out of them has been the general philosophy guiding the armed forces—accordingly, they may force recruits to eat sand or make them crawl naked over rough terrain or walk barefoot through thorny bushes. The price the boys pay for this initiation into adulthood has often been high. Those who cannot bear the psychological burden sometimes commit suicide, and those who survive are often left permanently scarred. Military service is also compulsory for eighteen-year-old women. But, unlike men, they serve only two years, mainly in noncombat functions, although recently, over the past five years, with the increased awareness of feminism, more and more female soldiers are in positions traditionally identified with men, such as tank instructor.

Military service in Israeli society is equated with a "license" to life. Those who have not served in the military, for whatever reason, are held back without the chance of getting many civilian jobs. Those who have served, preferably in an elite unit, will find it relatively easy to get a good job. Ex-soldiers from these elite units function as a human reservoir for Israel's extensive security industry and for secret services, especially the Mossad. This system works similarly to the British old boys' network: an Israeli who has been in the right army unit will easily follow the paved path to success.

The late 1950s and early 1960s brought economic wealth and military strength. Two billion dollars of German money, as compensation for the Nazis' crimes against Jews, brought previously unknown prosperity. The state of Israel was recognized as the legitimate heir of the Jewish people—both individual victims and survivors of the Holocaust—and the lion's share of the money was channeled to the government. This marked the end of a period during which food was rationed and distributed in exchange for food stamps. Meat became a regular part of Israeli diet. Israel, to some degree, was still a community of idealists, even though signs of materialism and greed were evident. The majority of Israeli youth still showed obedience and conformity and was ready to accept authority unquestioningly.

While young people in the West were disillusioned with consumer society and its materialism—while they became increasingly politically active, declaring war on the establishment—the youth of Israel were dreaming of becoming part of the establishment. As students mounted the barricades in Paris and fought against the police, their Israeli counterparts read about them in the newspapers and continued on their way to their lecture halls and seminars. At the very time when American students were protesting against the Vietnam war and burning their draft cards, their Israeli peers were looking forward to joining the army.

The adoration of the military reached its zenith after the victory in the Six-Day War. Unlike other armies, the Israeli forces do not take great pains to organize transportation for its soldiers on leave. As a result, it is common in Israel to see hitchhiking soldiers carrying their guns and kit bags. Normally, drivers do not stop to pick them up, but after the Six-Day War almost every car would pull over. The soldiers were regaled by civilians and given food and drink. Men dressed in prayer shawls blessed the forces. The press was full of features about army bravery, and fast-acting publishers produced "victory albums" with battle photographs. The generals stood in especially high regard and were worshiped. People stopped soldiers in the streets, gave them free meals in restaurants, and invited them to every party in town. Some enthusiasts refused to wash their hands for days after shaking the hand of a general.

The great icon of the 1960s was Moshe Dayan. After 1967 he became the idol of every Israeli. The antithesis of Eshkol, Golda Meir, and their generation, Dayan epitomized the spirit and myth of the Israeli-born sabra. Born in 1915 to pioneering parents on a Jewish farm, Dayan at an early age developed the traits of a farmer-soldier. His skin was permanently sunburnt and his hands, people said, were those of a farmer. Dayan joined the mainstream Jewish underground forces of the Haganah, and lost his eye in 1941 while fighting with the British against French pro-Nazi units in Syria. The black eye patch which he henceforth wore became his trademark.

Dayan gradually rose through the ranks of Israel's army, and by 1956 he had become chief of staff and the architect of the Sinai Campaign. Later, when he left the army, he became minister of agriculture in Ben Gurion's cabinet. In 1963, he followed Ben Gurion into the political wilderness, only to be salvaged by popular demand on the eve of the Six-Day War. Under public pressure Premier Eshkol appointed him defense minister.

Following the victory, which was wholly and erroneously attributed to him, Dayan's credentials in Israeli society took on mythological proportions. He was perceived as a demigod and Dayan knew very well how to exploit this idea. Lacking all inhibition and restraint, he publicly flouted the law. Sometimes, while driving in his official car, Dayan found the road barred by a police blockade. When this happened, he simply stopped the car and removed the obstacle in order to continue on his way. He abused his power as defense minister and employed soldiers and army equipment— including helicopters—in order to illegally indulge his hobby of archaeology. He was a professional collector of rare pieces of ancient pottery and artifacts. After his death, as instructed in his will, his second wife sold his collection—which was really state property— for over one million dollars to the Israel Museum in Jerusalem.

Dayan was a lone wolf. He had no real friends, and in the restaurant of the Knesset I saw him many times sitting by himself. People respected him, but he was an egotist and a cynic. Though he was a brave soldier, he was a coward in politics. He refused to take responsibility for his actions and allowed himself to be contradictory. Had he shown more leadership and political courage, he could have easily ended up as prime minister. But Dayan chose to be Eshkol and Meir's number two. A pragmatist and pessimist, he knew that maintaining the status quo in the territories following the 1967 war was potentially disastrous; nevertheless—like Ben Gurion, his mentor after the 1948 war—he sanctioned this status quo. For Dayan it had become a goal in its own right.

During the 1960s and early 1970s the electronic media were under the full control and supervision of the prime minister. Israel today has all of the advantages and disadvantages of multichanneled American and European television, from CNN to Geraldo Rivera. But twenty-five years ago there was no television in Israel. The government feared that the introduction of television would corrupt and poison the minds of its obedient subjects. They were unaware as yet of the enormous potential of television as a propaganda tool. Israel was one of the only countries whose citizens couldn't watch the box. Television sets were heavily taxed, and even the few people who could afford to acquire one had nothing to watch except fuzzy broadcasts from neighboring Arab countries.

The radio, under the watchful eye of the centralist, socialist government, played hardly any western pop music. When Israeli adolescents wanted to hear the latest music, they had to tune their radios to Arab stations. The Labor elders felt it was better for young people to listen to Israeli, Russian-inspired songs. The leadership wanted young people to join in folk dances and did everything in its power to prevent the opening of discotheques. This strict attitude led to the 1964 veto of a Beatles tour of the Holy Land. A private promoter had signed a contract that would bring the "fab four" to the biggest soccer stadium in Israel for a concert. The government worried that the concert would encourage Israeli youth to begin wearing long hair and jeans and listening to loud music. Thus, the veto was issued.

The intuition of Labor's fearful old guard was indeed correct. Following the Six-Day War, Israel and its army were greatly admired in the West. This brought tens of thousands of young tourists to Israel. These ambassadors of the swinging sixties introduced Israelis to drugs, drinks, and other expressions of the counterculture.

During the first three decades of its existence, Israel had hardly any bars and pubs serving beers or other alcoholic drinks. Bars and pubs were viewed as immoral, shadowy places frequented by criminals and prostitutes. Israelis hardly drank at all, except for the traditional sip of sweet, ritual wine after the Friday night's blessings or on religious holidays. Israelis were totally unfamiliar with the culture of drinking. In fact, in 1965 the finance minister in Eshkol's cabinet was invited for dinner at the castle of the Baron de Rothschild in France. In honor of his guest, the Baron ordered an especially exquisite wine to be brought to the table from his private cellars. The Baron proudly drew his guest's attention to the vintage wine, but the Israeli minister was not impressed: he poured himself half a glass of it, and filled the rest with soda water. Mixing soda with wine was very popular among Israelis and was considered the height of culinary sophistication. Over the years there has been a tremendous rise in the consumption of alcohol. Its use has become extremely widespread, especially among the young, though in 1990, the average Israeli spent annually only $4 on alcoholic beverages—which still falls well below the consumption level of Western Europe or North America. But clearly, drinking is catching on. One factor in this change is the rise in the Israeli standard of living: no modern host can give a party without serving plenty of alcoholic drinks. The new drinking habits have taken root in all social strata and are particularly visible among the young. Fewer and fewer of them join the youth movements, and increasingly they choose to spend their free time in bars and pubs. The worrisome increase in road accidents is partly caused by drunken driving—particularly among the young. This has created a real problem and has forced the police to prohibit people under the age of twenty driving after 1:00 A.M. on the weekends. Breathalizer tests are soon to be introduced.

Another foreign influence in Israeli society is drugs. According to statistics published by the Israeli Narcotics Authority, three out of every hundred Israelis today are addicted to drugs. The number of people using hard and lesser drugs totals 250,000, and many of them are under the age of twenty. Addiction to heroin and cocaine is still increasing and is a problem not limited to poor neighborhoods and slums. According to a study carried out at Tel Aviv University, there are areas in my own middle-class neighborhood that are considered hotbeds of drug use.

Israelis increasingly look to foreign travel for respite from the strenuous monotony of war. Soldiers hope that after the three years of their compulsory service they will travel far away from the burning battlefields of the Middle East. And when they finish their stint, they often realize their dream by setting off for exotic places. Travel before enrolling at the university or looking for a steady job has become almost a ritual: in groups or couples, they set off for the jungles of South America or the Himalayas in Nepal, carrying no more than a backpack and a few thousand carefully saved-up dollars. They tend to view the trip as something bordering on a religious duty: anyone who misses out on it is viewed as some sort of a deplorable loser. Over the last decade young Israelis have taken on jobs, all over the world, which they pass along to others—from one Israeli traveler to the next. Sheep farming in Australia, ice cream vending in Houston, fishing in Alaska, and house moving in New York City have all become new occupations.

Of course, it is not only Israelis who have come under the spell of the culture of travel—young people from all over the world can be found in the South American rain forests and on the roads of Asia. But unlike their European or American peers, whose escapism has a spiritual-intellectual side, young Israeli travelers go for sheer adventure, as if it were a physical extension of their military service. They don't make an effort to acquaint themselves with the languages of the places they visit, and they lack the necessary curiosity to become familiar with local customs and history or learn to respect them.

The most prominent symptom of the urge to flee can be found in the Israelis attitude toward their international airport. Israel has only one international airport, named after Ben Gurion, ten miles from Tel Aviv. The airport, buzzing with tension as armed soldiers are patrolling everywhere, could serve as a metaphor for the whole of Israeli existence. In a country whose citizens are deprived of the simple pleasure of getting into their cars and crossing borders, the airport is a powerful symbol of freedom. Entire families gather there to take leave of their loved ones or to welcome them on their return. Even if a person is only traveling on business, he or she will usually be accompanied by spouse and children, and often the entire extended family. The hostile reality—with the Mediterranean at their backs and antagonistic neighbors before them—creates among Israelis a strong sense of isolation and a siege mentality, which brings perpetual tension and claustrophobia.

However, foreign influence, disenchantment with the old culture of defense, and the wish to escape isolation have brought about, in recent years, a growing readiness to break the many myths of heroism—such as those about Moshe Dayan, Yosef Trumpeldor, and the saga of Masada. There is an increasing demand for a "new history" that offers a more comprehensive and complex representation of the past.

Nowadays Dayan is represented in books and newspaper articles as a shameless womanizer unconcerned about public opinion—in order to impress his mistresses, Dayan let them in on state secrets and occasionally lost classified documents in their beds. Dayan is portrayed as a greedy man who demanded money for interviews. When he was dying of cancer, he sold his last reflections to Israel's largest daily newspaper. His son responded to this by remarking cynically that his father had sold his intestines to the press.

These words are illustrative of the relationship between the father and his children. Dayan wasn't exactly a family man, and he neglected his three children. Upon his death, in October 1986, the gossip columns thrived on his children's accounts—so much so that the Dayan family story came to look like Israel's local version of a soap opera.

Today's iconoclasts mock Trumpeldor's famous last words. In an attempt to discredit his myth they have suggested that on his deathbed Trumpeldor probably cursed the world rather than agreeably accepting his fate. They imagine that Trumpeldor, the anti-hero, whose Hebrew was quite poor, would have voiced a juicy curse in his real mother tongue, Russian.

Since the Likud's enthusiastic exploitation of the Masada myth, left-wing intellectuals have woken up to the more offensive aspects of this symbol. After many years of silently accepting the convenient use of the story for Labor's purposes, they now seem to realize that it encourages nationalist chauvinism and identification with fundamentalist zealots.

Signs of discontent and challenge to authority can also be seen in Israel's cemeteries and memorials. Israel has about one thousand war memorials—which equals one memorial for every seventeen fallen soldiers. In contrast, historian George Mosse has estimated that this ratio would be something like one per ten thousand in Europe, and one per fifteen thousand in the United States. In this respect, Israel stands unrivaled in its idolatry. Perhaps it can be explained by the fact that the country is so small and so intimate that almost everybody knows everyone else. Each person has his own fallen soldier—relative, neighbor, or friend. Israel's culture of eternalization looks at the individual and does not attempt to obscure his identity. Elsewhere memory focuses on the collectivity, not the individual. In Washington, D.C., the Vietnam War Memorial carries the names of *all* the fallen soldiers; and on the headstones of European military graves, you will not find the soldiers' first names. As in the British military cemeteries in Israel—in which are buried soldiers from the First World War who fell against the Turks—all that remains of these soldiers' individuality is an initial: J. Smith, B. Jones.

Superficially, Israeli soldiers' tombstones, too, have a uniform shape, a style created by the Ministry of Defense. But Mosse's trained eye discovered, when he visited cemeteries and studied the Israeli practice of remembrance, that almost every grave has its own special character. One stone reads that the soldier "fell in battle," another that "he fell while fulfilling his duty," and yet another bears the words "during service." And as Israel is a small country, families can frequently visit the graves of their loved ones. They are entitled to keep them up and put fresh flowers in the vases or plastic beakers. Some graves are decorated to look like works of art. This contrasts quite strongly with foreign practices; this sort of thing is forbidden by the British, who go so far as to determine the kind of flower permitted.

In the Israeli graveyards, Mosse found not only first names, but also pet names. But a nine-year-long battle was fought by two families over another, more serious, privilege. The Israeli government, led by Menachem Begin and Ariel Sharon, insisted on calling the 1982 Israeli invasion of Lebanon, "Peace for Galilee." Accordingly, the gravestones of soldiers who died during this war read that they "died during the Peace for Galilee campaign." The Spiegels and the Zipkers, whose sons were killed during the 1982 Lebanon war, felt these words were hypocritical and deceitful. The Israeli invasion of Lebanon was the most controversial of all wars. It was not a war imposed upon Israel by the Arabs but a war initiated by Israel. The government's name for the war suggests that it was a military operation of self-defense, but many Israelis saw it as an unnecessary escapade, fought not for survival but for political aims. People felt deeply opposed to this war which took seven hundred Israeli soldiers. The Spiegel and Zipker families demanded that the word *Peace* be erased from their sons' gravestones and the wording changed to "died while fulfilling his duty in Lebanon." The government objected. The families turned to the Supreme Court and won. In June 1991, their appeal was accepted. Another brick in the bulwark of Israeli consensus had crumbled.

Mosse has concluded that Israeli war memorials and cemeteries express a desire for peace. An increasing number of parents are public questioning the sacrifice of their fallen sons. Young parents, looking nervously ahead to when their children will be called up, are afraid that their offspring will have to serve interests that don't represent their views. That is why more and more parents have become involved in changing school curriculums to reduce the level of state indoctrination. As a result, education is becoming more tolerant, liberal, and open-minded.

Israel in the 1990s, as never before, is haunted by questions that threaten to explode its deepest taboos. More people than ever want to dust off the history books and reconsider questions that have received only pat answers in the past. Is it really the case that all these wars were forced upon Israel? Were there not some wars that Israel initiated? Has peace always truly been our ultimate goal?

The truth is that Israel is a country where war and peace coexist symbiotically. And no place better represents the coexistence of war and peace than Tel Aviv's Shderot Shaul Hamelekh. Named after the first monarch of the ancient kingdom of Israel, Shaul Hamelekh is one of the widest and most elegant boulevards in the city. Both the Tel Aviv Museum and the Kirya, the nerve center of Israel's elaborate defense system, exist side by side on this boulevard. This contradictory juxtapositioning serves as a poignant reminder of modern Israel's desire to regard its tense and volatile existence as normal.

If the early Zionists perceived "normalcy" as something that would be achieved with the emergence of an indigenous Israeli class of thieves and prostitutes, the new Israeli normalcy is perceived as a thriving, internationally oriented cultural life, like the prestigious cultural capitals of the West: New York, London, Paris, or Rome. Today, for a million dollars, Tel Avivians can buy a glamorous apartment in an upscale residential and cultural complex which functions as a kind of annex to the museum. Residents enjoy living virtually under one roof with the opera and within walking distance of the home of the Israel Philharmonic Orchestra. The orchestra, established nearly sixty years ago, has gained worldwide acclaim under its Indian conductor, the flamboyant Zubin Mehta. The Philharmonic boasts one of the largest subscribing audiences in the world.

In addition, Tel Aviv has a plethora of jazz clubs, cafes, ballet companies, theaters, and dance groups. Tel Aviv's cultural zest has spawned about ten museums and attracts highly popular pop and rock performers. Famous pop singers from Tina Turner to Bob Dylan now include Israel on their international tours. On a per capita basis, Tel Aviv is, according to United Nations statistics, one of the largest art consumers in the world.

Other towns, not only Jerusalem and Haifa, but also the small, provincial ones, regularly run into serious budget deficits by trying to emulate big and rich Tel Aviv. During the summer of 1992, Israel had more than ten festivals dedicated to classical and Jewish music, jazz and rock, and folk dance. Most of these concerts were attended by large audiences of sometimes up to a hundred thousand people. The same crowd seems to move from one venue to the next.

In their desperate pursuit of fun and entertainment, the new Israelis have turned the long Middle Eastern summer into one protracted festival, apparently shrugging off, or perhaps sublimating, the acute existential problems of political violence, terrorism, and military tension that constantly face them. To a foreign observer this mania for culture may seem appalling or even perverse: Are cultural pursuits and war compatible? But to most of the new Israelis, this peculiar coexistence of combat and culture does not pose any serious contradictions. Israelis are used to having wars while also enjoying music, theater, and other kinds of entertainment.

At a different location on the south side of the Shaul Hamelekh Boulevard there is a large wall complete with concrete roadblocks and barbed wire: this area constitutes the outer perimeter of the Kirya. Male and female soldiers armed with Israeli-made Uzi submachine guns or American M-16 assault rifles patrol the length of the wall. It is the strictly segregated section of Tel Aviv that is home to Israel's Ministry of Defense. It also includes the tallest building in the entire country: the headquarters of the general staff of the Israeli Army. Its tower, crammed with antennas, satellite dishes, and other communications equipment is clearly visible from afar.

This complex is the heart of Israel's security system. Unlike the other buildings on the Shaul Hemelkh Boulevard, here you need a pass in order to get in. The contrast is sharpened by the architectural difference—the drab and messy Kirya, which could hardly be mistaken for anything but government offices, and its modern, steel and glass highrise neighbors.

Few people inside Israel know the inner workings of these buildings. Up until the late 1980s, one building on the boulevard served as the headquarters of the Mossad—the branch of Israel's renowned intelligence community in charge of foreign espionage. In the early 1990s, the Mossad's central command moved to a site north of Tel Aviv, but most of the offices of private businesses, middlemen, and arms dealers which had gathered there over the years remained at Shaul Hamelekh Boulevard. Selling arms and exporting security know-how has become one of the most lucrative areas of Israel's economy.

For some Israeli and Jewish intellectuals this is a sad twist of fate. Israel's resources and sophistication, instead of being channeled into progress and learning, are used to boost the culture of war. In spite of the recent changes in attitude, the painful reality of war, death, and bereavement, which inspired George Segal to sculpt his piece of art, still strongly mark the nation that was intended to embody the Jewish heritage.

NINE

The Rise of Political Extremism

DURING the 1992 election campaign, in order to boost the morale of its supporters, Israel's ruling Likud party distributed leaflets showing photographs of the former prime minister, Menachim Begin, and organized pilgrimages to the Jerusalem cemetery where he is buried. This campaign paraphernalia was intended mainly for the Sephardic community—avid supporters of Likud under Begin—to help influence the outcome of the election. What made this tactic so strange was the party's focus on the image of a dead leader rather than on the live, current prime minister who was actually running in the election.

It is no coincidence that the Likud was embarrassed by Yitzhak Shamir. They themselves acknowledge Shamir to be a cold, contemptuous, and unattractive personality—passive and ruthless at the same time. He was regarded as a liability to his party rather than as an asset. Nevertheless, the man had managed—though lacking in respect in Israel or throughout the world—to run Israel's government since 1983. Only David Ben Gurion, who was Israel's longest serving prime minister, has governed longer than Shamir; he had even outlasted the far more charismatic Golda Meir and Menachim Begin.

In the period since 1983, which has been marked by conservatism and an obsession with maintaining things as they are, Shamir's vigilant do-nothing political stance has matched the mood of the country. Shamir is known for his fear of change and his love of the status quo. According to *Yediot Aharonot,* Israel's largest daily newspaper, Shamir "is known for his hibernation, his hyper passivity: he does not merely keep the status quo, he is the status quo himself."

Under Shamir's Likud, Israel sank deep into the mire of political polarization in its relations with the United States, its strongest ally. In fact, Shamir's obsession with the concept of greater Israel—and his stubborn maintenance of all of the settlements in the occupied territories—has endangered the United States–Israel bond as never before in the country's entire history.

Shamir's apathetic leadership, which has brought the country into one of its most stagnant periods since independence, is in direct contrast to his dramatic and adventurous past. In my own conversations with him, Shamir has admitted that he lived his greatest moments of glory more than fifty years ago, when he was the leader of a small but lethal underground organization in Palestine and, later, an agent of the Mossad.

Shamir, an ardent Zionist in Poland, emigrated to Palestine in 1935. One year later he joined the Irgun, Jabotinsky's clandestine military wing, where he personally participated in attacks resulting in the deaths of dozens of Arabs. Later Shamir came under the charismatic spell of Avraham Stern. In 1940, Stern, a gifted poet, led a small breakaway group from Jabotinsky's Revisionists; Shamir was one of them. They called themselves Lehi—Israel's Freedom Fighters—but they were dubbed the "Stern Gang" by the British. Shamir and the other members of the Stern Gang accused Jabotinsky and his Irgun of being too soft and conciliatory toward the British. This was the same accusation that Jabotinsky had thrown at Ben Gurion and his mainstream Zionism in 1937. The Stern Gang believed that the

Irgun, at the outset of World War II, had wrongly suspended its military operations against the British rulers of Palestine and the Arab inhabitants.

Stern and his colleagues saw the British as more of a threat to the Jewish people than the German Nazis. Indeed, they dreamed of forging an alliance with Mussolini and Hitler. At meetings between Stern's emissary and Italian and German diplomats, the common enemy was the British; it was the understanding of Stern that Hitler did not intend to destroy the Jews but simply wanted to get rid of them. This astonishing chapter in Israel's pre-statehood history illustrates both the blind stupidity of Stern and his supporters and their lack of morality in initiating talks with the greatest enemy of the Jewish people.

The cold-blooded killing of Stern in 1942 by British plainclothes policemen led the group to reorganize under a new triumvirate. The most prominent member was Yitzhak Shamir. In 1942 Shamir had been detained by the British but escaped with a comrade, Eliahu Giladi. Upon his return, Shamir moved the underground in a new direction. The first victim of Shamir's new Stern Gang and its revolutionary zeal was Giladi himself. Most of the group perceived Giladi as a dangerous adventurer: he had suggested assassinating the entire Zionist leadership, including Ben Gurion. Shamir concluded that Giladi and his "insane" plans were a danger to the group and decided to get him out of the way.

In 1991 I discovered an old document in which Shamir acknowledged that it was his orders that killed Giladi. The only indication that Shamir's conscience may have bothered him about Giladi's death was the curious and unusual name he gave to his daughter, Gilada.

Under Shamir, the Stern Gang was small and highly secretive, consisting of no more than a handful of active members and several hundred sympathizers. Their unmitigated cruelty, however, terrified the British. They robbed banks, executed Jewish "traitors," and assassinated a British cabinet minister and other British officials and diplomats. They also murdered hundreds of Arabs in indiscriminate terror attacks by planting car bombs and booby traps in Arab markets and public places.

After an extensive manhunt, the British arrested Shamir in 1946 and deported him to a remote detainee camp in Africa, from which he escaped once again. In 1948, after Israel's Declaration of Independence, Shamir returned to the newborn state. His underground experience and self-discipline, and his obsession with secrecy and ruthless devotion to the cause, made him a perfect candidate for the secret service. In 1955, he was rescued from oblivion and joined the Mossad.

For a period of ten years, Shamir led Israel's small but highly effective hit squad. The unit carried out attacks on perceived enemies of Israel, including Arabs, suspected Nazi war criminals, and German scientists suspected of helping Egypt develop missiles. In 1965, when there was a reshuffling of the top ranks in the Mossad, Shamir and some of his old friends were forced to resign. He tried his luck in business, as he had once before, but failed again. In 1970, at the age of fifty-five, he joined Begin's right-wing party. Though it was a late age to begin a political career, Shamir succeeded beyond anyone's expectations. He was not offered a ministerial post, and he certainly never dreamed of receiving the prime ministership. Within a period of thirteen years he was elected to Knesset, became its president, then Israel's foreign minister, and, in September 1983, Israel's seventh prime minister.

Shamir's opportunity to rule Israel's government came one August morning in 1983 when Menachim Begin walked into his weekly cabinet meeting and astonished everyone by announcing, "I can't continue anymore." Begin resigned from government, from his party, and from political and public life entirely. He became a hermit, shut away in his Jerusalem apartment, his face overgrown with a wild-looking beard. In his morbid seclusion he refused to see anyone except his closest relatives.

I phoned him from time to time to get his reactions to political events. His answers were always brief, and he sounded like he was seriously ill. His family—particularly his son, Benjamin Zeev Begin—protected him from everyone, both those who might have been able to help him and those who could tarnish his name.

Begin's dramatic disappearance from Israeli politics remains an unsolved riddle. In March 1992 he took his secret with him to the grave. The country had never before witnessed an event quite like

Begin's funeral. All previous conventions and procedures of such state burials were changed. Tens of thousands of Likud supporters joined in the ceremony. The police had difficulty controlling the crowd: people were trying to pass the security barriers in order to touch the body and bid him farewell. It was closer to the mass hysteria of the funeral of Iran's Ayatollah Khomeini than to the poised and Western-style funeral it was supposed to have been.

Only Begin's son, who was closest to him, may be able to reveal the circumstances of his resignation. But so far he has shown no such intention. All else is guesswork and speculation: The death of his wife, which left him a broken man? His bad conscience about the war in Lebanon?

The Lebanese war marked the end of a wholly unpredicted period of peace that was fostered by Begin's signing of the peace treaty with Egypt in March 1979. Begin returned to his more familiar position as militant aggressor when, in June 1982, he ordered Israeli armed forces into south Lebanon. This was only the second time in its short history that Israel took the war initiative without provocation. Prior to that, in 1956, Israel, as an ally in the imperialist link with Britain and France, had attacked Egypt.

But the Israel of the 1950s was a very different place from the Israel of the early 1980s. Israel was no longer a cohesive society, and political divisions within the country led to deep disagreements about the rationale for the war. The declared objective had been "peace for the Galilee," i.e., to stop Palestinian terror groups in southern Lebanon from attacking villages and towns along the northern border of Israel. What Begin was really after, however, was the destruction of the Palestine Liberation Organization, the PLO. The mission failed and the price Israel paid was very high.

On the first day of the war, Begin made a statement in the Knesset promising that the campaign would take no more than forty-eight hours. However, days, weeks, and months passed by and Israel's soldiers became more and more entangled in the fighting, not only with Palestinian fighters and Syrian soldiers, but also with Shiite fundamentalists using unorthodox military methods: they sacrificed their own lives by acting as live explosives. More than seven hundred Israeli soldiers and thousands of Palestinian and Lebanese fighters and citizens died. Though the tendency in Israel has been to blame Ariel Sharon, who was the minister of defense, the truth of the matter is that Begin was well aware that no one could accurately predict the length or outcome of this or any war.

In 1983 the Likud chose Yizhak Shamir to succeed Begin as its leader and prime minister. This decision has helped to bring about perhaps the most divisive decade in Israel's entire history. Shamir's leadership represented a disorienting and destructive combination of passivity toward most of Israel's social and economic problems and an aggressive determination to maintain Greater Israel at any cost. Shamir, impatient and easily bored, can barely conceal his contempt for most people. He dislikes the media and publicity. An unsentimental man, typical of a kind of nineteenth-century Russian revolutionary, Shamir is a character Dostoyevski could have written—a person for whom the end always justifies the means. Unlike Begin, he has never spoken of his personal loss in the Holocaust of most of his family. His tough behavior is infamous in government circles. Some of his aides have reported being reduced to tears in his presence.

Shamir's period in office was marked by the rise of a younger generation of Likud. Some of these descendants of political families have come to occupy key functions in the party and government.

Unlike most western countries, Israel does not have a tradition whereby the children of government officials follow in the footsteps of their parents. While in America it is common for the son of a senator or governor to take their place, in Israel this has not been the case until recently.

This new young generation of Likud can be divided into two groups. One group consists of the sons of Ashkenazi fathers who had been leaders of the party. This group has been christened by the press, part mockingly and part sympathetically, as "the princes." The most prominent among them are Benjamin Begin, Benjamin Netanyahu—well known to American television audiences—Dan Meridor, and Ehud Olmert. All of these men are known internationally as Shamir government spokesmen. All of their parents, prior to the Likud administration, experienced some form of discrimination from Labor. The sons' routes to power have been smoother.

The other group are mostly Sephardis and represent the children of the massive wave of immigrants who arrived in the 1950s. Their background, as we have seen, was quite different. They lived in shantytowns and tent camps. The humiliation and deprivation they suffered was channeled into political activism, and they were motivated by a desire to be better, more like the sabras.

Meir Shitrit, who was my officer in the army in the 1970s, came from a family who had immigrated from Morocco and lived in a small absorption town. Though his family was extremely poor, they made sure that Meir received a proper education. He went to the army and later to the university, where he became politically active. Labor, however, was not prepared to take him seriously. The party already had its "Sephardi representatives," a bunch of yes-men who did exactly what the party expected of them. It was a paternalistic party, not keen on independent thinking or any show of initiative. Given this attitude, young people like Shitrit ended up joining Begin or Shamir's Likud, with no other real alternative. There they were received with open arms. Most Sephardis launched their political careers by representing the Likud at local elections; by 1973 they had already made considerable headway from the municipal level of politics into the national arena. This was the first sign of the change that culminated in the 1977 election.

Shitrit himself became mayor of Yavneh, a town fifteen miles south of Tel Aviv. In a few years time, he changed the small town, known for its high crime rate, unemployment, and socioeconomic depression, into a developing town with modern services and an extremely high level of education.

However, from the mid-1980s, with the resignation of Begin and the election of Shamir, a change came over Shitrit and his friends. When Likud came to power, some of its ministers, members of parliament, and mayors could not resist exploiting their privileged positions for the purpose of furthering their personal and party interests. As a result, political patronage and the squandering of government funds have been revealed at unprecedentedly high levels.

The style of the Likud party under Shamir has become a cross between an increased display of the Western trappings of power and a Middle Eastern chaos. Party members arrive at meetings in chauffeur-driven limousines equipped with cellular phones and beepers as symbols of their new status. After only fifteen years of government, Likud was manifesting the same arrogance, corruption, and complacency Labor had shown during the 1970s.

In the Israel of the early 1990s, there is a feeling that history is repeating itself. Likud, after recruiting Sephardis in order to build the party, was now accused of ignoring that population. This atmosphere of ethnic and racial tension came to a head during Likud's internal elections in early 1992. The supporters of vice premier David Levy—Likud's most senior representative from the Moroccan community—accused Shamir and his people—mostly of Ashkenazi origins—of treating him and their community as inferior. No wonder that in June 1992 Likud lost to Rabin's Labor. Though some of this can be seen as a natural desire for a political and historical change, much of the blame for losing the elections must be laid at the door of Shamir and his failure to act on any of the real problems in Israel today.

It is not surprising that the single most important decision of Shamir's entire career has been to not decide. During the Gulf War, his generals and some cabinet members put pressure on Shamir to order an attack against Iraq in response to the Scud missile hits on Tel Aviv. Shamir refused to make up his mind. He was afraid that Israeli intervention would go against the grain of the pro-Western Arab countries who were fighting against Iraq. A military response from Israel could have possibly collapsed the international coalition that President Bush had created; it would, in turn, have seriously soured Israel's already weakening relations with the United States.

But despite this attempt to please President Bush the irony is that never more than during Shamir's leadership Israeli-American relations have come apart. As foreign minister during the Begin administration, Shamir was against the peace treaty with Egypt. As prime minister, he has made every possible effort to torpedo any United States initiative to bring Israel and its Arab enemies to the negotiating table. Shamir, a rigid and suspicious man, has made no attempt to make a good faith effort toward the Arabs: he does not trust them. He still operates with the same beliefs of his Irgun and Stern Gang days: the Arabs are only interested in weakening Israel and in dealing it a fatal blow.

Shamir turned a blind eye to right-wing extremists, led by Ariel Sharon, when they continued building new settlements in the occupied territories. This kind of activity took place throughout Secretary of State James Baker's visits to Israel in 1991. As revenge and punishment for this behavior, President Bush rejected, in September 1991, Israel's request for a ten-billion-dollar loan guarantee that was intended to finance the absorption of Soviet Jewish immigrants. In a speech explaining his decision, President Bush said that Israel was not in a position to close its eyes and ears: every Israeli citizen owed $1,000 to the United States Treasury. But for Shamir, choosing between settlements and immigrants would be tantamount to cutting off his own hand. Shamir, who is a hesitant politician, tried to outmaneuver and foil the Americans, but he failed. He did not stop the settlements, and he did not get the money.

This tension between Israel and its most powerful ally has sounded historical echoes from the period of the destruction of the Second Temple nearly two thousand years ago. More and more often, analogies are made between Shamir's style of governance and the revolt of the Zealots against the Roman Empire. The opponents of the Zealots were in favor of maintaining friendly relations with the outside world. The Zealots, though, spoke in terms of honor and pride and believed in stressing their privileges as the chosen people. In A.D. 68 the Zealots succeeded in stirring up a popular uprising against the Roman Empire. After some initial Jewish success, their revolt was suppressed. The city of Jerusalem was taken by eighty thousand Roman soldiers in the year A.D. 70. They burned the Second Temple, and two years later, after the tragic conclusion of the siege of Masada, put an end to Israelite independence.

For the Jewish people these events constitute one of the greatest disasters of their history: occupation and exile eventually followed by two thousand years of diaspora. The trauma of this crushing defeat lingers on in the Israeli-Jewish collective memory. What they remember, too, is that even during the final stages of the Roman siege of Jerusalem, the rival Israelite camps were unable to reconcile their divisions.

Shamir's Likud and its consorts appear, more than ever, like the extreme Zealots; and Israel today—especially after the victory of the Labor party—is as dangerously divided as it was at that critical time. The ancient maxim that emerged after the fall of the Second Temple comes back to haunt us: "Those who will destroy and ruin you will come from amongst you. The Temple was destroyed because of vain hatred."

Every summer, according to the Hebrew calendar, the destruction of the Second Temple is commemorated in prayers and a day of fasting. In Israel, cafes, restaurants, and theaters are closed; radio and television broadcasts are devoted to discussions of the relevance, to contemporary Israelis, of the fall of the Temple and the loss of political independence. Could it happen again? Is modern Israel repeating its ancestors' mistakes—internal division, or, rather, inflexibility and suspiciousness?

Though this internal division and polarization first began to show itself in 1967, after the Six-Day War, the process came to a head during Shamir's period in office.

Despite the ubiquitous presence of political argument in Israel, the country has little forum for debate. Israeli politicians lack the education and background to use language in a sophisticated manner. The Knesset does not entertain displays of wit or humor that might broach uncomfortable subjects. The speeches of Israeli politicians are boring and overly serious and usually boil over into shouting matches between rival party members.

In 1990, Yitzhak Shamir accused Ezer Weizmann—one of his most seasoned cabinet ministers and a former defense minister in Begin's government—of treason because Weizmann had arranged to meet with Palestinians. On the night that Shamir raised the issue, Weizmann received threatening phone calls.

Begin, during his premiership, did not hesitate to use demagoguery in his fight against Labor. And it did not stop at verbal violence. The walls of buildings housing Labor and other left-wing clubs were covered in offensive graffiti, and attempts were made to set fire to the homes of left-wing politicians. Leftist leaders were pelted with tomatoes and their political meetings were attacked by Likud supporters who had taken Begin and other Likud leaders' messages literally.

To those with a sense of history, Israel's current state of affairs recalls not only the chaos before the destruction of the Second Temple, but also the conditions in the German Weimar Republic between the two world wars, when that country was in a recession with ravaging unemployment and lots of political violence, and the cabaret, theater, and nightclubs flourished. With the rise of political extremism in Israel, many fear that its democracy will eventually buckle under problems similar to those of pre-World War II Germany and be replaced by a dictatorship. Others fear a civil war.

In this tense and pessimistic atmosphere, the Israeli press has devoted attention to the question of what form such a war would take. The question, it turns out, is not whether Israel could sustain a situation in which brother would take arms against brother; rather, it is what would provoke such a conflict: Would U.S. pressure to evacuate settlements in the occupied territories turn one Israeli against another? Would social and economic tensions come to a breaking point? How would the army act in a civil war? Would it take sides, as in Yugoslavia? Would it preserve neutrality or split into factions?

The widespread preoccupation with these questions points to underlying psychological factors. Some believe that in discussing the questions, the entire situation can be averted. Others, however, have stopped believing that Israel's inner conflicts—between the religious and the secular, Sephardis and Ashkenazis, right and left, rich and poor, and the Palestinian problems—would find their solution only in such a war.

In the 1980s, many Israelis believed that if political violence were to erupt in a civil war, the catalyst would certainly be Rabbi Meir Kahane. Kahane rose to fame in America in the late 1960s with his establishment of the Jewish Defense League and his slogan "Never again." Never again would Jews be victims. Initially, the organization was providing security for New York Jewish communities who were receiving threats from surrounding ethnic neighborhoods. In time, however, the league became a group of Jewish thugs and hooligans who used guns and violence against anyone they considered an enemy of the Jews, from the Black Panthers to Soviet diplomats.

After becoming a nuisance to the FBI and an embarrassment to the Jewish mainstream establishment, Kahane emigrated to Israel in the early 1970s. Once there, Kahane channeled his violent activities into setting up a new movement in Israel. Known as "Kach" ("this is the way" or "thus"), the movement tried to establish itself as part of Israel's traditional right. Links were forged between Kach and the right during the peak of Kahane's struggle for the release of Soviet Jewry. As early as the late 1960s, rumors were circulating that right-wing Israeli businesspeople were helping to smuggle arms to Kahane's Jewish Defense League.

But Kahane was not born to operate within an organized political framework: he was a lone wolf. He thrived on fear, paranoia, and hatred. His movement in Israel came to stand for racial hatred against the Arabs and violent resistance toward political opposition. What Kahane and his people created was an antidemocratic, protofascist movement. Kahane's intense preoccupation with the prevention of mixed marriages—he objected to even the most innocent associations between Arab men and Jewish women—together with a call to maintain the purity of the Jewish race, was a cynical reminder of Nazi racist theories. At some point, when Kach violence was taking on serious proportions, members were put under constant police surveillance and some, including Kahane, were thrown in jail.

Nevertheless, in 1984 Kahane was elected to parliament because he had managed to gain a foothold among some segments of the Sephardi population. Even at the height of his popularity, when twenty thousand people voted for him, Kahane was seen as a stranger in Israeli politics. His American accent, foreign political style, and deranged demeanor during speeches made him and his group look like thugs. After his election, he refused to pledge allegiance to the state, claiming he would only declare loyalty to his God. His parliamentary career came to an end when the Knesset declared his party illegal and passed a law forbidding incitement to hatred, racism, and violence.

Interestingly, the initiative for this new law did not come from the left—who supported it, of course—but from Likud and the other small parties on the far right who grasped that Kahane's status might come to endanger their own position and rob them of precious seats.

Two years later, in November 1990, Kahane was assassinated in a Manhattan hotel during a lecture to his American supporters. The man suspected of murdering him—an Egyptian fundamentalist living in the United States—was acquitted for lack of evidence. With Kahane's death, the remaining fragments of his Kach party have disintegrated. Kahane's lasting achievement, no doubt, is his exposure of the darkest side of the Israeli psyche—anti-Arab racism.

This racism exists in the political concept of *transfer,* which literally involves the resettlement, by their own decision, of all Arab communities out of Israel. Mainstream Zionists called for financial incentives and compensations to encourage Arabs to leave their homes and resettle in neighboring Arab countries. Nothing practical ever came of the massive plans, but the notion of Arab transfer—the idea that Palestinians must somehow make way for Jews—has survived. However, transfer has become a very marginal concept in the Zionist discourse and a taboo topic.

Had Kahane been the only modern supporter of transfer, then the concept would have died quickly. Once other right-wing parties, even some elements in the Likud, started employing the term *transfer,* it became clear that this disturbing idea had somehow caught on. No longer was this the ambition of a marginal splinter group: now respectable mainstream Israelis concurred.

Upon outlawing Kahane's group in 1988, an entirely new party was established whose single preoccupation was the advocation of transfer. The Moledot movement—or fatherland—was led by ex-general Rehavem Zeevi, previously identified with Labor. The party gained three seats in the Knesset in 1992 and participated in Shamir's coalition government with Zeevi functioning as a minister. In effect, by allowing this to happen, Shamir legitimized the concept of transfer.

Those who use the word *transfer* today do not refer to its original meaning: a *voluntary* movement of the Palestinians that would operate under international supervision. Transfer now stands as a codeword for the expulsion of the Arabs from Israel and the Palestinians from the West Bank and the Gaza Strip. The leaders who believe in this kind of extreme have brought Israel to the heart of their own darkness.

TEN

"Our Arabs"

"THIS is my village," says Abd a-Salam Manasra, pointing in the direction of a small hill. There are no buildings, no streets, no signs of life—just the fields, greener after the last rains. Wheat covers the hills from horizon to horizon. Manasra touches his white woolen cap with his hand, gazes at the hill, and sinks into deep thought as he recollects images of the village where he was born more than fifty years ago.

The hill is situated in the Valley of Jezrael, not far from the mountain district Armageddon, the Greek name for Megiddo. This crossroads, because of its geostrategic position, has seen many great battles, including invasions by Egyptians and Babylonians into what was the ancient kingdom of Israel. Christianity appointed this as the place where the last decisive battle was to be fought on the Day of Judgment. In 1948, during the War of Independence, Manasra's village was taken by Israeli soldiers. The village inhabitants, including the seven-year-old Manasra and his large family, escaped. Later, the village was wiped off the face of the earth by Israeli bulldozers.

"We were a militant village," he admits, "and as we were

exchanging fire with the Jewish forces there was a growing fear that the Jews would seek revenge. So it was decided to evacuate women and children first and, after a week, the fighting men also retreated and abandoned the village. Actually, we were the only village in the vicinity that acted in this way: all the others stayed intact. Our babies, children, and some mattresses were loaded on a few donkeys, and we walked all the way—more than ten miles to Nazareth."

In many ways, Manasra's fate was not unlike that of another six hundred thousand Palestinians who fled or were expelled from 450 villages in the heat of the war. The big difference is that his family did not escape to the other side of the border, but remained inside Israeli territory. Thus, instead of becoming refugees residing in a tent in Jordan, Egypt, Syria, or Lebanon, the family moved to the nearest large town, Nazareth, from which Jesus' family originated.

Manasra's traumatic childhood has made him a bitter man: "The journey shaped my life. Since then I lived with a sharp sense of disorientation. I feel like a dispossessed person, as someone who's lost his land, his house, his roots. My family was well off, and suddenly, overnight, we became penniless."

One of the most painful events for Manasra was his first visit, during his teens, to the site which had once been his village. "Our houses were completely destroyed, erased, and our fertile lands were now being cultivated by members of the neighboring kibbutzim. I even managed to identify the exact spot where our own family house used to stand. Walking on the land which used to bear my village only deepened my trauma. Since then, I have made it a habit, a pilgrimage, to pay a visit once every so often to my old village." Manasra's recollections are part of a growing nostalgia among Israeli Arabs for the land they left behind. In their memoirs, Israeli-Arab and Palestinian authors write longingly and mournfully about a world that has disappeared.

Even though the majority of those uprooted in 1948 were villagers, the greatest damage was sustained within the urban fabric of Palestinian life. In large towns like Yafo or Haifa, a lively urban Palestinian society with healthy trade and culture had developed. Active political life with many parties was flourishing. These urban centers were slightly less advanced than what the Jews had built up in

Tel Aviv under British rule, but they were a lot more developed than most towns elsewhere in the Arab world. With the 1948 "disaster" the Palestinian Arabs lost their elite—the intellectuals, the leadership, the political structure—and their economic base.

The old photographs shown in Palestinian memoirs date back to the 1948 war and earlier. These yellowing pictures are vivid, and they seem to give off the fragrance of the country. You can easily make out the mountains, the plains, the valleys and hills, the curving rivers, and the ancient castles and fortresses. The photographs also show the variety of Arab building styles. The villages are situated on hilltops—they seem an integral part of the topography. Yet in today's pictures of the same areas, it is hard to distinguish the course of rivers because many of them were diverted and turned into sewage channels by overzealous Israeli construction. The hilltops, too, were rearranged by bulldozers and transformed into urban conglomerations with tediously uniform houses. The modern standard housing complexes look alien and forced onto the landscape.

Still, relatively speaking, the Manasra family might be considered better off than the majority of the Palestinians who ended up in refugee camps in neighboring countries. At least, that is how it might seem to the cool, objective observer. But for the Palestinians it is a tragedy that was often marked by three successive phases: frustration, reconciliation, and return to roots. Manasra himself has gone through all of these. His personal experience, therefore, can be seen as a reflection of the political experience shared by many of his people.

When he was young, Manasra joined the Israeli Communist party, which had a strong appeal for Israeli Arabs.

The Communist party was the only Israeli party that preached peaceful coexistence of Jews and Arabs and accepted both as its members. All other Jewish-Zionist parties refused to receive non-Jewish membership. The Communist party was also the only one which, at least in the first years after the Palestinian tragedy in 1948, managed to reflect the genuine national aspirations of Israel's Arabs. Many of those supporting the Communist party were not, in fact, communist.

During the first months after the War of Independence, most

Palestinian refugees were still convinced they were going to return home and that the new reality in which they had been forced to live was only temporary. Abd a-Salam Manasra remembers some protests among uprooted Palestinians within his own family, in which people refused to wash or change their clothes as long as they could not return home. A small minority of Communist voters entertained secret hopes for a miracle by which an Arab state would materialize where the Jewish state is now. But by far, most Arab supporters of the party were giving their vote to the Communist party more as an act of protest than because they identified with its ideology.

During the first eighteen years after the war, the Israeli Arabs were under military administration despite the fact that they were legally equal citizens. Arabic was even made an official language, along with Hebrew. In reality, though, Arabs were discriminated against wherever they went and for whatever they did. Their movements were severely restricted. Discrimination against Arabs is still glaringly evident today, twenty-six years after the military administration was lifted. Arabs are barred from most civil service jobs. They are also exempt from the obligatory national service. This decision was mutually agreed upon: the Israeli authorities did not want to recruit Arabs, whom they suspected of being disloyal to the Jewish state; and the Arabs did not want to be mobilized and forced to face the dilemma of serving a state that was at war with their own brothers and sisters.

Viewed as the ultimate litmus test of identification with and loyalty to the state, very small groups within the Israeli Arab minority are encouraged by the Israeli authorities to volunteer for military service. Bedouin tribes, whose nomadic existence has kept them somewhat apart from the farmers and townspeople of Arab origins, have long been a party of the military. The Druze community—Muslims whose faith requires that religious secrets be kept from ordinary people—also served in the Israeli army. The rationale behind Israel's policies in this matter is the ancient Roman dictum "Divide and rule."

Unemployment among Israeli Arabs has always been higher than among Israeli Jews. In 1992 Arab unemployment was double that of the Jewish population. In addition, Israel does not have even one

Arab university, although it does have six Jewish universities plus another ten or so colleges of higher education. Arab students who graduate from these Jewish institutions have a much harder time finding appropriate work than do their Jewish classmates. Apart from jobs in the civil service, they are also unable to obtain positions in institutes for higher education, science, and research. They have no access at all to the sprawling military-industrial complex. Forty-two percent of all Arab university graduates of the last decade have remained unemployed. Only fifteen percent of the Jewish graduates have not found work. It is, in fact, only in the educational services that Arab university graduates are not prevented from practicing their profession.

Moreover, life expectancy among Israeli Arabs is seventy-one years, which is three years shorter than among Israeli Jews. The Arabs live in poor housing, and the level of municipal services in the average Arab village falls well below that in Jewish towns and villages. The government provides resources and funds for the development of industries in Jewish areas, while preferring to see the Arab sector continue its dependence on agriculture. In fact, the substandard conditions in many Arab towns and villages are reminiscent of the squalor in America's inner cities. Neglect is rampant: sewers are blocked and flooded; roads are unpaved; and there are insufficient sidewalks and community centers, clinics, and schools. Correspondingly, crime rates are high and drug abuse is on the increase.

In shrill contrast to the supersensitivity displayed toward the Jewish Orthodox, the government ignores Muslim sentiments: roads and houses are built on the grounds of former cemeteries, mosques, and other Islamic holy places. For instance, Tel Aviv's Hilton Hotel, one of Israel's most luxurious, was constructed in the early 1960s on the site of a Muslim cemetery.

The Israeli Communist party did try vigorously to fight this discrimination and called for the practical implementation of the principles of equality. These principles are expressed in Israel's Declaration of Independence—but to no avail.

The Communist party, in the eyes of the Israeli government, stood for Arab nationalism. It is therefore not hard to understand why the

Communist party—which was tied strongly to the Soviet Union—
had such difficulty attaining its goals. Repeated calls since 1949 for
an end to military rule had no impact whatsoever on the government. Military administration was eventually halted, when the
Labor party decided in 1966 that the Arab minority could no longer
be considered a serious security risk.

After the first years of rage and frustration, most Israeli Arabs
started to believe that they should reconcile themselves to Israel's
existence. They recognized that neither they nor their Palestinian and
Arab brethren on the other side of the border stood any realistic
chance of achieving a state of their own at the expense of Israel. Israel
was powerful, with a modern army that had proven itself in wars
with neighboring Arab states. Agriculture blossomed and industry
was doing well. Jewish-Israeli modernization began to penetrate and
strike roots in the Arab community. Israel's Jewish sector had
become a sort of role model for some of Israel's Arabs. Many,
especially the young, tried to emulate and become a part of Israel's
Western way of life. Abd a-Salam Manasra was one of these youths.
He changed his traditional clothes for fashionable Western costume.
He became fluent in Hebrew, complete with slang. Manasra was a
builder and worked for a Jewish contractor. "I believed in a peaceful
coexistence between Jews and Arabs, and as a political activist, I
worked for it," explains Manasra.

It was not exactly a chosen integration, but a product of the
circumstances. Many Arabs found work with Jewish employers, and
this led to increased contact between the two communities. It did
not bring about any new social or cultural exchanges, nor did it
change or remove prejudice and stereotypes. But it did force both
communities to adjust to the fact that they were living side by side,
mingling with each other daily.

Young Israeli Arabs today have shown an increased desire for
excellence. When Rifat Turk, a young teenager from Yafo, played his
first game for the national team in the early 1970s, many eyebrows
were raised among the twenty thousand spectators. Many of them
could not adjust to the spectacle of one lonely Arab playing
alongside ten Jewish players. Some of the crowd did not hesitate to
reveal their bias and prejudice. They called him derogatory and

racist names. "It was not easy," Rifat Turk recalls, "but after a while I decided to ignore the crowd, and eventually, after a few more games, the crowd accepted me and even started liking me."

Now a successful and popular coach on one of Israel's prestigious soccer clubs, Turk can watch with satisfaction as other Arab players follow in his footsteps. Occasionally, they too have a rough time: some games turn into humiliating events with curses and obscenities filling the stadium. Nevertheless, the majority of Israeli Jews now accept Arab players. This "acceptance," however, seems more like that of the average white racist who hates blacks but recognizes their sportsmanship and doesn't mind them if they play for his team. Politicians also exploit the appearance of Arab actors and sportsmen by pointing out that, despite everything, Jewish-Arab cooperation is possible.

Beside the basic impulse to better oneself, many Israeli Arabs seem to express a need for "copying the master." In the first twenty years of statehood, Arab protest usually expressed itself in peaceful political rallies, marches, and demonstrations. Then the protest patterns of Arabs changed drastically. The Arab population did not hesitate to turn to violence when protesting the discriminatory practices of Jewish authorities by blocking roads, burning tires, and clashing with the police. This experience gave young and radical Israeli Arabs the confidence to call for changes in outdated political structures and destructive old habits within their own community.

Modernization introduced socioeconomic change in the Arab community. Most left farming to become wage earners in local industries, trades, or services in the Jewish sector. This brought with it a tendency to urbanize the Arab communities: the standard of living rose, and the first signs of consumerism and affluence started to appear. These changes, however, happened at the expense of old traditions.

The Hamula, the extended family, has been one of the pillars of Arab community life. Kinship still plays a major role in Arab politics. Most of the electoral lists and political movements in the 1989 municipal elections were Hamula-based. The Hamula, which functions as a political, social, and economic network, is still most obviously present in Arab villages and towns. Yet, despite its continued existence, there are clear signs that the power of the Hamula is diminishing. The central role of the father in Arab families has eroded; family members now tend to make decisions based upon practical considerations rather than family commitments.

The status of women is still quite inferior in Arab-Israeli society. It's true that the role of women in some orthodox Jewish groups is in many ways equally backward. What makes Arab women more vulnerable than their Jewish counterparts is the phenomenon of "family revenge"—murders which are committed to save the "honor" of the family. When an Arab woman has an extramarital affair or loses her virginity before marriage, she runs the risk of being killed by her own father or brothers. Nevertheless, with the passage of time, more and more Arab women have been leaving their family homes and redefining their traditional housekeeping duties. More Arab women have entered the job market, more Arab female students are seen at the universities, and a growing number of Arab women are involved in politics. The first feminist organization among Israeli Arabs emerged in 1992 and called for tougher measures to be used against "family honor" crimes.

Israeli as well as Arab sociologists have called this new Arab westernization and move toward modern technology and democratic values "the process of Israelization." This is by no means an unmixed blessing for the Arab community, as it brings in its wake a profound identity crisis—one which in some ways mirrors the Israeli Jews' own identity problems.

The Arab community has to live with the consequences of the contradiction between the Zionist-Jewish nature of Israel and its democratic values. This contradiction would seem primarily to involve and affect the Jewish majority, but in reality it has an enormous impact on the Arab minority. While the Arabs have had to come to terms with the fact that they are citizens of the state of Israel, they also must accept that, as such, they will never receive full and equal treatment.

In the Jewish state, Jews enjoy certain privileges—foremost, the Law of Return. This substantial advantage over non-Jews does not seem to satisfy Israel's decision-makers. Using all kinds of gimmicks, they have managed to pass additional laws in their favor, such as laws regarding child allowances and mortgages. In order to remain legally in the clear and still not have to pay a child allowance to Arab citizens, the Israeli legislators and politicians invented the notion of "ex-military allowance." What this comes down to is that only the child whose head of family has served in the Israeli army is entitled to the money. Thus, since the vast majority of Arabs cannot and do not serve in the army, they are ineligible for the allowance. A similar, legally instituted sleight of hand is designed to make Arabs ineligible for state-subsidized mortgages.

Of course, these laws also exclude anyone else who has not served: the disabled, those who have been disqualified on other medical grounds, and the Orthodox, who protest loudly against this injustice. What infuriates Israeli Jews who can't qualify for the allowance, perhaps even more than the financial loss, is that they fall into the same category as the Arabs—a serious stigma. But it seems that the decision-makers, in their obtuseness, prefer to tolerate this drawback (though from time to time attempts are made to find an even more sophisticated legal manipulation whereby the Arabs, finally, would be the only ones excluded from these basic social benefits) rather than spending millions of dollars in comprehensively extending the welfare system to Arabs.

Clashes between Jewish and Arab culture and questions of divided loyalty all cause the Arabs who live within Israel's borders to agonize about their identity. Are they Israelis? Are they Arabs? Can they possibly be both? Or neither? The truth of the matter is that Israeli Arabs live in limbo: The Arab world calls them "the Arabs of 1948," or more obviously derogatorily, "the Israelized and Judaized Arabs." Israeli Jews refer to them as "the minority," "the Arab sector," or simply, and patronizingly, "our Arabs." Israeli politicians categorize Israeli Arabs as "moderates" or "extremists." This division is aimed at rewarding the "good Arabs" and discriminating against the "bad Arabs." In practice, this system of identification does not work.

In addition to this, Israeli authorities pursue Bedouin shepherds and their herds who trespass. The shepherds are constantly arrested and their herds confiscated. By confiscating their land, too, the authorities have been trying to force Bedouin tribes to leave their areas and abandon their nomadic life, taming them into town dwellers. Even the individual Arab groups who are considered "moderates" have fallen victim to Jewish insensitivity.

Arabs who have tried their best to live harmoniously with Jewish Israelis, to sublimate or ignore their identity problems—even those who had almost no doubts about their political sympathies—have had to realize that there was a limit to their capacity to blend in with Jewish Israeli society. Like most of the Bedouins who volunteer for military (army) service, Khaled Nimer Sawad was a scout. Bedouins, who live close to nature, make excellent navigators and guides. After completing his military service, Khaled returned to the Galilee intending to become a farmer. He settled on a hilltop not far from Safed and the tombs that have become pilgrimage sites to modern Israelis. He lives, along with his wife and four children, in a little hut. "I didn't choose to live here," he points out. "I was born here, and so were my parents and grandparents. My father is buried here, and my family has been in this area for hundreds of years. We never budged." Israeli bureaucracy, in an ill-disguised attempt to make Kaled move away, has been giving him a hard time. He has no electricity, and to get water, he has to take his pails to the nearest community.

What hurts Khaled most is how well the state of Israel has taken care of his neighbors. Right next door to him, at the end of his field, a fence has been erected to stake out the border of the Jewish community, which has long had electricity and running water. The crackling sound of electricity passing through the cables and the murmur of water flowing through the pipes serve as a continuous reminder that Israeli discrimination remains strong. Though some of Khaled's Jewish neighbors help him and let him fill up his buckets with water, they still won't accept him as a member of their community. Segregation, fear, and prejudice don't allow Arabs and Jews to live together in one community—even when the Arab in question has paid his full debt to society with the currency considered most valuable in Israel: serving in its armed forces and fighting alongside his Jewish comrades and against his Arab brothers.

Jewish landlords are reluctant to rent their property to Arabs. There are very few mixed neighborhoods in Israel, and they exist only in such towns as Yafo, Acre, and Haifa, where the Arab population has remained since 1948. Except for one experimental project, there is not one rural community where Jews and Arabs live and work the land together.

The case of Majid Khader is an even sadder one. I first got to know Majid by his other name, Amos Yarkoni. I was a timid recruit and he was the admired officer of our unit. The unit was in charge of reconnaissance missions, intelligence gathering, and patrols along Israel's long borders with Jordan and Egypt. Those who served with and under Majid can tell endless, amazing stories about his military excellence.

Majid was born in the late 1920s in a Bedouin community in the valley of Jezrael. However, unlike the people of Manasra's village, Majid and his kinsmen struck an alliance with their Jewish neighbors during the 1930s and supported them in the 1948 war. When the state of Israel was officially declared, Majid and his tribesmen volunteered to serve in the new Israeli army. Majid had a long and outstanding career. He was promoted to colonel in charge of our unit, which was one of the army's elite units. He was wounded in fights against Palestinian terrorists, Arab infiltrators, and smugglers, and he lost an arm as well as a foot. He received the highest decoration for his service. He also received an Israeli name, Amos Yarkoni, but he never actually changed his Arab name, nor did he renounce his religion. He was a proud Arab and Muslim and an Israeli patriot.

Given Majid's impressive biography, one would think that Arabs in Israeli society can serve the nation and live in equality. Sadly, the rest of his life story betrays that notion. When Majid finished his military service and retired, he was given a civil service job and took up residence in a southern Israeli town, among the Jews. His Jewish friends from the army, some of whom had become government ministers, continued to respect him, but, said Majid-Amos, "it wasn't the same." His son, Majid junior, wanted to serve in an elite marine unit, but his request was refused because of his Arab origins.

Perceived as potential security risks, Bedouins, the Druze, and other Arabs who volunteer for the army are not assigned as air force pilots, submarine crews, or fighters in special forces and are usually confined to their own ethnic units. Even the support and intervention of his father's influential friends did not prevail—bureaucratic paranoia was stronger. Both father and son were deeply wounded by the incident, and Majid's son left the country for the United States as soon as he finished his regular stint in the army. Disappointed by Israeli reality, Majid Khader died in February 1991, after a long illness.

It's not surprising that ideological confusion, political frustration, widening socioeconomic gaps, and the constant search for identity have caused a resurgence of Islam within the Israeli-Arab community. The Islamic movement has emerged as a need for Israeli Arabs to "return to their roots." The attraction to Islam is the third phase in which Manasra now finds himself.

"For more than thirty years of my life I was a Communist who believed in peaceful coexistence with the Jews," he confesses, "and who hoped that my Israeliness and my Communism would work as tools toward our development and advancement. Now I'm disappointed in that hope. In Islam I've found the new way. Today I believe that my secular political ways led me to an evil culture. I abandoned the religion with which I grew up. I renounced God and began to feel like I was an orphan. Communism functioned for me like a religion and a family. When I left Communism and politics I understood that what I needed was another faith."

"I tried to find a religion that would suit me. I began reading the Bible. I even considered converting to Judaism. After that I looked for the light in Christianity, the New Testament, but in the end, I saw that my old religion really was the best for me. Not because I was born into it but because I made my choice. I became religious because I want to look for justice and truth."

Manasra now belongs to a small sect of the Islamic movement which occupies itself mainly with philosophical discourse and the search for life's meaning. But for most of the Arabs who have returned to the fold, Islam became attractive for less metaphysical and more urgent reasons. The Islamic movement provides Israeli Arabs with a valid interpretation of their aggravating situation, and with a comprehensive set of norms and values that are well anchored in their political-religious heritage.

The Islamic movement in Israel was established about twenty years ago by a group of young people who, at the time, were beginning to return to their religious roots. Most were educated urban people familiar with both their own Arab society and the state of Israel. They speak Hebrew fluently, know the nuances of its slang, and in many ways behave like their Jewish peers. The only difference seems to be in their outward appearance—long caftans, caps on their heads, and short beards—which marks their return to Islam.

Sheikh Abdallah Nimer Darwish is the most prominent among the young leaders of the Islamic movement. His village, Kafar Kassem, is a typical community fifteen miles east of Tel Aviv that has grown into an urban center. In his remote past, Darwish spent some time in an Israeli jail for committing "security charges." This is the legal term for the association with a Palestinian or Arab organization outside of Israel. After his release he "saw the light of Islam" and studied with an elderly sheikh in the mosque, until he was eventually ordained. Sheikh Darwish is an impressive man. He speaks fluent Arabic and Hebrew. He stresses that the Islamic movement calls for Muslims to return to Islam and abandon Western culture, but he expresses no desire to achieve this by force, coercion, or violence, as was done in Iran. Darwish also argues that he is in favor of democracy and believes in the right of Jewish statehood. In his view the phenomenon of the return to religious roots is not just local or even regional, spreading as it has through neighboring Jordan and Egypt and also into the more remote Sudan and Algiers, but worldwide.

Ironically, it is therefore not surprising that he and his colleagues in the movement have found common ground with Orthodox Jews of their age, notably those from the Shas party. Sometimes it is hard to distinguish between the Muslim and Jewish fundamentalists, since they both wear beards and strikingly similar skullcaps. They share, at least, one common aim: to set up a theocracy.

Despite the reassuring message of Sheikh Darwish and his colleagues, most Israelis fear the rise of the Islamic movement. Rightly or wrongly, the Israeli Jews identify the movement with Iranian-style fundamentalism. The perception among many Israeli Jews is that hatred of Israel and Jews is inherent in the Islamic movement. In February 1992, this perception was strengthened when members on the fringe of the Islamic movement murdered three recently recruited Israeli soldiers. This was the worst political crime ever committed by Israeli Arabs against Israeli Jews.

Secular Muslims and especially Christian Arabs in Israel also fear the growing power of the Islamic movement. In the local elections of 1989 the Islamic movement defeated the Communist party in some towns and large villages. The Islamic movement has changed the face of the "Arab street." In many places, over the last few years the conspicuous green flag, the color of Muhammad's banner, can be seen flying over recently built mosques. Friday prayers are now attended by hundreds and sometimes even thousands of young worshipers. Shops selling holy books and religious articles have been mushrooming. The movement has opened schools and kindergartens which—like their Jewish Orthodox counterparts—strictly separate boys and girls. Education is alarmingly doctrinaire, and is conducted mainly through recitation of verses from the Koran, the Muslim holy scripture. Wherever the movement gains hold, the few women who wear modern Western-style dress are told to change back into the traditional, "modest" female style. Some of the sports organizations have been persuaded that their players should only appear in long trousers.

The consolidation of the Islamic movement in Israel is indicative of the depth of traditional-religious sentiment within Arab society in general and within the Israeli Muslim community in particular. It attests to the strength of Islam as a cultural and historic badge of identity. Nevertheless, it would be a mistake to judge this phenomenon only on its historic, religious, and cultural merits. The Islamic movement also represents a cohesive social force, with a deep involvement in community life. It organizes community centers, job training courses, and medical emergency training and is committed to fighting crime, prostitution, and drug abuse. The movement also aims to improve the local infrastructure: to replace the old sewage pipes with a better system and to build roads. In other words, through fundamentalism, Israeli-Arabs are attempting to restore their national identity while reconciling it with the Jewish character of the Israeli state.

While the Islamic movement is a popular protest movement, it is impossible to ignore the fact that it was established only a few years after the Six-Day War. This war and its aftermath contributed at the same time to the development of certain tendencies within Jewish Israeli society: Sephardi self-awareness, political radicalism, and fundamentalism. Just as the opening of the old borders, between the West Bank and Israel, enabled Jews to reach places that historically and biblically had been a part of their collective national memory, it also helped Israeli Arabs to reunite with their Palestinian brothers on the other side of the pre-1967 borders and to visit their holy places. Israeli Arabs could now pray on Fridays in their holiest mosques on the Temple Mount in East Jerusalem, exposing them to a religious influence that was much stronger on Jordan's West Bank and Egypt's Gaza Strip than inside Israel's borders.

Sociologists call this process of change the "Palestinianization of the Israeli Arabs" and contrast it to the earlier mentioned "Israelization." The connection to their Palestinian brothers sharpened the national-religious consciousness of Israeli Arabs. This awareness might be summarized as: We are Arabs living in Israel, our nationality is Palestinian, and our religion, mainly, is Islam.

As the Israeli Arabs enter the nineties, their identity problems and the inner contradictions with which they live are more complicated then ever. They are walking a fine line between their "Israeliness," their "Palestinianness," and their "Islamicness."

Information reported about current tendencies in any community is colored by the political views of the sociologist or researcher. Jewish sociologists—or those Arab sociologists who believe that peaceful coexistence is still possible—will stress a connection between Arab and "Israeliness." The assumption is that Israeli Arabs, who have grown used to the Israeli pace of life, will prefer Western-style modernity over a separate Palestinian state. In this view, the Israeli Arabs will form a bridge of peace between Israel and the Arab world. Arab and Jewish nationalist sociologists, however, will attempt to prove that the Israeli Arabs will choose to live among their Arab-Palestinian brothers.

Whatever the case may be, one thing is clear: the future of the Israeli Arabs, and the solution to their manifold problems, is closely linked to the difficult question of what is to become of the Palestinians who still live under Israeli occupation on the West Bank and the Gaza Strip.

ELEVEN

The Arabs Over There

ONE EVENING in March 1992, a young couple was walking quietly along one of the main streets in an affluent Tel Aviv suburb. The sun was low in the sky, but it was still light. This was the evening of the Jewish Purim festival, when families put on fancy clothes or costumes, go to parties, and have a good time. Usually the costumes reflect popular television programs, current politicians, or folklore traditions: that evening one might have seen numerous Ninja turtles, President Bushes, Saddam Husseins, cowboys and Dutch flower girls. On the sidewalk opposite the young couple, two men in costume were approaching. One was wearing a monkey's mask and the other had covered his head with a kaffiyeh, the Arab headdress, and was wearing a traditional Arab gown. As the two men came face-to-face with the young couple, the man who was dressed up like an Arab was shot at close range. He collapsed and was taken to a nearby hospital with minor injuries. Within a few days he was able to go home. The assailant was taken to a local police station for questioning. "I thought I had shot a terrorist," he explained. The young man turned out to be a soldier on leave. According to Israeli army regulations all soldiers remain armed whether they're in their base or on a short leave.

The incident, which occurred in the heart of Israel, is symbolic of our times. Aside from its tragicomic aspects, it contained all the elements that characterize the special relations that have evolved between Israelis and Palestinians, between the Jews and the Arabs of the occupied territories: fear, suspicion, hatred, stereotyping, and a violent volatility.

A lot of these emotions have accumulated and developed over the quarter of a century of Israeli occupation—a period during which most Israelis generally believed that it was possible to live like this and continue doing so indeterminately. This illusion, however, was shattered on December 8, 1987.

When, in June 1967, Israel seized the West Bank and the Gaza Strip—home to 1.2 million Palestinians—it hadn't intended to stay there. The majority of Israelis were convinced that soon Israel would be forced to return the newly occupied territories to the Arab states, either because of international pressure or as part of a peace agreement.

When the Israeli presence in the territories lasted for one year, and then two, some Israelis became ashamed or embarrassed by the state of affairs. To deflect their shame they denied that the Israeli presence actually constituted a military "occupation." Instead, other less charged terms were invented. They called the military rule "enlightened occupation" and created an equally absurd fantasy about how life would be in the occupied territory. Their military would be a caring, considerate administration: occupation with a human side. The subjects of the occupation, "the Arabs over there," would run their own lives, as if there was no occupation at all—these were not relations between the occupier and the occupied but an example of real equality between Jews and Arabs.

It had not been long since the Jewish people themselves had been exposed to occupation and victimization. Surely after what happened in the Second World War and during the British mandate of Palestine between 1917 and 1947 they could not now be on the side of the oppressor? Most Israelis refused to consider the possibility they were now causing the suffering. The contradictory notion of "enlightened occupation" had to fall flat on its face.

For nearly twenty years, from 1967 until 1987, Israel managed to conceal this failure, partly in order to maintain a sense of order. It achieved control over the occupied territories through methods similar to those practiced by any colonial power of the nineteenth and twentieth centuries. The job of keeping the Palestinians quiet was given to Israel's General Security Service (GSS), Shabak in Hebrew. GSS men, known in Israel as "Shabakniks," became the "kings of the territories." Just as under the medieval feudal system, every Israeli agent ("lord") was assigned an area of land that thereby became his "estate." Usually this area consisted of one or more villages in the West Bank or on the Gaza Strip. It was the agent's responsibility to know everything that was going on in his area. Known to the local people by an Arab code name and their military rank—resulting in such odd combinations as Captain Yussuf—the agent knew some rudimentary Arabic and was instructed to get acquainted with all the inhabitants of his "estate."

Not even one Palestinian could enter or leave the particular latifundium to which he belonged without the knowledge and assent of the Shabaknik-lord. In order to keep a finger on the pulse of his vassal population, the agent would select informers from among his subjects. The informers were pressured into taking these positions. If a Palestinian applied for a building permit, his "lord" would decide the matter. A Palestinian tradesman who wished to export oranges from Gaza, tomatoes from Jericho, or olive oil from Nablus, could only obtain the necessary papers through the GSS. Almost every daily routine, almost every minute of the lives of the local Palestinians, fell under the scrutiny of his Shabaknik-lord and the intelligence apparatus that backed him up.

If the aim of all this control was to maintain order and silence, it was attained very quickly. When they recovered from the first shock of defeat and occupation, the Palestinians attempted, during the first months following the 1967 war, to rebel against the Israelis. Their plan, devised by the PLO, was to make the territories ungovernable for the Israelis. What the guerrilla groups had in mind was a "popular liberation struggle," similar to the ideas of Mao Zedong and Fidel Castro. Militant PLO factions, armed with guns and explosives, entered the occupied territories and set up command posts under the noses of the new Israeli administrators. Guerrilla factions were dispatched on hit-and-run operations against army vehicles and patrols. The Palestinians staged ambushes in the narrow streets of West Bank and Gaza Strip towns. Inside other parts of Israel, the Palestinians began a campaign of indiscriminate, bloody terror by detonating bombs in markets, schools, cinemas, bus stations, and restaurants.

By the end of 1967, however, the Palestinian rebellion was crushed by the combination of efficient Israeli security operations and the amateurism of the PLO. The Palestinian communications system was primitive, the codes simple. No escape routes were planned. Their safe houses were only nominally protected. Members of the guerrilla squads were not trained to withstand interrogation techniques. As soon as they were picked up by GSS agents, they would tell everything they knew. Consequently, their codes were cracked, their weapons and explosives confiscated. One after the other, like dominoes, the cells collapsed. Above all, failing to follow Mao Zedong's dictum that the guerrilla fighter must have the support of the population and feel "like a fish in the water," the Palestinian fighters could not "swim" unnoticed among their fellow people, who swept them to the GSS. Motivated by Israeli incentives, the local populace preferred peace and quiet and relative prosperity to risky collaboration with their own underground.

The Palestinian resistance against the Israeli occupation continued to exist throughout the years but at a level that was too insignificant to inflict any serious damage and disruption on Israel's daily routine. Indeed, the manageability of Palestinian resistance allowed the Israelis to positively reap the fruits of their occupation. They considered the Palestinian population of the occupied territories cheap labor and developed an attitude of superiority and contempt toward them. Every morning, before dawn, tens of thousands of Palestinians from the territories left their houses like industrious ants—on foot or in vans and buses—to go to work in Israel.

Young and old Palestinian workers, with nothing but a bag holding a meager meal (usually pita, olives, and a piece of cheese), would crowd the Israeli roadside in hopes of being picked up for work by a Jewish contractor. Any car that stopped would be stormed by tens of Palestinians eager for a job for the day—shoving each other, pleading, kissing the hands of the Jewish employer, offering themselves cheap. In these virtual slave markets you could find children no older than ten or eleven who, instead of going to school like normal kids their age, were sent to work to contribute to the family's income. Palestinians were almost everywhere. They were washing the dishes in Tel Aviv's restaurants, tending gardens in rich Haifa suburbs, standing at the production line in a Beer Sheba factory, and balancing on the scaffolds in the expanding neighborhoods of Jerusalem.

Over the years, Israelis have grown used to the presence of Palestinians in their homes, gardens, and offices: they have come to regard them as part of the furniture of their living space. The floor cleaner in our apartment building was, as in most similar Israeli buildings, a young Palestinian boy from a small village in the West Bank. Every morning, when residents were leaving for work, he would appear in the hall with his pail, broom, and rag. People would pass by this slight, stooped figure as if he were invisible. Not even one of them knew his surname, only a few were familiar with his first name—Kassem—and even fewer took the trouble to greet him. Only in rare outbursts of compassion, occasioned by a bout of bad conscience, would some good souls bring Kassem some food, old clothes, and leftovers that would have otherwise have ended up in the garbage pail.

Israel's success in pacifying the territories came at a price, however. At a time when booby-trapped cars were exploding and hotels and airplanes were popular terrorist targets, it was essential to extract information quickly and efficiently. The Shabakniks learned the hard way what occupation meant. Theirs was dirty work in the service of a noble cause: defending their country and its people. But security methods followed a double standard of justice. Democratic justice was available to Israeli citizens, and a totally different standard—

operating in the gray area between the permissible and the forbidden—was used against Palestinian suspects in the occupied territories. Whenever Palestinians were arrested, they were immediately
taken to separate detention centers or special wings of the Israeli
civilian jails. Neither the police nor the National Prison Authority
knew what was happening behind these walls.

I spent part of my military service during the early seventies in the
Gaza Strip. During the day we would patrol the narrow alleys of the
refugee camps. We were greeted by the women with looks full of
hatred and fear. Many of us behaved like brutes when we broke
furniture, smashed crockery, and left a house looking as if it had
been visited by a hurricane. Only a very few among us were aware of
the fact that we, boys of about eighteen, were the representatives of
the occupation in the eyes of the Palestinians.

In the night we would accompany the Shabak officers as they
rounded up new Palestinian prisoners. The Shabakniks were always
joined by Palestinian informers, who covered their faces in order not
to be recognized by their own people. The role of the informer was to
betray his friends and deliver them into the hands of the administration. He would whisper the suspect's address into the Shabaknik's
ear. Some of us would surround the apartment or house, while others
would gain access to the property by smashing the door. The usually
large families would wake in a panic. The informer would step into
the scene and point out the suspect. Immediately, we would tie his
hands and sometimes his feet, too, while brandishing our weapons.
The family's shouts and cries reached the sky as we dragged the
suspect outside and threw him into the car.

Next we would drive off to the Shabak wing at the nearest jail. The
arrested man would be delivered at the entrance. We, the soldiers,
were not allowed to enter. But on our nightly visits we always heard
the terrible screams that came from these wings. It was clear that the
Palestinian detainees were being beaten and tortured.

Later on, I learned that it was common practice for the Shabakniks
to cover the Palestinian prisoners' heads with a black sack stinking of
urine. Later, with their heads still covered, they were exposed to the

unbearable Israeli sun. Suspects were usually deprived of sleep for hours on end and were sometimes soaked with cold water to prevent them from falling asleep.

I witnessed a few particularly sadistic and violent incidents while in the army. During one of its patrols my team came across an Arab man who was quietly walking in an orchard. We shouted at him to stop, and he, of course, immediately obliged. Had he refused to obey we might have fired at him. Next, following standard procedures, we put him in front of a nearby wall with his arms high above his head. We searched his pockets and his body, requested his identity card, and asked him for his name. After this, one of the soldiers decided it was time for some fun with the victim. He made him march to a nearby tree and told him that he had been found guilty of terrorist activities and would be executed. The Arab man began to weep bitterly. The soldier tied him to the tree and blindfolded him with a handkerchief. The man's sobs increased. He begged for his soul and his family and screamed that he was innocent. Now the soldier was joined by two of his mates. Quietly they slipped the magazines out of their rifles, counted in Arabic, "One, two, three...", and noisily pulled their triggers. Of course, there was no actual shooting as the rifles were not loaded. We all burst out laughing. The first soldier walked up to the Arab, took off his blindfold, and untied him. The Arab's trousers were wet. He fell to his knees, his entire body shaking, and kissed the feet of the "liberating" soldier. The soldier gave the Arab man a contemptuous kick and ordered him to get up.

Some hours later, as I lay down on my bed in the army base, I reflected on the terrible incident in which I had just participated. I had been a passive witness, and I had not joined in staging the execution, but my conscience disturbed me. I could have reported the whole affair to my superior, and the soldier who had invented the "game" probably would have been punished. If I had done this, however, I would have been considered an informer, and my mates would have ostracized me. I decided to keep my mouth shut.

I had also heard about a case in another unit in which a young Arab man had been stopped and ordered to kiss the genitalia of the donkey on which he had been riding. In a different incident, soldiers had shaved off the pubic hair of an Arab man whom they had halted in the street for a routine search.

Only toward the end of my stint in 1971, when I had come to the conclusion that I could swallow no more, I phoned a prominent journalist who was known to have a strong moral commitment to truth and wrote about this kind of injustice. Had the authorities known about my deed, they would no doubt have taken me to court and given me a prison sentence. It is strictly forbidden for any soldier to report, without army permission, on anything he has witnessed during his service. On the phone I identified myself as a soldier on leave, who was posted in Gaza and who had important information. The journalist was reluctant to meet me. Only after begging him and repeating my request several times did he soften—but not before warning me that his time was limited and that he would be able to see me for only a few minutes.

We met in a Tel Aviv cafe. I told him briefly of what I had seen and heard during my stay in Gaza. He made a few notes in his book and promised that he would deal with the issue. We met for only a few minutes. For weeks I closely scrutinized the newspapers for the story. Gradually, it became clear that the journalist had not bothered to write one.

At this time, there was a national consensus in Israel that such excrescences of the military occupation should not be made public. Everyone was still convinced that the occupation was a temporary matter and that Israel was conducting an "enlightened occupation." Only years later, when the Likud rose to power, did the press gather its courage and begin reporting on real events in the territories. Indeed, since then, Israel's press has openly covered news about the effects and implications of the occupation. But as one senior editor put it, "Nobody wants to read about it."

For a period of about twenty years, it seemed that the entire country was in a trance. People lived their lives as if there was no occupation. Denial, sublimation, and alienation allowed Israelis to ignore the virtual slave markets that existed in their towns. They did not want to know about the tortures the Shabakniks were inflicting on their behalf, and in the name of security. They averted their eyes when they approached army roadblocks, which they could speed right through while Arab cars were stopped. In order to facilitate identification, cars from the West Bank and the Gaza Strip have license plates that are easily identified.

The Palestinian during these twenty years, however, could neither forget nor repress. For years they quietly worked for the Israelis for low wages and without benefits. Many of them were young and well-educated people with university degrees. A shortage of jobs, especially for university graduates, meant that many thousands of bright and able Palestinians were either unemployed or hauling crates of citrus fruits at the Haifa market or sweeping up a Tel Aviv restaurant after closing time. After work they slept in old, dilapidated sheds on the kitchen floor of the restaurant or beside the machines in the factory where they worked by day. Even the "robber barons" and the worst capitalists in American would have been ashamed to employ their workers in such conditions. After a week's hard menial work, Palestinians returned to their families for the weekend. On their way home they passed the clean, wealthy Jewish settlements that had been built near their villages.

Over these last two decades, the Palestinians have become closely acquainted with Israeli society. While Israelis on the whole do not make the effort to learn Arabic, the Palestinians have had to learn Hebrew for survival. It's nearly impossible for them to find work without speaking Hebrew. Young Palestinians have come to imitate their Israeli peers. They adopt similar manners and idiosyncrasies of speech, and they even dress like Israelis. But there are distinct differences: the Palestinians are still the servants of the Israeli masters. It is not surprising that their view of Israeli society is dominated by hatred and envy.

In December 1987, these feelings peaked as a rumor spread like fire on an oil slick that "the Jews had killed in cold blood." Word spread from the narrow alleys of the shantytown of Jibalyah refugee camp in northern Gaza, to the equally poor but less crowded town of Rafah, on Gaza's border with Egypt. The Palestinians of Gaza were saying that the recent deaths of four Arabs, run down by a truck, had been "the revenge of the Jews." On the main road linking Gaza with Israel, an Israeli driver had lost control of his heavy truck and plowed into a crowd of Palestinians on their way home from work. Hundreds of Palestinians witnessed the incident and were convinced it was murder: a tragic road accident became a historic incident.

Spontaneous demonstrations broke out and moved quickly through the entire Gaza Strip. These actions initiated the Intifada, the Palestinian uprising, which continues to this day. The word *intifada* literally means "shaking off," and is applied by Palestinians who intend to "shake off" Israeli military rule and occupation. The protesters demanded an alternative system of government, run by the Arab population, and hoped for a future Palestinian state.

Prior to the Intifada, there had been little Palestinian action against the Jewish occupation. In fact, most of the guerrilla violence was caused by a few individuals. The Intifada involves also, as in the past, explosives and weapons, but it is a popular revolt. Popular methods such as protest demonstrations, strikes, and even the throwing of stones, have succeeded in uniting most sectors of the Palestinian population in the occupied territories. Even though the strikes hit Palestinian businesses much harder than Israel's economy, most Palestinians are prepared to pay the price.

The Intifada also embraces conflicts within the Palestinian community: the social revolt of the poor Palestinians against the rich; the protest of the young against their elders; and the outcry against the impossible living conditions of many Palestinians, especially those in the refugee camps of Gaza. Those who live in the refugee camps survive against impossible odds. In the winter their dirt roads turn into huge muddy pools that block the roads to pedestrians and cars alike. The houses, built close together, are made of clay and are always on the verge of collapse. Open sewers pollute the air, and many cats and rats scavenge the never-emptied garbage containers.

The Intifada has, above all, given the Palestinians a sense of pride. It has strengthened their nationalist consciousness and has improved their international image.

Such an uprising was precisely what Shabak was meant to prevent. The network of informants was employed to alert them to any significant attempts to organize dissent. The several thousand informers throughout Palestinian society, from factory workers to intellectuals, were paid anywhere from fifty to two hundred dollars per month. Their job was to keep Shabak informed of political activism.

Reports of activism or trouble by the informers would lead to detentions, interrogations, and the filing of more reports. However, the larger picture was overlooked—Shabak lost the forest in the trees. Their obsession with each terrorist act made them unable to analyze the larger picture: the political tendencies of the Palestinian population.

In the early eighties, there was a unique attempt, undertaken jointly by Shabak and the military authorities in the territories, to learn about and to understand what was happening among the Palestinians, but this attempt failed.

In this period, because of the increasing strength of the national elements among the Palestinians, the military authorities decided to encourage the formation of a Palestinian agrarian league. The authorities thought that these groups would function as an alternative to PLO-dominated factions. With the support of the Israeli government, the Agrarian League was established on the West Bank. Members of the league had permission to carry weapons and enjoyed certain privileges from the Israeli authorities. All of this was done in hopes that it would lead to a new and pro-Israeli Palestinian leadership. The league, however, failed, and its members were considered traitors by other Palestinians: they had sold their souls to the Israeli occupier and were no longer to be trusted.

The second organization, which was indirectly supported by the Israeli authorities, was the fundamentalist Hamas movement. While the military authorities severely restricted the movement of any Palestinians who maintained connections with the PLO, the Islamic movement was cautiously supported by the Israeli government. The Hamas people went to Saudi Arabia, Kuwait, and the other rich Gulf Emirates and raised funds. Shabak and the military authorities allowed them to import this money into the West Bank and Gaza, where it was used to build new mosques, schools and colleges, religious community centers, and clinics.

The relative wealth of the Muslims, combined with their message about a return to religious roots, appealed strongly to young Palestinians. Thousands of them turned up for Friday prayers and joined Koran study classes. Entire families made use of the clinics for medical care, and their children went to the community centers. The mosques and schools became hotbeds of religious agitation.

In this sense, those Shabakniks who believe in "divide and rule" may view the creation of Hamas as a success story, since it threatens the political hegemony of the PLO nationalists in the territories. With the help of Israel, Hamas has developed into a political power with broad popular support. The rivalry between Hamas and the PLO often is violent and has already led to the deaths of hundreds of Palestinians. Both sides, especially Hamas, enlist their own people to kill "collaborators," drug pushers, or prostitutes.

The consolidation of Islam has created great apprehensions among Christian Palestinians. Tens of thousands of families from Christian population centers on the West Bank emigrated to the United States, Canada, and Europe in the 1980s. Venerable families with eight-hundred-year histories were among those who departed. Due to this wave of emigration, the town of Bethlehem, which is so closely linked to Christian history, lost its Christian majority and has become an Islamic stronghold. Prominent Christian leaders warn that if this trend continues, Bethlehem might eventually become a kind of "Christian Disneyland or reserve to be visited by tourists."

The crumbling of the Christian-Palestinian community has weakened the moderate and Western-oriented elements in Palestinian society—a sector with which Israel might have more easily found a common ground. On the other hand, Israel has not the slightest chance of reaching any understanding with Hamas.

Just as Shabak and the military authorities desired, the fundamentalists have indeed weakened the nationalist element in Palestinian society—but their hatred of Israel and the Jewish people is profound and uncompromising. The hostility between Hamas and the PLO is one of principles: While the PLO is basically willing to come to a peace agreement with Israel, Hamas simply does not acknowledge the right of the Jews to a state of their own. Unlike the nationalists, Hamas looks at the conflict with Israel as a religious and cultural struggle and not as a political argument over territory. More than any other movement in the occupied territories, the Palestinian fundamentalists believe their struggle is part of an old conflict between Islam and Western culture, spearheaded by Jews and Zionists.

To bring home their point they use the medieval crusaders as a parallel: Israel, Zionism, and Judaism are the new crusaders. Like the crusaders who journeyed to the Middle East between the eleventh and the thirteenth centuries, the Jews came from Europe too. Like the crusaders, the Jews too were a minority and subjected the land to their rule by war. They confiscated land from the local inhabitants but never succeeded in mixing and integrating with their environment. They always remained strangers and did not belong to the place. They spoke a foreign tongue, dressed differently, and had different habits and another religion. As with the crusaders, the Jews have not been accepted by their Arab-Muslim surroundings, being forced to live in fortresses in perpetual fear for their lives.

Thus the fundamentalists conclude that the Jews' fate will be like that of their predecessors. As the crusaders were eventually chased back to Europe, the Jews will be driven out as well, back to their countries of origin in Europe. This rather simplistic way of seeing things ignores the historical background: the bond the Jewish people feel with the land, and the fact that Zionism is no less a movement of national liberation than its Palestinian counterpart. Young, fanatical Palestinians, brainwashed with religious propaganda, go out and buy kitchen knives and stab innocent Jewish pedestrians on the streets of Tel Aviv or Jerusalem. They yell the opening words to every Muslim prayer: Allahu Akhbar—God is Great!

As is conveyed by the Jewish legend of the Golem, the Israelis have unwittingly helped to consolidate the fundamentalists' power. In that legend, a great rabbi in sixteenth-century Czechoslovakia molded himself a clay figure that he subsequently brought to life by means of his supernatural powers. He hoped the creature would become his obedient servant, but the magic creature rose against its master and ran amok in the city of Prague.

But despite the violent elements in their struggle and the rise of fundamentalism, the Intifada has generally helped the Palestinian resistance movement to obtain a certain legitimacy in world public opinion and among many governments in the West. This sympathy stands in sharp contrast to the deep repugnance aroused by the brutal methods that had earlier been employed by the Palestinians. The world could not support the Palestinians as long as they seemed to view innocent citizens as legitimate targets in their struggle. The world grew profoundly outraged when Palestinian "freedom fighters" would force their way into houses in the middle of the night and take four- and five-year-old children hostage. In the winter of 1974, not far from the border with Lebanon, the terrorists—surrounded by Israeli security forces—crushed the skull of one of their child hostages. No one could call men who were capable of such atrocities "freedom fighters" nor praise their actions as part of a "national struggle."

Through the media, the Intifada introduced a different picture of Israeli behavior for the "global village." Young Israeli soldiers were seen dispersing protesting children and cruelly beating a stone-throwing young Arab. Young Palestinians were photographed standing fearlessly—their chests bared—against the armed occupiers. The film footage, which precisely embodies the change that has taken place, was shown on Israeli television during one of the first weeks of the Intifada. In this scene an Arab teenager went face-to-face with a group of Israeli soldiers in one of the towns in the Gaza Strip. He cursed and taunted them in fluent Hebrew, which he must have acquired while working for a Jewish employer. The expletives he used were the latest popular Israel slang. The boy was not afraid to come within a few yards of the soldiers. Suddenly, a short fat officer—his belly bursting through his shirt and trousers—stepped forward and started running after the Arab boy. The images on the screen were pathetic and grotesque: the young boy moved easily, and, far behind him, the chubby soldier plodded after him. Out of breath and embarrassed, the officer rejoined his mates. To me this scene symbolizes the entire Palestinian-Israeli conflict—its irony and its historic reversal. It was the Palestinian who had become little David, and big Israel had turned into a helpless, clumsy Goliath.

Israeli society has been judged by the world for what was revealed about its security policies, and it has rapidly lost its good name. Having once enjoyed the highest status in Western public opinion, the Jewish state has fallen among the lowest. The victorious underdog of 1967 is now perceived as the ruthless occupier of another people's land.

December 8, 1987, also brought to a conclusion the desperately fostered notion of the "enlightened occupation." Those, like myself, who had served in the territories had given up on it twenty years earlier, but most Israelis continued to believe an illusion. Once the Intifada broke out, it was clear that the "enlightened occupation" didn't exist. And now, just as the Intifada was allowing the Palestinians to vent their frustration and rage, it unleashed similar feelings among the Israeli population toward the Palestinians. Thus, the vicious cycle of violence and counterviolence continues.

Israeli authorities do not allow the Arab press in the territories to run articles that have appeared in Israel, even though many Palestinians can now read Hebrew and have access to the Hebrew newspapers. Books printed and sold in Israel are forbidden to be printed or sold in the territories. The works of Karl Marx, for instance, are considered to be "subversive." The authorities have no qualms about closing down newspapers without providing any explanation. Every printed word—even the crossword puzzle, the weather forecast, and the sports page—must be submitted to the military censor.

This is not just a question of the freedom of speech and the right of the public to know—both fundamental elements of democracy—which have obviously been crushed under military occupation. What we see here is also evidence of Israel's paternalism: a view of the population in the occupied territories as insufficiently mature to decide what it does and doesn't want to read.

This double standard is also reflected in the choice of language itself. From as early as 1967, Israel has been operating a kind of "language laundry" wherein it uses cleaner sounding language that trivializes and obscures what is being described. Since the onset of the Intifada, the language laundry has been working overtime. The rhetoric of occupation favors words like *purifying* rather than *attacking* enemy positions. In police reports of traffic accidents, Jewish victims are always named, while Palestinian victims are referred to as Arabs. When the occupation authorities expel Palestinians from their residences, these activities are called "evacuations." This language creates the illusion that the "evacuation" is conducted to the advantage of the "evacuees." When Palestinians are injured or killed during demonstrations, the military spokesman will always explain that Israeli soldiers "fired shots in the air."

In 1990, a Palestinian woman called Safia Saliman Jarjon was killed in the Gaza Strip. After chasing a group of youngsters who had been throwing stones, the army entered Safia's house. The soldiers found her there, and one of them pushed her so that she fell to the ground. When her husband and daughter arrived about a half hour later, they discovered Safia on the floor with blood flowing from a wound in her back. She was pronounced dead at the hospital, and the death certificate stated that the cause of death was a gunshot wound to the back. Safia's husband and children applied for compensation from the state. The Ministry of Justice, however, came up with quite an original line of defense: the husband and his children were told that they had only gained by the death of the wife and mother. During her lifetime the husband had been obliged to support her: a burden from which he was now released. This is one of the ugliest examples of language manipulation.

The Israeli army has turned into a policing force. It furnishes young men with clubs, handcuffs, and helmets and obliges them to chase children their own age or younger, and sometimes even to shoot at them. During the first five years of the Intifada the Israeli security forces killed about eight hundred Palestinians. Ninety thousand Palestinians were put under arrest without trial. That means one in every fifteen Palestinians has now experienced Israeli prison.

When a Palestinian is seized for a violent action that resulted in injury or death, his house is destroyed by the security forces. This is done without any trial, even if the house is inhabited by the perpetrator's family. During the Intifada one incident occurred which was particularly indicative of the obtuseness and evil of the system. A Palestinian murder suspect was killed in a shootout with the Israeli security forces. As if this wasn't enough, his family residence was also demolished. Since occupation began in 1967, about five hundred houses have been razed, while an additional three hundred have been sealed off—leaving thousands of elderly people, women, and children on the street. All of this destruction is caused because a member of their family stood up against the oppressive Israeli regime.

When pro-Palestinian graffiti appear on the walls of a house, the inhabitants will be visited by an army patrol that will get them out of their beds in the middle of night and force them to erase the slogans. The next morning new graffiti will appear on the same walls. Needless to say, Palestinians are forbidden to convene political meetings, nor are they allowed to publicly display national flags. As a way around this prohibition, young Palestinians can often be seen dressed in their national colors of green, black, and red.

The Intifada adds a new dimension to the old Israeli-Palestinian conflict, which it has changed from a political struggle to communal, sectarian strife. The use of stones and knives by the Palestinians has bothered the Israelis. They are used to another game with different rules and would prefer to fight the Palestinians with "cleaner" weapons with which they are more familiar. More importantly, the use of these weapons actually scares the Israelis.

Employers now think twice before taking on a Palestinian worker; there have been incidents where a Palestinian worker suddenly got out his knife and stabbed his boss. Mothers are afraid to send their children on their own to school or the playground, because there have been such attacks. Under the pressure of their customers, supermarkets and other shops have had to fire the Palestinians who worked there and made home deliveries. Residents of towns and neighborhoods demand that people from the territories should not be allowed into Israel.

The occupation and its attendant fear have turned Israeli society into a defensive one, dominated by issues of self-preservation. In 1967, a Palestinian terrorist managed to surprise all of Israel when she planted a bomb in a Jerusalem cinema. The security forces invented a solution which, at the time, seemed clever: a security guard was posted at the entrance of every movie theater to check the bags of everyone who entered. Now, an armed guard can be found at the gate of every public building in Israel: kindergartens, schools, and, of course, movie theaters.

The increasing fear of Palestinians felt by Israelis has also whipped up emotions of hatred and revenge. This leads to expressions of intolerance and racism. In Ariel, one of the largest Jewish settlements on the West Bank—a town with nearly ten thousand Jewish inhabitants—it was suggested in 1990 that the entry of Palestinian workers be controlled by forcing them to wear a plastic card. The proposers of this plan—among them the town's mayor—were of the Likud, and not sufficiently sensitive to realize the horrible connotations: only sixty years before, the German Nazis had forced European Jews to wear yellow stars. And then there was Tel Aviv's chief of police, who helpfully suggested, in mid-1991, that any bus driver who set his eyes on "an Arab face" should head straight for the nearest police station. There the suspect would undergo investigation and be released only if he was an Israeli Arab or, alternatively, one—of the awkwardly many—Oriental Jews with an Arab/Mediterranean aspect. The powerful outcry from Israeli liberals and the media has prevented the full use of such strategies. But beyond the manifest lack of sensitivity and sense of history, such attitudes also reek badly of the kind of racism found under South Africa's old apartheid, which the white majority itself eventually chose to abolish. Despair and frustration about finding a reasonable political settlement to the Palestinian-Israeli conflict have confused many Israelis and made them susceptible to oppressive solutions, but even more widespread has been the choice of political extremism.

On the other hand, Israel's left and liberals had for years been calling for a separation between the two communities, but their voices had been lost in the wilderness. Recently, though, the Israeli majority has been returning, metaphorically speaking, to the green line—the old border of Israel prior to the Six-Day War. Out of fear Israelis pragmatically avoid visiting the occupied territories, and they do not want to see Palestinians in their streets any longer. More and more Israelis are reaching the conclusion that there is no alternative but to create a political separation between the two communities. This new position is seen as a solution offering the least of all evils.

TWELVE

Death of a Dream

SHMEUL Hadash has no more illusions: "The kibbutz as an idea has failed," he says, seated on the volcanic stones in the cemetery of Kinneret, his kibbutz. On his right, the tranquil waters of the Sea of Galilee, and facing him, the graves of the founders of the kibbutz. "They"—Haddash points to the engraved names on the head-stones—"tried to change human nature and to create a new man. To my regret, the kibbutz did not succeed in this task, because man's nature is stronger than his deeds. In the kibbutz, as in any other human society, people like to sow the minimum and reap the most."

Recounting his personal history, Shmuel Hadash, in his blue overalls and high boots, could be portrayed as the epitome of the average old kibbutznik. His father, buried in the cemetery of Kinneret, was among the founders of the first kibbutz in 1911.

A group of young Halutsim, pioneers from Eastern Europe, arrived during the wave of immigration known as the Second Aliyah. They started working as hired laborers at a dreary farm, a few yards from the place where the cemetery stands today. Eventually, disappointed in both their physical and spiritual conditions, they decided to establish a commune, a collective settlement that would be self-managed. The pioneers moved two miles down the road, along the shore of the lake, and set up Degania, the first kibbutz in Palestine.

More than anything else, the kibbutz is Israel's most authentic contribution to twentieth-century human experience. During my travels even in the most remote and obscure parts of the world, where the locals had never heard of Israel, the Middle East, or Jews, there was always someone who knew what a kibbutz was. Young people from all over the world are still attracted to the idea, and so are educators and sociologists. The kibbutz was established as an experiment in human coexistence. As with any empirical experiment, the results were meant to be used to achieve an improvement. In this case the improvement was to take place in people: the kibbutz was conceived as an instrument to change human nature.

Influenced by socialist writings and by the great Russian writer Lev Tolstoy, the kibbutznikim aspired to create a utopian society. What they had in mind, like the communist philosophers who had also inspired them, was summed up in one thought: contribute according to your ability and receive according to your needs. The kibbutz strove to alter the old image of the shtetl Jew: from trader, merchant, or moneylender to a farmer and pioneer, working the land.

The best recruitment tool for the kibbutzim was the Jewish youth movement system. The destination of any member of Labor-oriented youth organizations was settlement in a kibbutz. There, the ultimate synthesis was to take place—combining one's national contribution to Zionism and Israeli pioneering with the pursuit of socialist ideology to create a better and more just society. The youth movement was supposed to be a corridor leading to a better life in the kibbutz.

Like almost every Israeli child, I was a member of one of these movements. Mine was called Hashomer Hatzair, the Young Watchmen, an organization to the left of Israel's Labor party. As a young boy and a new immigrant, nothing seemed more Israeli than Hashomer Hatzair. All I wanted was to be an exact copy of my friends, something I tried to achieve by putting on shorts and sandals—the trademarks of the pioneer and the kibbutznik. I studiously imitated the way they talked. I never missed out on a hike. All of this was to prove to them and to myself that I was no longer a diaspora child, a Polish immigrant, but an Israeli through and through. For the same reason, I went "to fulfill my Zionist self" in the kibbutz. Once there, however, I lasted for no more than one year; my return to urban life was a defeat. My conscience would not leave me in peace: I had failed to "fulfill myself" in the way I was conditioned and indoctrinated to do. Still, the relatively short time I spent in the kibbutz significantly marked my character, my values, and my basic political outlook.

Building kibbutzim as rural outposts became the main vehicle shared by all branches of the Labor movement in their aim to spread socialist Zionism to new frontiers. It strengthened the security of the Jewish community in prestatehood days and especially after independence in 1948. The kibbutz's strongest impact on Israeli society was felt in the 1950s and 1960s. Although at that time the one hundred thousand members of the movement amounted to three percent of the country's Jewish population, their various important contributions to the state of Israel are still held in high regard. In the air force and special units (the most important links in Israel's defense) kibbutz members represented about twenty percent of the pilots and fighters. A significant portion of the country's leadership during the nearly thirty years of Labor's political hegemony, originated in the kibbutz movement. It produced fifteen percent of the country's industrial exports and provided fifty percent of its agricultural needs.

Participants in and observers of the Bolshevik revolution believed they saw the future in their struggle. A similar sense was shared by many admirers and members of the kibbutz. They looked at it as the most noble effort in human history to implement the ideals of communism: social justice, welfare, and mutual dependence.

Now all of this has dramatically changed: the kibbutz movement faces a serious crisis. After the 1960s, the kibbutz gradually lost its sense of purpose. Israel already had a strong army that could defend its people, and so the vital position of kibbutzim defending remote

frontiers diminished. Urban youngsters imitated the young kib-
buznikim in their zeal to volunteer for elite units in the armed forces.
And when the Labor party lost power to Likud, kibbutz input into
the political sphere also dwindled. In the heyday of its political
influence, the kibbutz movement had nearly twenty members in the
Knesset. It now has only four.

Their situation worsened in the 1980s. Due to bad management,
lack of motivation, and the loss of state subsidies, Israel's kibbutzim
sank into a deep economic depression. In a desperate move to survive
Likud's hyperinflation of the 1980s, the kibbutzim made poor
speculative investments in the stock exchange. This raised the total
debt of the kibbutz movement in the early 1990s to ten billion
dollars.

The economic collapse has added to the kibbutz's ideological
vulnerability and decline. The unselfishness and idealism, which
once were the pride of kibbutz society, are quickly evaporating.
Many young kibbutznikim no longer volunteer for elite units in the
army, and many do not return home to the kibbutz upon concluding
their three-year national service. Some of the youngsters simply
abandon their past and leave the kibbutz for the materialistic
temptations and the greater individual freedoms offered by Israel's
urban life. For others, however, replacing kibbutz rural society with
Israel's urban life is not enough—they may wander to Kashmir,
India, Cuzco, Peru, or, like the Rappoport brothers, to Los Angeles.

Gabriel Rappoport and his family live in Beit Alfa, "my" kibbutz.
It was established in the early 1920s and is one of the oldest and most
highly regarded kibbutzim in Israel. Situated at the foot of the Gilboa
Mountains, Beit Alfa used to be one of the most flourishing
kibbutzim in Israel. Gabriel Rappoport is another example of the
pioneer-farmer-soldier whom mainstream Zionism strove so hard to
create. A kibbutz member and a senior army officer, he embodies the
typical, mythical sabra. He is the son of pioneers who were among
the first settlers at Beit Alfa. Before Independence, he fought with the
Hagana underground and helped in the 1948 siege of Jerusalem.
Later he was promoted to colonel in Israel's armed forces. When he
left the military service, Rappoport returned to the plough and the

fields of Beit Alfa, where he raised his children with the same socialist Zionist principles that had guided him. But it didn't work.

When they were still young he taught them how to shoot, and they learned to drive a tractor at an equally early age. Though children under sixteen are not legally permitted to drive a tractor, kibbutz children can be seen regularly in the driver's seat. Taking your place behind the wheel of a tractor is considered a kind of initiation rite by which the young take their place in adult society.

Not one of Gabriel Rappoport's children stayed in the kibbutz. One daughter became a born-again Jew and married a prominent right-wing activist. Gabriel's three sons went, just as their father had wished, to elite combat units. But then, failing to return to the kibbutz, they left the country to settle down in Los Angeles. One of the brothers died of an illness, and the remaining two were joined in the United States by Gabriel's fifth and youngest child, a daughter.

Like so many of their age group, the Rappoport children experienced the kibbutz as a constriction on their individuality and freedom. Their financial dependence on the kibbutz, too, must have played a role: these young people wanted to earn a lot, and fast, believing that money would bring them happiness or whatever they could not get in the kibbutz. There was a time in the early 1980s when there were about thirty young people, all ex-members of kibbutz Beit Alfa, living near or in Los Angeles. They stuck together and worked together—it seemed as though they had transplanted communal life from Israel to California.

As the kibbutz movement in Israel is approaching its eighty-fifth anniversary, heretical voices like that of Shmuel Hadash or the actions of the young Rappoports are felt throughout its ranks. The wind of change is shaking all of Israel's kibbutzim. In the effort to save itself from idealogical decay, economic depression, social decline, and a steady drop in population, the kibbutz movement has made some changes. In order to keep its young members, the kibbitzim allow them to acquire higher education in universities and colleges and to take a year's leave within Israel's urban centers or even abroad. The dining hall, once the heart of community life, has lost its centrality. Before the decline, members of the kibbutz had all their meals together in the dining room. Now they are allowed to take the food from the communal kitchen and dine in their homes. Only those of the older generation who can still make their way to the communal dining room persist in eating together.

Despite the anger of the true believers in ideological purity, changes have also been introduced in the communal education of children. Kibbutz children formerly grew up from birth with their peer group in separate children's houses until the age of eighteen, when they went to the army. They were raised by members of the community who were especially assigned to this task. Although their respective parents and families lived within walking distance, the children could only see their families for up to two hours a day and on the weekends. This special method, according to the late psychologist, Bruno Bettelheim, was "remarkable and the most unique contribution of the kibbutz."

As part of this education and value system in the early days, showers were taken together—mixing female and male, children and adults. Unisex showers were the only available ones. This communal bathing was a revolutionary idea in the early 1900s. The reason for the unisex showers, however, was not economical but psychological. The founding fathers truly believed that if women and men had joint showers, then this would help to reduce sexual tension and create a generally healthier atmosphere in gender relations. But the experiment didn't work and in the early 1950s showers were taken separately.

Yet young females and males continued to share bedrooms. I was shocked upon arrival in my kibbutz, when I realized that I would have to share my bedroom with two female peers. Initially, I felt very clumsy in their company when I wanted to dress or undress. It took me a while before I got used to their constant presence and picked up the rules of the game: whenever one had to dress, the opposite sex was asked to turn his or her face to the wall. Today, kibbutz children, like other children elsewhere, live with their parents, brothers, and sisters.

Other major changes introduced by many kibbutzim would undoubtedly have caused the founding fathers to turn in their graves. These days the movement is prepared to try anything that might alleviate its economic burden, even if this results in the abandonment of major symbols that have come to be identified with its way of life. In the 1960s, the introduction of industry caused many kibbutzim to feel it was a "betrayal of traditional values."

Agriculture in the kibbutzim is still considered to be advanced and innovative. Near the Dead Sea, soil which was full of salts and minerals was made fertile by a special washing process. Because the climate in this part of the country is very hot, fruits and vegetables, such as tomatoes or cucumbers, can be cultivated there in the winter to supply the northern European markets. Using advanced research, new strains of fruits have been developed and grown commercially. The latest successful idea is to grow, in the occupied Golan Heights, various types of berries. Since berries do not grow naturally in Israel, exporting them to Europe is as strange as offering to sell ice and snow to Alaska. Yet the combination of Israeli chutzpah and agricultural innovation makes this possible.

Today the prevailing mood in the kibbutzim is to move from agriculture and industry to services. In Upper Galilee many kibbutzim are renting cottages for bed and breakfast and operating fast-food restaurants. In central Israel, not far from Tel Aviv, one kibbutz opened a beauty parlor; in a neighboring kibbutz, there are architectural and law firms. Another one opened an advertising agency that promotes itself as "the only agency in the world that comes with a barn." A fashionable trend in many kibbutzim is to open pubs and bars with alcoholic drinks and music. Still others have capacious supermarkets that stock almost everything from chocolate chip cookies to dog food.

In their effort to survive, the kibbutzim are even ready to open their once-segregated schools to the children of nonmembers. They also have opened their graveyards. A wealthy French industrialist whose brother lived in the kibbutz bought his plot of holy land in Kinneret's cemetery by donating a quarter of a million dollars for the maintenance of the site. Another prosperous German Jew who wanted to be buried in his ancestral land, but wished to avoid the unaesthetic religious burial ceremony provided by the state, cut a deal with a kibbutz near Jerusalem: a plot for himself for thirty thousand dollars.

But one of the biggest departures from the past was introduced in Neot Mordechai, forty miles north of the Sea of Galilee. A few years ago, the general assembly decided to separate economic activity from social and cultural life. Every kibbutz traditionally provides its members with clothing, food, and furnished housing, as well as cultural and social needs. In addition, a small personal allowance is provided.

At one time, neither the quantity nor the quality of labor was supervised. Now every member of Neot Mordechai is obliged to work at least 275 days a year; whoever does not meet this require- ment is financially penalized by a reduction in his personal allowance.

Similar to the reforms introduced by Mikhail Gorbachev under perestroyka, those of Neot Mordechai and other kibbutzim began to decentralize their economic activities. Each economic branch, whether in agriculture, industry, or services, is now considered an independent entity. Each branch is no longer linked with or budgeted by the community as a whole. It has to prove its economic viability and efficiency—the name of the game is sink or swim.

No less dramatic has been the decision by some kibbutzim to pay overtime to their own members. Members' refusal to work overtime or volunteer for special seasonal projects, like picking oranges, often results in rotten crops and the loss of money. Therefore, the need arose to offer incentives to meet the seasonal demands. Although a very small amount of money—no more than five hundred dollars a year per working member—is spent on overtime and wages, this still results in the emergence of two classes inside the same kibbutz: the wage earners and the non-wage earners.

There is yet another trend that departs from tradition. The need for economic survival has driven the kibbutzim to offer their industries for sale or to enter into joint ventures with outside investors. Their aim is to become more efficient, to make money, and to brave the crisis. For this purpose, experts and managers from outside the kibbutz are paid large salaries. In the past, industry was introduced solely to provide jobs for kibbutz members and to make them less dependent on agriculture.

Now circumstances have changed, and industry has become a necessity for its own sake: it is no longer a means to provide work but a purely commercial enterprise. As a result, a strong capitalist wind has been blowing into the quiet kibbutz yard. Shareholding companies have been set up, with all the attendant paraphernalia such as boards, directors, board meetings, and expense accounts. In fact, this has created the emergence of another class in the kibbutz community, which has taken the top place on the social ladder. Now, there are not only wage earners and non-wage earners, but also a new class of managers and directors. Some of them keep to a certain kibbutz-style profile: the modest sandal-clad directors. But the majority have rapidly acquired the manners of corporate executives and have proven to be a thorn in the side of the rest of the kibbutz membership. Their perks are the envy of other kibbutzniks: cars, mobile phones, fancy restaurants, and business trips abroad. If at one time there seemed to be a point in preserving a facade of egalitarianism, they've now given up trying.

These changes have seriously eroded the basic principles of the kibbutz. "When wages are introduced and industries are manned by hired employees," say the old-guard forces, "what is the difference between us, with our historically unique experience, and any other Israeli way of life?"

As further ammunition against what is perceived to be the rapid withering of the kibbutz movement, the traditionalists point to the example of North American communes. "There is a striking similarity," observes historian Yaacov Oved, himself a loyal kibbutz member, "between certain trends among us and these communes." Oved particularly refers to the fate of the Amana Church Society, a religious commune in Iowa. During the depression of the thirties, the Amana Church reorganized and restructured itself. First, they moved from agriculture to industry, then introduced wages and eventually redefined themselves as a shareholding company. "The act that symbolized the change was the abolishment of the communal kitchens and dining rooms," says Oved. Thus, the notions of collective and social life were replaced by concepts emphasizing the centrality of the individual and his nuclear family. Amana stopped being a commune and became a corporation, almost like any other American corporation, worshiping profit and talking the language of balance sheets, sales figures, efficiency, and work force. By now the name means refrigerators, air conditioners, and ovens.

Unless the course of the kibbutz is changed, many fear that it will eventually go the way of Amana: from an idealistic, pioneering community to a materialistic commercial venture; from a rural commune to a privatized complex of industry and services; from the vanguard of socialist Zionism to another bastion of capitalism and modern consumerism offering its inhabitants nothing beyond luxury goods and convenient living, as in any other affluent suburban neighborhood.

THIRTEEN

The Subaru Syndrome

SUBARU is known worldwide as a Japanese car, but in Israel the name also serves as an epithet for the average, suburban Israeli. Subaru, manufactured by one of Japan's leading corporations, was the first Japanese car on the Israeli market in the early 1970s. Today, almost all Japanese companies have Israeli dealers, but more than twenty years ago—because of threats of Arab boycotts on international firms—the Japanese refused to do business with Israel. Only Subaru chose to ignore such pressure—perhaps because, at the time, it was a small, largely unknown company. Thus, Subaru became the first Japanese company in the Promised Land. However, the Israeli's support of Subaru is not merely an expression of gratitude. The car arrived at a watershed in the gradual transition of Israeli society from productive pioneering austerity to Western consumerism.

Israel in the 1960s was a modest society with limited financial means and resources. There were very few wealthy people. The prevailing mood cause the wealthy to take an apologetic stance, as if they were ashamed of their own affluence. Many homes, indeed, had no refrigerator—a serious problem in the country's subtropical climate. I remember how my mother would rush downstairs when the iceman rang his bell. He came to our street with his horse-drawn cart once a day, and in the summer, even twice. He would chop the ice blocks with his sharp knife and sell them to the local residents, who then covered them with a piece of cloth to carry them home. They were stored in wooden boxes called refrigerators. The average Israeli at that time did not dream of air conditioners or washing machines—a car seemed the pinnacle of luxury. In 1966, there were five cars, including government and company cars, to every one thousand citizens. The most popular means of transport was the public bus. Traveling from Tel Aviv to Jerusalem for a visit to friends was considered a great expedition: the forty miles between the two cities took nearly two hours, one way.

This situation suited the government well. Since people had no cars, they tended to stay at home in the evenings. With no television they went to sleep early and rose bright and early for work. The government liked its citizens to work and produce more. Israeli society in those early years loyally reflected Labor's socialist ethos. The individual's wishes were wholly subject to the needs of the community. Thus the phrase "consumer goods" was considered obscene in the national vocabulary. Instead of consumerism, what was preached were the ideals of moderation and austerity.

To implement this ideology the government took steps that prevented Israelis from obtaining basic Western consumer goods. It added huge taxes and levies of up to three hundred percent to the basic price of appliances like fridges, washing machines, irons. An Israeli laborer had to work three years to be able to afford, for example, a washing machine or a television set. The Israeli attitude to these fairly basic goods is still reflected in the translation of the Hebrew words for them: luxury articles.

The Six-Day War and its aftermath, however, changed the perception. The newly occupied territories provided Israelis with economic opportunities to boost their standard of living. There was a boom in the construction industry: in order to defend and control the territories and keep an eye on the Palestinians, military camps, roads, and settlements all had to be built. As is the case with all colonizers throughout history, the Israeli conquerors exploited the

Palestinian minority as cheap labor. All this labor brought Israel the prosperity that paved the way for the country's first "nouveau riches."

The small building contractor who prior to the war had had a difficult time feeding his family and making it through the month suddenly found himself in great demand to build roads and army barracks in the territories. He became a rich and powerful man overnight. His new money rippled through the economy—a new, larger apartment for him meant more money for another contractor. Now he could finally afford a washing machine, a refrigerator, or any other "luxury articles." The purchase of these items brought new money to the manufacturers, importers, and retailers. All of these new middle-class people, of course, employed lawyers, accountants, and insurance brokers—and on and on. And when one of the family fell ill, our contractor could, for the first time, pay for private medical treatment—thus indirectly contributing to the income of the physician. Many of these transactions involved moonlighters. Large parts of the Israeli economy practically went "underground," turning many jobs, professions and even entire industries into "black market" activities. The treasury neither knew about nor benefited from them.

My family, too, shared in this chain reaction. My father's business started flourishing after June 1967. For the first time in the decade since we had arrived, my father managed to buy a small, old car. The event marked the entry of my family into Israel's growing middle class. Soon our situation improved and my father could buy larger and newer cars, at ever shorter intervals. My family realized their Israeli dream at the same time as tens of thousands of other Israelis or newcomers who succeeded by hard work and by exploiting the political-economic system. This process was, of course, accelerated in 1977 with the election of Begin and the Likud.

The continuous improvement was also made possible by another fact: Israel is basically a classless society. Both the relative newness of Jewish Israeli society and its socialist doctrines and ideology have served to keep class distinctions to a minimum. But mainly, Israel cannot afford to have the kind of visible socioeconomic gaps like those, for instance, in the United States between rich and poor, between the haves and the have-nots. This is impossible, not only because Israel is a small, intimate place in which everyone knows everyone else, but also because it is a strongly mobilized society: a society that demands each of its citizens—rich and poor—serve actively and for a long time in the army, as a conscript and later as a reservist. Large and unbridgeable class distinctions would prevent the government from maintaining its citizens' high level of motivation. For how could a poor, lower-class person feel himself to be the partner—in defending their shared country—of a well-off, upper-class person who has so much more?

The Labor and early Likud governments did their best to keep Israel an equal society in order to allow ample space for social mobility, to create the feeling that despite hardships, everyone would have the same potential for advancement. In this way, there was created a society which probably has, proportionately, one of the largest middle classes in the world.

Today, the average middle-class Israeli—who has already succeeded in realizing his middle-class dream—continues to feel himself deprived. Israelis of today do not regard freezers, dryers, and color televisions as appliances that make life better and more comfortable. Rather, they are seen as status symbols. At social gatherings in households all around the country, guests spend a great deal of time boasting about their new fridge or the latest electronic gadget on the market. Israelis have a love for these items that borders on obsession: electric appliances make many Israelis today feel prosperous and proud.

This new consumer culture provides the backdrop for the average Israeli's greatest obsession: his car. On Friday afternoons, tens of thousands of Israeli families wash and polish and buff their cars. This tradition was not created to save money at the car wash—the Israelis simply worship their cars. Of course, to own a Subaru is considered the ultimate Israeli dream come true. The acquisition of a Subaru is a sign that connects the purchaser to the entire Israeli middle class.

In a rather ambiguous way the ownership of a Japanese car, and its association with the United States, has become the true realization of the Israeli dream. Although Subarus are made in Japan and have nothing to do with the United States, the middle-class Israeli, the Subaru man, sees this ownership as making him like an "American consumer." Besides, these days even Americans find Japanese cars more economical. America, in the eyes of Israelis, is much more than a geographic notion: it is the synonym for "quality of life," a place where all dreams come true. In spite of what may be true, whenever an Israeli treats another person politely and deferentially he is admired for behaving "like an American."

The process of Americanization has been a slow and gradual one. At the inception of statehood, Israel was almost completely against such a trend. Moreover, due to historical and political circumstances, Israel was initially exposed to mostly French and British culture. Though the British had ruled over Palestine, the Israelis did not resent them—once they left. They copied and emulated the British—the English language became the first and only foreign language taught at elementary schools. The Israeli legal system is partly rooted in the British tradition. Public and government-owned services like the police, radio broadcasting, and even the military were based on their British counterparts, during the 1950s and 1960s. London was considered the center of the world and, generally, anything that smelled or tasted of England was enchanting to Israelis—from English clothes to English universities.

Later, the Israelis discovered France. More French-made cars gradually appeared on the roads, and the radio started broadcasting French music and songs. French was soon taught in schools as the second foreign language, and French films and restaurants became popular. The French influence coincided more or less with the diplomatic honeymoon between the two nations in the first half of the 1950s. The moment the diplomatic-military relations cooled off, French cultural influence in Israel waned.

And so Israel looked to the United States to fill the vacuum left behind by France. At first, though the bond tightened between Israel and the United States, the influence of American culture was not substantial. While American money and military assistance were well received in the Israel of the 1960s, the Israelis were less receptive to American music, food, sports, and consumerism. The American life-style was still viewed then as inferior to its European counterpart. Europe was identified as a land of solid tradition, rich culture, and a well-established civilization, while America was still identified as the land of Mickey Mouse.

Feelings of contempt for American culture kept the Israeli public out of Tel Aviv's first supermarket, "straight from America." The government, of course, had different reasons for holding the reins on such American cultural influences as television and radio commercials. However, as was the case with most Western European countries, resistance toward "American cultural imperialism" did not last for long. In 1960, the first radio commercials were broadcast. In 1968, Israeli television was introduced, first in black and white, without commercials, and later in color, with commercials. In the same year, the Coca-Cola Company agreed to sell its product, which perhaps more than anything else is the quintessential export of the American way of life. Until that time, Coca-Cola had yielded to the Arab boycott, stubbornly and systematically refusing to do business with Israel, for fear that its large Arab market would suffer. I still have sweet memories of my first few Cokes in the heat of the Israeli summer. I was then a regular conscript, and our insatiable desire for the fizzy brown drink exceeded the thirst we endured on our long, tough desert marches. There were plenty of other cold drinks made in Israel. I have no doubt that the attraction of the beverage had less to do with its taste than with its associations: Coca-Cola was America. It was the drink of the big world outside Israel.

Slowly, America and its culture were accepted. This was due partly to the influx of young American volunteers—Jewish and non-Jewish—who came to work on a kibbutz or to visit Israel. They smoked joints and were sexually liberated and they left a deep impression on their Israeli peers. The immigration of American Jews to Israel also brought a change in attitudes in Israel—though the American expatriate community in Israel is extremely small.

By far the most influential means through which Americana was brought to Israel was, undoubtedly, television. American soap operas, news, and music have left an imprint on all Israelis. Many American words entered the Israeli vocabulary, including a colorful repertoire of curses that have replaced the earlier Yiddish and Arabic oaths. Owners of Israeli shops are convinced that if they call their business "New York" or any other American-sounding name, they will do significantly better.

In terms of sports, British games have been replaced by American ball games. Almost every Israeli child was shocked to hear about Magic Johnson's HIV-positive diagnosis, and all know the NBA teams by heart. Even football and baseball—games which very few Israelis play or understand—have recently become extremely popular events on television. In January 1992 tens of thousands of Israelis watched the Super Bowl at one A.M. local time.

Of course, in addition to imitating American taste in sports, Israelis have also adopted its food fads: TV dinners, popcorn, potato chips, and beer are now favorite snacks while one is watching televised ball games. The new Israelis eat too much and, obviously, produce more trash and waste than ever before. According to a study, every Israeli produces a daily average of one pound of waste. Another study concluded that, because of their unhealthy food habits, Israelis are in very bad physical shape.

Today, there is hardly any major American company or product that is not represented or available in Israel. In the last few years American hamburger and pizza chains have opened branches. Israeli entrepreneurs travel to the United States, browse for ideas, and imitate them back home. In 1992, Pepsi Cola started selling in Israel, too, which leaves Mcdonald's as the one American "cultural" export not yet to have reached the Holy Land.

Having adopted almost every American habit and style, Israel has become a consumer society, a quintessential leisure-time nation. If certain particulars of the American dream are more difficult to realize in Israel, then local adjustments are made: the American suburban house becomes an apartment in the affluent Israeli suburb.

Israel's economy has recently switched from a six-day work week to five. Leisure time is now spent shopping. Recent years have seen the opening of numerous American-style shopping malls—more than the Israeli population really needs. Plastic credit cards are already in wide use throughout the country; when the children of the suburban Israeli get bored, they can go around the corner, slide their parents' magnetic card through the machine, and borrow a videocassette. Israeli children read fewer and fewer books and watch lots of television—four hours is the daily average. Half of Israel's households are already linked up to cable television. Donahue and Oprah Winfrey are a regular part of the Israeli television schedule. When videos and television are exhausted, parents can always send their bored teenagers to special discotheques that cater to the restless youth of the wealthy suburbs.

Today one in five Israelis owns their own car. Compared to some leading Western nations this is still insignificant: In the United States almost every person has a car, and in France there is one car for every two people. But when you look at Israel's rate of increase in privately owned cars over the last ten years, it has a place among the leaders: while this rate was only five percent in the United States, in Israel it reached seventy percent.

For an industrial, pluralistic society, Israel is still remarkably family oriented. Compared to most Western countries, the divorce rate is low—eighteen percent compared to fifty percent in the United States. The influence of religion, the centrality of the family in Jewish tradition, and the rigidity of rabbinical family laws all contribute to this stability. However, since 1970, tradition seems to have been weakening. Recent research on family trends already shows certain similarities in marriage and divorce patterns between Israel and the West. From the early 1970s, divorce figures have been rising persistently, as has the average marrying age for both sexes—twenty-six for men and twenty-three for women. The transition from traditional values has manifested itself in the rise of one-parent families—from less than one percent before to two percent in 1990.

Tel Aviv, more than anywhere else, is where Israel's culture of excess flourishes. Tel Aviv represents one face of Israeli society: an openness to the world in general and a wish to belong to the West in particular. Jerusalem is the opposite of Tel Aviv. Jerusalem is historic while Tel Aviv is contemporary. Jerusalem's seriousness is often contrasted with Tel Aviv's lightheartedness. Of course, Jerusalem has its blatant signs of Americanization and culture of abundance, but when compared with the vitality of Tel Aviv, Jerusalem seems a sleepy town. After nine P.M. the town closes down.

Tel Aviv spreads the message of Israel's modern culture, and to Tel Aviv come the world's fashion trends. In Tel Aviv a small colony of what might be called Holy Land Yuppies resides. This phenomenon, too, is a recent American import.

Israel's yuppies keep their fingers on the pulse of the latest developments in the larger world. They often introduce the latest American manners, fashions, cuisine, and culture. Like their counterparts in the West, they are well informed about the latest trends. If they're wearing all black in Greenwich Village, chances are everyone in the popular pubs and cafes of central Tel Aviv will be wearing black. It's a way of pretending that they are not actually living in Tel Aviv, but in New York. But for some, waking up and realizing that they are not living in the comfort of America leaves them frustrated and empty. With these feelings gnawing at them, many young Israelis are emigrating: escaping Israel. Of course, it is not merely the young people, or the yuppies among them, who leave the country to try their luck in the United States. There are no precise figures, but the number of Israelis who have left the country for America since 1948 is between one quarter million and a half million. Most go to New York or Los Angeles.

During the early days of the state, only those who had failed, or felt they had failed, or claimed that they felt they had failed to make the Israeli dream, left the country. Twenty or thirty years ago, the reason for moving from Israel to the United States was the same as that offered by other groups of immigrants, the Irish, the Italians, or the Poles: financial hardship. Over the years, though, some uniquely Israeli motives for emigration have emerged: fear of war and the reluctance to go on reservist service, at least once per year, until well into middle age.

What was typical of all the Israelis, unlike other immigrants, was their feeling of shame. They were ashamed of having left their country of origin, and they took every opportunity to apologize and explain that they were going to go back "very soon" (even if that "soon" often stretched into eternity).

The Israeli community in the United States is the only expatriate group which argues that their place is not there, that they are in America only temporarily. Over the last few years, however, a new kind of Israeli immigrant appears to have arrived: the one who is no longer embarrassed or ashamed of what he has done. This immigrant does not leave Israel because he's having a bad time there, he leaves simply because it's not good enough. After living a fake American existence in Israel, he wants to try the real thing. In Israel he has, on average, a three-bedroom apartment; in the United States, he knows, or believes he knows, that he might get a five-, six-, or even seven-bedroom house with a private swimming pool in his yard. In Israel his annual salary amounts to twenty or thirty thousand U.S. dollars, while in the United States he hopes to earn about two to three times as much. This new generation of immigrants are professionals and business people—the cream of Israeli society. In fact, in America an Israeli culture of immigration has been emerging: the immigrant settles and then is joined by his brothers, sisters, mother, father, and the rest of his relatives.

Israel is a nation of extremes: the moods of its population swing widely and nervously between a sense of catastrophe and intense enjoyment of celebrations and festivals. Perhaps this absence of balance can be found within the Jewish religion itself, which views Jewish existence as a movement between destruction and redemption. Or maybe the loss of old values of equality and social justice have left Israeli society unhinged.

Along with the fun and comfort of American life, Israel now also faces America's problems. In the past, Israel could hardly conceive of any of its people being so poor that they had nothing to eat. When, in 1965, a twelve-year-old girl from a small development town announced on a radio program that she was starving, the entire nation went into in shock. This piece of information led to Knesset debates and media pressure on the Labor government to investigate the case. Though it turned out to be a false alarm—she was not starving—opposition propagandists were able to exploit this highly charged issue. Today, though, real cases of hunger exist.

By the end of 1991, the number of poor in Israel had risen to a half million. Israel's poverty line is reached when a single person earns 220 dollars a month or when an entire family's income doesn't exceed 400 dollars a month. Since the average monthly rent for a small flat is 300 dollars, and the rest of an average income doesn't suffice to cover other essential expenses; it is no wonder that so many people are slipping below the poverty line. Every seventh Israeli is living below the poverty line and fifty percent of these poor are children. Another official figure estimates that the children of eighty thousand families are currently suffering malnutrition.

Israeli welfare officers argue that they have come across horrific cases in which—in Dickensian scenarios—young children are found rummaging for scraps of food in garbage pails or doing odd jobs for a pittance. Today, however, hardly anyone is taken aback by these revelations. The public remains unperturbed.

A few months ago I saw a woman in her fifties who was rummaging around in the garbage cans of our building. It was in the morning. She was wearing a gray dress and a red coat, frayed and full of holes. From time to time she looked anxiously around to see if anyone had noticed her. She probably had figured that the morning hours, when most residents were out at work, would be the best time to do her job unnoticed. After a few minutes of poking around in the cans she collected some used objects in her basket, some rotten vegetables, and a half-eaten carton of cheese. Since then, I have seen her a few more times: now her behavior and movements are not quite so nervous. She works as if she has all the time in the world. I am ashamed on her behalf and my own. I never would have imagined that Israel would offer me the spectacle of poor people living on the edge of starvation, trying to salvage a crumb from my garbage.

These appalling circumstances put Israel with other Western nations that regularly assess their poverty. Israel has relatively more poor than Canada, Britain, and Germany. Only the United States, where about twenty percent of the population exists below the poverty line, has a higher percentage of poor citizens than Israel. Not even in their worst dreams could Israelis imagine that, in Tel Aviv, Jerusalem, and other towns, there would be poor people spending the night in the shivering cold, covered with rags and huddling in cardboard boxes. This situation, for now, is still limited—but the once-socialist society has turned harsh and cruel and has abandoned its poor, old, and weak.

The Israel of the past served as model for the modern welfare state. The state took care that no one should ever be deprived of a home or medical care or lack enough money to supply basic needs. In its transition from socialism and the welfare system to a free market and privatization, Israel's social fabric has frayed. The by-products are the same as those of other Western nations who have traveled the same road: unemployment, poverty, and deep social division. The baby of social justice has been thrown out with the bath water of economic efficiency.

All Israelis have medical insurance and are eligible for equal treatment in hospitals. This has been the theory and practice since independence, but recently serious cracks have appeared in this foundation. For instance, today whoever is unable to pay his medical insurance is likely to end up either without any treatment or with second-rate health care. In 1988, my father had to undergo open heart surgery with four bypasses. He had paid medical insurance for thirty years, since our arrival in Israel. When the time came and he needed his insurance, the bitter truth emerged: due to the long waiting list for surgery, he got his appointment a year later. His physician, who was doubtful whether my father's heart would hold out that long, argued that he needed surgery within weeks. "What can I do?" my father asked. "Go private," he was advised. My father had no choice, and he had private surgery that cost him $20,000. Two years later, my mother had to undergo similar surgery. She was a little luckier and was not forced to have her operation done in a private hospital. Still, to be operated on by the best team of doctors and nurses available in the hospital, she had to pass $3,000 "under the table" to the surgeon. These payments, which are illegal, are called by various names: contribution to the ward, or consultancy fees. The truth is, it is through bribes that you jump the line, get to see your choice physician, and receive privileged hospital treatment. This is not to say that the entire Israeli health system is corrupt, but over the last years it shows more and more signs of moral decay and cynicism.

Similar forms of corruption are found in all walks of Israeli life. In the late 1980s there were reports of judges who received kickbacks. In recent years scandals have erupted in the armed forces involving kickbacks, fraud, and the theft of tens of millions of dollars by senior officers.

All this is evidence that the idealism of the past has made way for a materialism of such proportions that it borders on sheer greed and extreme hedonism. Israelis want to make a lot of money, and fast. Since 1967, Washington has provided Israel with seventy-seven billion dollars in economic and military aid. If you will, each Israeli man, woman, and child has received almost seventeen thousand dollars from American taxpayers. The United States saw Israel as a reliable ally and a strategic partner in the struggle against the Soviet Union. The alliance was further cemented by Israel's democratic institutions and by the work of the pro-Israel lobby in Washington and the influential Jewish community. This special relationship between Israel and the United States has enabled the country to create a unique situation in which—despite its basic poverty—the population has been affluent and living well beyond its real financial means. The Israeli economic "miracle" has been made possible by the generous support of the United States.

Without this American support the country would have looked like any other third-world nation. It is therefore thanks to the Americans that Israel has become a country that consumes more than it produces.

Since the occupation of the territories in June 1967, successive Labor and Likud governments have been spoiled by American generosity and have not been asked to give anything tangible in return. Although all American administrations from Lyndon Johnson to Ronald Reagan railed against the construction of Jewish settlements in the West Bank and the Gaza Strip, they took no significant diplomatic action. President Reagan went farther than any predecessor to make Israelis feel secure. He did not hesitate to pour more and more money into the Israeli economy in the form of military aid. That kind of generosity understandably led Israelis to believe they could do no wrong in American eyes.

However, since January 1989, when President George Bush entered the White House, the Israelis have come to realize that the party might be over. The president and his secretary of state, James Baker, lack their predecessors' emotional and ideological commitment to Israel. With the collapse of the Soviet Union, Israel's strategic importance, as a bulwark against the spread of communism into the region, has virtually disappeared. Seeking to bolster America's new position in the region and to contain the spread of Arab nationalism and Muslim fundamentalism that threatens the West's oil supplies, the Bush-Baker team is trying to appease the Arabs at the expense of Israel.

Thus the Bush administration decided to demand a freeze on Jewish settlements in the West Bank, which has become the most politically and emotionally loaded issue for Israelis and Palestinians alike. Nearly 120,000 Jews already live in these settlements. The United States government demanded a halt to construction of new ones and a limit on building within existing settlements. Hoping to be financially rewarded for the restraint it had shown during the Gulf War, Israel asked the United States government to guarantee loans amounting to ten billion dollars for five years. The borrowed money would help to absorb nearly one million Jews from the former Soviet Union, which the Israeli government saw as a humanitarian issue that should not be linked to politics. But Bush and Baker did not agree. "If you want the money," they told the Israelis, "stop the settlements, which are obstacles to peace." For the first time in American-Israeli relations, financial sanctions were used as political leverage. Moreover, America's own economic slump has made it harder to pour unlimited resources into what has come to look like a bottomless pit. With the change in governments in Jerusalem, and with his own standing with the American people low in the face of the approaching presidential election, President Bush reversed his original decision. In August 1992 he told Israel's new premier, Yitzhak Rabin, the United States would guarantee the loans.

But the already stunned Israelis are realizing that a country's finances, like a family budget, must have a certain set of priorities. For many years, Israeli leaders tried to wave several banners at once: one banner promised maximum security, another a high standard of living; one banner stood for occupation and the repression of Palestinians, another for an enlightened and democratic society; one for settlement building, the other for pretending simultaneously that Israel only wanted peace.

It is dawning on the new Israelis that their Subaru connection has metamorphosed into a two-edged sword: while it might help them lead their local version of American life, it may, equally, hurt them by forcing them to declare their priorities. The 1990s have punctured the Israeli Subaru dream balloon: Israel, as a small and poor country, cannot expect to conduct its affairs as it has done. If more immigrants are to be absorbed in the future—as part of the lifeline of the Zionist dream—Israel will need all of the foreign assistance it can get, especially from the United States. In order to obtain this help, however, it is clear that Israel will have to stop occupying, dominating, and colonizing the territories.

The Israeli dilemma is a simple but cruel one: to continue with Zionism as it has always existed—or to prepare to sacrifice the traditional Zionist ethos of immigration on the altar of land and to forget about peace.

EPILOGUE

EVERY Friday afternoon, at Gan Hakovshim, the Conquerors Park in south Tel Aviv, a line of Russian immigrants waits for food distribution. Right next to the park is the bustling Carmel Market, an anarchic maze of little streets filled with food stalls. It is a chaotic place, crowded with people and filled with noise and the smell of fruits and meats. All the various and opposing cultures within Israeli society today can be found here. The market serves as a blender, mixer, and shaker. In the streets of the market you can find Orthodox Jews in their traditional long black overcoats, Arab heads wrapped with kaffiyehs, young men and women in jeans and T-shirts, and older people in shabby suits.

But in Gan Hakovshim you will find a different mood among Israel's most recent immigrants from the former Soviet Union. On late Friday afternoon, when thousands of them gather near the market, you might expect the atmosphere to be calm and perhaps even festive: the Sabbath is Israel's main day of rest. This, however, is not the case. The people in Gan Hakovshim are waiting not for the Sabbath but for food. After a one-hour wait, each person receives a small bag with fruit and vegetables. The Tel Aviv municipality which sponsors this charity no doubt had the best of intentions in initiating such a program.

Before the program, the food situation was even worse. Immigrants would take possession of the market after closing and collect garbage and any leftovers they could lay their hands on. Journalists and photographers from all over the world have come to report on the tragic face of these new immigrants whose dream has turned into

223

a nightmare. In an effort to minimize the damage done by such news reports, Israel's absorption authorities have persuaded some of the market vendors to contribute food and distribute it in a more dignified way. But even this method does little to change the humiliation suffered. Functionaries ask each person requesting food to show an identification card verifying their status as a new immigrant. Whoever is unable to show a card is given no food. Such behavior brings back the memory of the cold bureaucrats who received me and my family upon our entry into the country thirty-five years ago.

The Jewish immigration from the former Soviet Union could have become one of the most fascinating chapters in the Israeli saga—with all the ingredients of a fairy tale.

From the Bolshevik revolution in 1917, the Soviet Union did everything in its power to suppress and uproot nationalist sentiment. For a period of almost fifty years, Soviet authorities denied Jews and other ethnic groups the right to their religious culture. The teaching of Hebrew was forbidden, synagogues were closed, and Zionism was pronounced a public heresy.

Yet somehow a form of Jewish tradition was maintained—much of it through the work of Israeli intelligence. For years, a secret body called the Liaison Bureau worked alongside the Mossad with the sole purpose of supporting Jewish and Zionist consciousness among the three million Jews of the Soviet Union. The Bureau dispatched its agents to trace Jewish communities throughout the Soviet Union. Once found, the agent would disseminate prayer books, Bibles, Hebrew dictionaries, and tape recordings of modern Israeli music.

By the late 1960s, the first buds of Jewish activism emerged in the Soviet Union. Their slogan invoked the Bible once again: "Let my people go." The Soviet dictatorship tried to fight the Jewish dissidents with the same methods used against other "troublemakers"—KGB agents hunted them, had them fired from their jobs, and even put some in jail for long periods of time.

Eventually, however, these measures proved to be counterproductive. Inspired by Israeli initiatives, Jewish organizations joined the struggle to free Soviet Jews. Once again, the Zionist credo of helping Jews in distress came to fruition: Soviet Jews were brought to Israel.

Eventually, when this well-oiled campaign succeeded in mobilizing the United States administrations of Presidents Nixon and Carter, the Soviet authorities yielded to diplomatic pressure: the Americans continued to supply grain to the USSR as long as Jewish emigration was allowed. In the 1970s, under the label "family unification," the Soviets allowed nearly a quarter million Jews to leave. Two thirds of them settled in Israel, and many adjusted successfully to their new lives. The rest either dropped out en route or left for other destinations, mainly the United States.

This wave of immigration, however, came to a halt with the deterioration of United States-Soviet relations in the early 1980s. The Soviets viewed the Jews as hostages whose fate was entirely tied to the mood of Moscow's complex relationship with Washington. The Soviet attitude could be summed up in one line: no grain, no Jews.

When Mikhail Gorbachev became the leader of the Soviet Union in 1985, he introduced reforms and historic changes that would lead to the abolition of Communism and the collapse of the Union. Policies regarding the Jews changed once more: they were allowed to leave for Israel without any limitations. Within two years, in 1990-1991, about four hundred thousand Jews left the Soviet Union. At the height of immigration, nearly fifty thousand Jews arrived in Israel within one month.

Though this mass emigration can be seen as the by-product of historic, diplomatic, and strategic interests, many Israelis regard it as a victory for the Likud and Israel's right-wing government.

Likud's luck, however, was soon to run out. In early 1992, immigration from the former Soviet Union began to take a decisively less dramatic form. The flood subsided into a trickle. Forecasts had been made that within the coming five years at least one million immigrants would come to Israel, adding twenty-five percent to its Jewish population. Only a few hundred per month, however, were now coming in. Even during the Gulf War, when the country was being shelled with Scuds almost daily, more Russians were arriving on average than later in 1992. What caused this abrupt and dramatic decrease was the failure of Shamir's government to properly absorb all the new people.

Unlike previous groups of Soviet immigrants in the 1970s, those of the 1990s were not motivated by Zionist ideological passions. Their reason for coming to Israel was the same as the Sephardis of the 1950s: to escape danger and deprivation. Only Israel was prepared to take them in without question. During this period, in the early 1990s, when Israel was the only refuge for Soviet citizens, many rushed to the Israeli consulate to receive immigration papers. Israeli diplomats at the Moscow consulate had, of course, no way of checking up on applicants who claimed to be Jewish. They simply approved almost every application. The Law of Return stipulates that Israel is allowed an unlimited number of Jewish immigrants. As a result, in the years between 1990 and 1992, the Soviet Union witnessed a flourishing trade in forged Israeli immigration papers. Among these immigrants were a considerable number of non-Jews married to Jews. One estimate says that about a quarter of all Soviet immigrants and applicants have been non-Jews.

A new, private topic of conversation among Orthodox circles in Israel is the "new demographic danger" posed by these non-Jewish Russians. If Israel, they argue, does not find a way of identifying and taking action, million of non-Jews are likely to pour into the country and outnumber its Jewish population. To control this tide, the Orthodox establishment has demanded that a requirement be made that all male immigrants undergo circumcision. Traditionally, the operation is performed on the eighth day after the boy's birth, but those who weren't circumcised at birth may undergo the ritual at any other age. Often the immigrants themselves ask for circumcision as a way of identifying with their new homeland. But, in many cases, they undergo the operation because of Orthodox pressure—in the form of dire forecasts about the future of Isarel's children and that of their own if the ancient rite is to be performed. In 1991, fifty thousand circumcisions were performed in hospitals under the supervision of rabbis paid by the state. These rabbis also take the opportunity to press for a name change as well—first as well as family—into "proper" Jewish names.

Ask any immigrant and you will be told that integration into any new country is neither smooth nor easy. Cultural transplantation and differences in language, attitudes, and life-styles all make the transition difficult. But never in their worst dreams did the Soviet Jews foresee the problems they would be confronted with in Israel.

The government did its best to help, and attempts were made to learn from the mistakes of previous mass immigrations. Unlike the 1950s, immigrants today are not put up in transit camps—they are absorbed more directly. Once they touch down at Ben Gurion Airport, they are free to go anywhere they wish. They are given money immediately and, later, a regular monthly stipend for the first six months of their stay. They can make tax-free purchases and their children receive state-supported help at school. The Shamir government supported the building of cheap housing.

All these good intentions amounted to nothing, though, when the Soviet immigrants could not find jobs. Over half of the immigrants have received a higher education; many are trained in areas that are either not in demand—mining engineers and metallurgic technicians—or are in oversupply already—physicists, chemists, and physicians. In order to create sufficient employment, Israel desperately needs foreign investment. However, the Israel market is small and offers only limited opportunities. And because of the country's security problems and the political instability of the Middle East, foreign investors are not easily attracted. This situation has resulted in the need for a ten billion dollar loan guarantee. Without this money, Israel will not be able to support such a huge new population. Unemployment is already up to forty percent; immigrants are left without money as soon as their monthly allowance runs out. They cannot pay rent and so entire families have been left homeless by greedy landlords. For most of the 1980s—before these population changes—Israel was in a recession. Apartments that could not be sold or rented remained empty. The Russians, though, grabbed many of these apartments, and that, in turn, led to rent increases. Even poor shacks in decaying urban areas, not good enough to house animals, suddenly were part of the housing market.

Even those Russians who manage to find jobs, usually don't work in their own professions. The Israeli market needs cheap labor in industry and services. Because of the Intifada, many Israeli employers are afraid to employ Palestinian laborers. In place of them,

Russian immigrants have been hired, and they are exploited and paid low wages as well. As a result, a former rocket engineer may find himself washing office floors; a physician may clean the streets; others may sell flowers door-to-door.

The economic hardship of the Russian immigrants, combined with the shock of seeing Israel's culture of plenty, makes them ready to do almost anything to survive well in the new Israeli jungle. Some women, in fact, have resorted to prostitution to keep their families going. Supermarket managers in areas with many Russian immigrants complain of the rise in theft. "We're hungry. Our parents didn't have the money to buy bread so we have to steal," said two boys who were caught taking bread from a supermarket in my neighborhood. The manager, who was visibly moved, let them go but not before giving them some more food. In most cases, though, the police are called in. It's no wonder then that a study published in 1992 by Israel's absorption authorities shows that close to twenty percent of the Russian newcomers now want to leave Israel. This deprivation is, of course, also fertile ground for all sorts of social problems: there is an increase in the divorce rate among immigrants and a rise in alcoholism and crime. The Israeli press already speaks of a "Russian mafia" that has taken root in Tel Aviv's criminal underworld.

Against this background a not-so-new phenomenon has surfaced: despite their good will and their awareness that "immigration is Israel's oxygen," many established Israelis have lost interest in the newcomers. There are some who do voluntary community work to help them, but old behaviors are rising to the surface; many violent attacks are made on them. Recently, some Israeli boys were found beating up Russian boys at the beach. Many Israelis would not consider renting their property to the newcomers or giving them a job. Some of these incidents against the Russian Jews involve Sephardi Jews. Not surprisingly, there is resentment among the Sephardis for the relatively easy absorption process the Russians have enjoyed, in contrast to their own early humiliation at the hands of the Ashkenazis. Moreover, the Sephardi community harbors suspicions that the enormous resources invested by the government in the latest wave of immigration has been taken away from them. This suspicion has given rise to a new political party. Though it is an insignificant one in many ways, its slogan, "Stop the Soviet Immigration," was striking enough to speak to the mood in Israel today.

The Sephardis also fear that, after a decade's progress into the country's mainstream culture, they might once again relapse into second-class citizenship. This is a fear that is not without merit. Already the Soviet immigrants have managed to bring about one significant change in Israeli society: for the first time since the 1960s, after a quarter of a century, the Ashkenazi population once more outnumbers the Sephardi. In May 1992, Israel's Bureau of Statistics recorded that there were one hundred thousand more Ashkenazis than Sephardis. There is a snag here, though: the Bureau counts all Soviet immigrants as Ashkenazi, whereas, in fact, those who come from the Asiatic republics should actually be considered Sephardi.

To this already complex fabric another problem has been added. The Russians are not the only immigrants to have arrived in Israel in the 1990s. The black Jews of Ethiopia have also arrived—their move to the land of their forefathers representing a "dream come true."

Legend has it that the black Jews of Ethiopia are the descendants of the ten lost tribes who went into exile over twenty-six hundred years ago and were lost without a trace. For hundreds of years they managed to preserve their ancient customs while living in remote mountain villages. These customs were clearly based on a Judaism of a very different form. The establishment of the state of Israel in 1948 roused their hopes, but the political interests of the Labor government resulted in total unconcern for their plight. Labor premiers from Ben Gurion to Golda Meir bowed to Orthodox pressures based on the rabbis' refusal to recognize Ethiopians as Jews. Successive Israeli governments were also reluctant to alienate the friendly Ethiopian emperor. Only when both countries saw a change of government did the Ethiopian Jews' situation improve. In place of the ousted emperor came a Marxist-oriented and anti-Israeli military regime. At the same time in Jerusalem, Menachim Begin and the Likud came into power, and they were prepared to act on behalf of their black brethren and get them to Israel.

As in the past, Israel's intelligence service moved into action. Agents were sent to Ethiopia and neighboring Sudan to bribe politicians and senior officials. Israel supplied arms, and, in return, the military government agreed to ignore the departure of the Jews. Under the auspices of international organizations and supported by the CIA, the Israeli agents began to smuggle out the Ethiopian Jews on charter flights via Europe and on boats that sailed directly to Israel. In this way, up until 1985, about ten thousand black Jews got to Israel in an action code named "Operation Moses." In June 1991, another twenty thousand were flown over to Israel during a three-day-long campaign code named "Operation Solomon." This was the result of a favorable trade: forty million dollars for the Ethiopian treasury and some of its corrupted officials in exchange for the release of the Ethiopian Jews. During the operation, Israel and the entire world held its breath and watched in disbelief as the first pictures of thousands of people in traditional dress boarded the airplanes for the first time in their lives. The initial fascination, however, soon waned, and Israel's Ethiopian Jews were left to deal with their own copious problems.

In the span of one four-hour flight, the Ethiopians were moved from the African Middle Ages to Western civilization of the late twentieth century. It wasn't merely that the airplane was a mystery to them, they were not even familiar with a toilet and how to flush it. Officials in charge of the Ethiopians' absorption agreed that in their case—unlike that of the Soviet Jews—there was no point in direct absorption. The Ethiopians needed guidance. Thus, they were enrolled in absorption centers and transit camps. The ideas was to keep them there for some months and them to offer them permanent housing. This plan, however, did not work.

Most of the Ethiopians have already spent nearly two years in transit camps. They may not be living in tents like the Moroccans and Yemenites of the 1950s, and the food they get is better, too; but some of the similarities between those camps and today are striking. The Ethiopians have no work, and unemployment among them is even higher than among the Russians. There are also cases of alcoholism and suicide. And there is hardly any integration between them and their environment. The established Israelis don't want them. Rumors are spread among the Israelis that many Ethiopians are AIDS carriers. When a camp for them was erected on the outskirts of a prosperous rural community in the Galilee, there were protests from the local population. When Ethiopian children arrived at a kindergarten, Israeli parents rushed to move theirs to another place.

There was one attempt made to introduce the Ethiopians to the Russians—but within days the differences between them erupted into violence. The Soviet immigrants asked to be transferred elsewhere so that they and their children would not have to live under one roof with these "blacks." The Ethiopian transit camps are turning into full-blown black ghettos. Like the Moroccans before them, they are becoming the subject of ethnic jokes and stereotypes fed by racism.

The Ethiopians—like the Yemenites and the Moroccans—are being pressured into abandoning their ancient traditions. In the 1950s, the Ashkenazi Orthodox establishment took the North African youngsters and put them into their black suits and hats. Today, Israel's Orthodox—Ashkenazi and Sephardi alike—put skullcaps on the heads of Ethiopian boys, which is not a part of their tradition. Soul hunters working for various political parties still prowl about the immigrant neighborhoods with the hope of gaining new votes.

It was not surprising at all, in the end, that the majority of the new immigrants punished the Likud government in the June 1992 election for abandoning them. In the minds of the Russians the Likud is remembered for their inhospitable goverance, just as the Moroccans and Yemenites remember Labor as their oppressors. Labor realized it did not have to wait twenty-nine years—the time it took the Sephardis to seek revenge in the form of voting for Likud—for another party switch to occur.

Nevertheless, there is no question that the immigrants will contribute to Israel's social, cultural, and ethnic life. This will become clearer with the passage of time. Even now, Russian is heard increasingly in the streets, and restaurants now serve Russian food.

The influence of various immigrant populations will also be felt in politics, the army, the business community, and everywhere else in Israeli life.

Israel has often been called a place where dream and myth live on as reality. Historically, immigration has always somehow energized the country with the influx of new skills, vigor, and newcomer determination. Immigration is still going on and constitutes the hope that the building of a Jewish nation won't be stopped or arrested.

But Israel's destiny does not depend only on immigration. On November 8, 1917, the *London Times* carried two headlines—one about a major event, the other about something quite marginal. The big news concerned the takeover of the government of St. Petersburg by the Bolsheviks. The small item reported on a letter from the British foreign minister, James Balfour, which announced, in the name of His Majesty's Government, support for the Zionist enterprise. Seventy-five years later, St. Petersburg—whose name had changed to Leningrad—became St. Petersburg again, and the communist Bolsheviks were sent packing. By contrast, the small announcement on the front page has become a big and important story. All of the great revolutionary movements of the twentieth century have failed—socialism, communism, fascism, and liberalism. Only Zionism has stayed strong and alive. Zionism began with a small number of people with a religious tradition but without a territory and made them into a nation. Zionism grew up on the big ideologies of the century and has adopted them through synthesis. In it socialism and humanism have found a place beside nationalism, religious clericalism, and even fundamentalism.

We should not, however, forget to look at the other side of the coin. Zionism uprooted Jewish people from their ideological and cultural habitations and transplanted them to foreign soil. Zionism and Israel have not yet succeeded in bringing together and reconciling all the resulting contradictions and ambivalences of such ventures. Every so often the seams open and Israel's immigrant nature becomes evident. Israel is a nation which has difficulty defining its identity; a society which tries to live in Western style in a Middle Eastern environment; a society which essentially depends on its openness and connectedness to the world at large, but which periodically retreats into self-imposed isolationism; a society which was built on voluntarism and mutual dependence but has adopted eogotism and hedonism as its modern credo; a society which demanded and achieved through bloody struggle independence and the right to self-determination but which stubbornly refuses the same rights to its opponents; a society which claims to long for peace but continues to live by the sword.

In the last decade of the millennium Israel finds itself at the most decisive crossroads of its short existence. As the world changes and adjusts to the twenty-first century, Israel too, will have to move on. In fact, most of the old political and social definitions of the past have lost their relevance. Israel's two largest political parties are viewed in terms of "left" and "right" or socialist and conservative—but in reality they have become ideological supermarkets, each of which stores something for everyone. In the Likud, it is now possible to find brands of old-fashioned socialism and readiness for an agreement with the Palestinians. Labor, on the other hand, has often become the home to old capitalist notions, extremism with regard to the Palestinians, and radical nationalism. The old divisions between the Sephardis and Ashkenazis are also becoming indistinct. Israel's new social stratification exists along more economic lines—according to income and standard of living—and is less based on ethnicity.

The most critical problem facing Israel, both today and in the future, is how to reduce the friction and tension between Israel and the Palestinians and Arab states. In November 1991 Israel attended the Madrid Peace conference. The irony of the Madrid Conference and Israel's presence there is that it was accomplished by the most right-wing premier of all, Yitzhak Shamir. In spite of their appearance, though, the Likud government did not plan to change its settlement policy in the occupied territories and was not willing to enhance peace. But with the election of a new government and Rabin's readiness to make concessions to the Palestinians and the Syrians, encouraging steps are being taken. There should be no hesitation, however, about making further dramatic and brave decisions: without them, Israel may well find itself lost in the shuffle of new political developments. Instead of moving with history, Israel may find itself lagging behind or, worse, losing its political direction and ultimately dropping out.

Past experience shows that Zionist and Israeli leaders are usually realistic and can react accordingly. During its most crucial moments Israel has always pulled together and found the strength to regenerate itself. The recent victory of Labor might be indeed a reaction in that direction. Occasionally, as in the case of Meir and Shamir, Israel's leaders have been rigid and determined to maintain untenable positions, but when the situation demanded it, they, like Ben Gurion and Begin, showed flexibility and moderation. There is room for optimism.

Source Notes

Prologue
Between April and June 1990, I published several articles in the *Washington Post*, *Los Angeles Times*, *Boston Globe*, and the Israeli daily, *Ha'aretz*, in which I warned against Saddam Hussein's nonconventional military buildup. Other observations recorded in this chapter are based on the impressions I gathered during the Iraqi Scud attacks on Israel during the 1991 Gulf War, and on articles I wrote for the above mentioned newspapers in January-May 1991.

Israel's other dailies, especially *Yediot Aharonot*, *Ma'ariv*, and *Davar*, provided raw material for some anecdotes.

No Other Place: On Literature and Society is a collection of essays by Gershon Shaked, Hakibbutz Hameuchad Publishing House (Tel Aviv, 1983).

Chapter One
Among the many books dealing with the question of the Zionist leadership and the Holocaust, I would like to mention three: Walter Laqueur, *The Terrible Secret: Suppression of the Truth about Hitler's "Final Solution,"* Penguin (Middlesex, England, 1982); Dina Porat, *The Blue and Yellow Stars of David: The Zionist Leadership in Palestine and the Holocaust*, Harvard University Press (Cambridge, Mass., 1990); Walter Laqueur and Richard Breitman, *Breaking the Silence*, Simon and Schuster (New York, 1990).

David Ben Gurion's biographer, Shabtai Tevet, on April 25, 1991, explained in an elaborate interview that appeared in the Israeli daily *Ha'ir* the notion of power as perceived by Ben Gurion.

The most valuable documentation of how the Sephardis were absorbed in Israel's first years of independence can be found in Tom Segev's excellent work, *1949: The First Israelis*, Domino Press (Jerusalem, 1984).

The phrase, "he was born from the sea," referring to the notion of the sabra, is taken from Moshe Shamir's elegy on his brother, *With His Hands*, Am Oved (Tel Aviv, 1975).

Chapter Two
Due to space limitations, I will mention here only a few books out of the dozens which I have read on the history of Judaism, Jews, Zionism, and Israel: *A History of*

the Jewish People, edited by H. H. Ben Sasson, Harvard University Press (Cambridge, Massachusetts, 1976); Howard M. Sacher, *A History of Israel*, Alfred A. Knopf (New York, 1987); Abba Eban, *Heritage: Civilization and the Jews*, Stematzky (Tel Aviv, 1984); Paul Johnson, *A History of the Jews*, Weidenfeld and Nicolson (London, 1987); Walter Laqueur, *A History of Zionism*, Holt, Rinehart and Winston (New York, 1972); Amos Elon, *The New Israelis: Founders and Sons*, Penguin Books (London 1972); Theodor Herzl, *Old-New Land ("Altneuland")*, Bloch Plublishing Co. (New York, 1941).

Chapter Three

For information about Ben Gurion I relied on Michael Bar Zohar, *Ben Gurion: A Biography*, Adama Books, (New York, 1986).

For the descriptions of the first pioneers and their colonies in Palestine I found most useful material in David Vital, *The Origins of Zionism*, Am Oved (Tel Aviv, 1978) and *Eretz Israel in the 20th Century: From Yishuv to Statehood, 1900-1950*, edited by Mordechai Naor and Dan Giladi, Ministry of Defense (Tel Aviv, 1990).

The notion of changing names appears in Elon's *New Israelis*, pp. 124-125.

On Zionist socialism see Anita Shapira, *Visions in Conflict*, Am Oved (Tel Aviv, 1988). Also see Anita Shapira, *Berl Katznelson: A Biography*, Am Oved (Tel Aviv, 1980).

On the notion of organization and the Histadrut, see Yonathan Shapiro, *The Organization of Power*, Am Oved (Tel Aviv, 1975), and *Trouble in Utopia: The Overburdened Polity of Israel*, edited by Dan Horowitz and Moshe Lissak, Am Oved (Tel Aviv, 1990).

David Horowitz, *My Yesterday*, Schocken Publishing House (Tel Aviv, 1970), provides insight into the development of the youth movement in general and Hashomer Hatzair in particular.

Chapter Four

On the origins of Arab nationalism, see Yehoshua Porath, *The Emergence of the Palestinian-Arab National Movement 1918-1929*, Hebrew University Press (Jerusalem, 1971).

On Jewish-Arab relations, see David Fromkin, *A Peace to End All Peace: The Fall of the Ottoman Empire and the Creation of the Modern Middle East*, Avon Books (New York, 1989).

There are many books on the war of 1948. However, most of them provide a one-sided version. For the Israeli version I used the official history known as *The History of the Wars of Independence*, published by the Ministry of Defense (Tel Aviv, 1962). Arab historiography is less fortunate. There has never been a coherent effort to record the Arab version in a similar way. Nevertheless, two good works can be mentioned: Aref, el-Aref, *The Disaster*, six volumes, Al Maktabel al Asriya (Beirut and Sidon, 1956-1960). For a more balanced and less "official" description I used *Both Sides of the Hill*, by Jon and David Kimche, Secker and Warburg (London, 1960), and Nadav Safran, *From War to War*, Keter Publishing House (Jerusalem, 1969).

On the special relations between the Zionists and the Hashemites, see Avi Shlaim, *Collusion Across the Jordan: King Abdullah, the Zionist Movement, and the Partition of Palestine*, Oxford University Press (Oxford, 1988) and Yossi Melman and Dan Raviv, *Behind the Uprising: Israelis, Jordanians and Palestinians*, Greenwood Press (Westport, Conn. 1989).

On the question of Palestinian refugees, see Benni Morris, *The Birth of the Palestinian Refugee Problem, 1947-1949*, Am Oved, (Tel Aviv, 1991), and Danny Rubinstein, *The Fig Tree Embrace*, Keter Publishing House (Jerusalem 1990), which cites the study of Bir Zeit University.

After 1948, the efforts to reach peace treaties are described in Itamar Rabinovich, *The Road Not Taken: Early Arab-Israeli Negotiations*, Maxwell-Macmillan-Keter Publishing (Jerusalem, 1991).

Most of the information about Levi Eshkol I gathered in an interview with his widow, Miriam Eshkol.

The story of the team of experts who explored the mood among Palestinians after the 1967 war appears in chapter 8 of Dan Raviv and Yossi Melman, *Every Spy a Prince: The Complete History of Israel's Intelligence Community*, Houghton Mifflin (Boston, 1990).

For more understanding of Yeshayaho Leibovitz's views, see his collection of essays *Judaism, Jewish People and the State of Israel*, Schocken Publishing House (Tel Aviv, 1975). His article on "The Territories," pp. 418-422, is particularly interesting.

Chapter Five

My capacity as a journalist in the period 1975-1983 provided me with many opportunities to witness most of the events described in this chapter.

Several meetings with Sara Rehavi, gave me sufficient information about her mother, Golda Meir.

The material for the question of Israel's nuclear capabilities is based on the relevant chapters (3 and 9) from *Every Spy A Prince* and also on my interview with Shimon Peres, a former prime minister and one of the architects of Israel's nuclear program.

The portrait of Menachem Begin is based upon my meetings and phone conversations with him and on his autobiography, *The Revolt*, Steimatzky (Bnei Brak, 1990).

On Jabotinsky, see Joseph Schechtman, *Rebel and Statesman: The Vladimir Jabotinsky Story*, Karni Publishers (Tel Aviv, 1959).

On Sharon, see Uzi Benziman, *An Israeli Caesar*, Adama Books (New York, 1985).

Chapter Six

This chapter is based mainly on my visits to the "holy" graves and meetings with some of the "saints."

Chapter Seven

The Israeli daily *Yediot Aharonot* in its April 1991 issues had several news items covering the story of Alexander Basov.

A History of the Jews has a vivid description on pp. 267-274 of the story of Shabtai Zvi.

On the question of religion, God, and the Holocaust, see Eliezer Schweid, *Wrestling until Daybreak*, Hakibbutz Hameuchad (Tel Aviv, 1990), pp. 21, 170-173.

Trouble in Utopia: The Overburdened Policy of Israel has a good analysis of the status and role played by religion and the religious parties in Israeli society. *1949: The First Israelis*, substantiates these topics with some fine examples.

Aharon Amir, a poet and writer who was a member of the Canaanites helped me to understand the history of the movement. *Jonathan Ratosh: Letters*, Hadar Publishing House (Tel Aviv, 1986) provided further material on the subject.

The material on the Block of Faithful is based on my own journalistic coverage, as well as Hagai Segal, *Dear Brothers*, Keter Publishing (Jerusalem, 1987) and interviews with the writer Haim Be'er.

Chapter Eight

I learned about the case of George Segal from the Israeli artist Danny Karavan.

On the historical origins of the notion of remembrance, see George Mosse's excellent essay "The Cult of the Fallen Soldier National Cemeteries and National Revival," in *Zmanin*, vol. 6 (Tel Aviv University, 1981).

On the importance of Masada in the Jewish and Israeli history, see Avirama Golan's article in *Ha'aretz*, May 7, 1992.

On Dayan, see *Moshe Dayan: Story of My Life*, Edanim Publishers (Tel Aviv, 1976).

Tom Segev sponsored George Mosse's visit to Israel's war memorials. His findings were published in *Ha'aretz*, April 24, 1990.

Chapter Nine

I have had seven personal interviews and participated in a dozen meetings of social and political nature with Yitzhak Shamir in 1984-1992.

On the Stern gang, see Joseph Heller, *Lehi: Ideology and Politics, 1940-1949*, Keter Publishing House (Jerusalem 1989).

On Sharon's role in Lebanon, see Shimon Shiffer, *Snow Ball: The Story Behind the Lebanon War*, Yediot Aharonot (Tel Aviv, 1984).

The Israeli daily *Davar* on September 7, 1989, devoted a special supplement to the question of how close Israel is to civil war.

Chapter Ten

During the research for this book and for my daily journalistic work, I conducted several interviews with Adb a-Salam Manasra at this Nazareth home and in Tel Aviv.

The nostalgic views of Palestine are found in Valid Khalidi, *Before Exile*, Center for Palestinian Studies and Bir Zeit University, 1991, and in Binyamin Zeev Kedar, *A Glance and One More Glance*, Ministry of Defense (Tel Aviv, 1991).

One of the best and most moving descriptions of the Palestinian tragedy in 1948 can be found in the writings of Emil Habibi, a former Communist member of the Knesset.

The basic data about Israeli Arabs: Population: 800,000; 77% Muslims, 13% Christians, 10% Druzes. 88% live in urban centers. Unemployment in 1992: 17% among Arabs, 12% among Jews. Education: 8.6 years for an average Arab, 11.5 for a Jew. Students: 5.2% in the Arab sector, 16.4 for Jews. Number of persons per family: 6 Arabs, 3.4 Jews. Life expectancy: Male: Arabs 71.5 years, Jews: 73.5 years. Female: Arabs 74.2 years, Jews: 77.1 years.

Majid al Haj, *Social Change and Family Process: Arab Communities in Shefar-Am*, Westview Press, 1987, deals with questions of modernism among Israeli Arabs.

The story of Rifat Turk is based on my own conversations with him and many newspapers articles, television, and radio interviews.

The notion of "Copying the Master in Arab Protest" was presented by Dr. Sam Lehman-Wilzig from Bar-Ilan University during a conference on "The Arab Minority in Israel: Dilemmas of Political Orientation and Social Change" in June 1991.

The case of Khaled Nimer Sawad was reported in *Yediot Aharonot*, December 28, 1992.

Politika, Israel's political magazine, vol. 21, had an interview with Sheik Nimer Darwish.

Nadin Ruhana, an Israeli-Arab sociologist at Boston College, claims that "people known as Israeli-Arabs are, according to their definitions, first of all Palestinians." He represents the opposing view of scholars such as Sami Samocha, who argues that Israeli-Arabs see themselves, above all, as citizens of the state of Israel.

Chapter Eleven

The Purim shooting was reported by several Israeli newspapers on March 17, 1992.

According to the *New York Times* (December 20, 1992) nearly forty-five thousand Palestinian-Christians left Bethlehem in the years 1987-1991. George Kerry, the Archbishop of Canterbury, was cited as a resource for the article.

On the rise of fundamentalism and Hamas, see Dan Sachs's article published in *Politika*, March 1992.

On the notion of "laundering words," see Amos Elon, *A Certain Panic*, pp. 264-265, Am Oved (Tel Aviv, 1988).

The case of Safia Saliman Jarjon was investigated by "Betslem," an Israeli-Palestinian organization for human rights.

Chapter Twelve

I am most grateful to Sima Kadman of the Israeli daily *Ma'ariv* for her permission to quote from her excellent articles on the Rappoport family, published during 1987.

Bruno Bettleheim, *Children of the Dream*, Avon Books (New York, 1969) is still considered one of the best studies of the kibbutz education.

For the comparisons between the kibbutz movement and American communes, see Yaacov Oved, *Two Hundred Years of American Communes*, Yad Tabenkin (Tel Aviv, 1986), pp. 120-130.

Chapter Thirteen

All data and statistics used in this chapter were taken from the official publications of Israel's Central Bureau of Statistics.

The study about Israel's trash and waste habits was conducted in 1991 by Tel Aviv's sanitation authorities.

Figures and information regarding family trends were taken from a research study conducted during 1991 by the Center for Family Study at the University of Haifa.

Zvi Sobol, *Migrants from the Promised Land*, Am Oved Publishers (Tel Aviv, 1986), deals with the emigration of Israelis to the United States.

Index

Abdul Hamid (Turkish sultan), 32
Abdullah, King, 59, 63, 77
Absorption, 17–19, 226–231
   see also Immigration
Absorption camps, 18–19, 230
Agrarian League, 189
Agriculture, 168, 203
Agudat Israel, 112–113, 119, 124, 125
Air force, 199
Alcohol, 140–141, 228, 231
Aliyah, 14, 43
   see also First Aliyah; Immigration;
      Second Aliyah
Aliyah Rishona see First Aliyah
Aloni, Shulamit, 126
Alon Moreh, 89
Alterman, Nathan, 133
Amana Church Society, 205–206
Americanization, 210–215
Anti-Semitism, 25, 27, 36
Appliances, 208, 210
Arabic (language), 166
Arab-Israelis see Israeli Arabs
Arabs, 31, 37, 53–56, 62–65, 71, 83
   see also Christian Arabs; Israeli
      Arabs; Palestinians; specific
      Arab countries
Ariel (West Bank), 196
Ashkenazis, 13, 19, 20–22, 97, 101,
      102, 104–105, 119, 229
Assad, Hafaz, 80
Ateret Kohanim Yeshiva, 122
Atrocities, 61

Automobiles see Cars
Autonomy, 92–93

Baker, James, 157, 219–220
Balfour Declaration, 54
Balfour, James, 232
Baruch, Baba, 100–101
Basov, Alexander, 107–108
Bedouins, 166, 171–172, 173
Be'er Haim, 123
Begin, Benjamin, 154
Begin, Menachem, 68, 75–76, 85,
      87–95, 106, 152–154, 158,
      229–230
Beit Alfa, 200–201
Ben Dov, Meir, 98
Ben Gurion Airport, 142
Ben Gurion, David, 17, 35, 41–42, 44,
      56–58, 66, 94
   aversion to Revisionist movement,
      86–88
   and nuclear weapons, 80–82
   reaction to Holocaust, 14–16
   and religious right, 112–114
   and socialism, 47–48
   and War of Independence, 63–64
Ben Maimon, Moses, 127
Ben Porat, Yoel, 40
Berenson, Zvi, 113, 115
Bethlehem, 56, 190
Black market, 209
Borders, 113–114
Bribery, 17, 218

241

Britain *see* Great Britain
Buber, Martin, 49
Bureaucracy, 44–45
Bush, George, 156–157, 219–220

Camp David accords, 91–92
Canaanites, 116–118
Capitalism, 205
Carmel Market, 223
Cars, 208, 210
Carter, Jimmy, 91
Casualties, 131–132
Charlatans, 100–101
Child allowances, 171
Children, 202, 217
Christian Arabs, 176
Christianity, 99, 109
Christian Palestinians, 190
Circumcision, 108, 226
Civil war, 159
Class distinctions, 209–210
Coca-Cola Company, 212
Cocaine, 141
Collectivism, 45–46
Commando units, 57
Communist party, 165–168, 176
Conservative congregation, 128
Constitution, 113–114
Construction industry, 208–210
Consumerism, 207–215
Corruption, 47, 126, 218
Credit cards, 213
Crime, 167, 228
Culture, 145–146, 212

Darwish, Abdallah Nimer, 175
Davar (newspaper), 47
David (Biblical king), 23
Dayan, Moshe, 68, 71, 76, 79–80,
    82–84, 89–90, 138–139, 142–143
Declaration of Independence (Israel),
    16, 58, 113–114, 115
Defense, culture of, 131–147
    see also Military service
Defense, Ministry of, 146
Degania (kibbutz), 198
Deir Yassin massacre, 61–62
Demagoguery, 158
Der Judenstat (Herzl), 27–28
Deterrence, 9
Diaspora, 16

Dimona (atomic site), 80
Discrimination, 166, 170–172
    see also Prejudice; Racism;
        Segregation
Divorce, 214, 228
Dreyfus, Alfred, 27
Drug abuse, 141, 167
Druze, 166, 173

East Jerusalem, 68, 69–70
Eban, Abba, 92
Ecology, 48
Education, 104, 112, 124, 132, 136,
    145, 167, 176, 202
Egypt, 40, 62, 65, 67, 68, 78, 81, 83
Emigration, 215–216
England *see* Great Britain
Entertainment, 146
Environment, 48
Eretz Israel *see* Palestine
Eshkol, Levi, 66–68, 71–72, 76, 139
Ethiopia, 230
Ethiopian Jews *see* Falashas
Etzel *see* Irgun
European Jews *see* Ashkenazis
Expulsion, 60, 161–162
    see also Transfer
Extended family, 169–170
Extremism, political, 149–162

Falashas, 17, 126, 229–231
Family revenge, 170
Fanaticism, 126
Farmers, 40
Fascism, 86
Feminism, 170
First Aliyah, 36–39
Food fads, 213
Foreign aid, 33
France, 27, 81, 82, 211
French Philanthropic Alliance, 38
Fundamentalism, 126, 175–176

Gan Hakovshim (Conquerors Park),
    223
"Gates of Aliyah, The," 18
Gaza Strip, 43, 62, 68, 69, 71, 92, 95,
    180
General Security Service (GSS) *see*
    Shabak
Germany, 4

Ghettos, 25
Giladi, Eliahu, 151
Ginzberg, Asher *see* Ha'am, Ahad
Golan Heights, 43, 68, 71, 80, 83
Goldberg, Leah, 20
Gorbachev, Mikhail, 225
Grave worship, 98–99
Great Britain, 15, 33, 55–56, 81, 151, 211
Gruen, David *see* Ben Gurion, David
Gulf War, 1–9, 156
Gurevitz, Adolph, 117
Gush Emunim, 120–122, 126

Ha'am, Ahad, 39–40
Hadash, Shmeul, 197
Haifa, 1
Halacha, 114, 119
Halperin, Uriel *see* Ratosh, Jonathan
Halutsim, 37, 197–198
Hamas movement, 189–191
Hamula, 169–170
Hashomir Hatzair, 49–52, 198–199
Hassan II, 17
Hatzera, Abu *see* Baruch, Baba
Hebrew (language), 25, 30–31, 166
Hebron, 71–72
Heroin, 141
Herut, 88
Herzl, Theodor, 26–34, 53
Histadrut (labor organization), 45–48, 76
Hitler, Adolf, 151
Hit squads, 152
Holocaust, 4, 14–16, 57, 82, 88
Homelessness, 217
Horowitz, Dan, 50
Horowitz, David, 50, 105
Hovevey Tsion, 36
Hussein, King, 79
Hussein, Saddam, 3

Identity registration, 115–116, 119
Ilia Capitolina, 24
Illiteracy, 100
Immigration, 14–22, 36–39, 43, 102, 223–231
Industry, 168, 203, 204–205
Informers, 181, 184, 188–189
Insurance, 218
Intelligence service *see* Mossad

Intifada, 188–196, 228
Investment, 227
Iraq, 2–9, 17
Irgun, 87–88, 150–151
Islam, 99, 174–178
Isolation, 25
Israel, 6, 10, 31–32
    Arab minority in, 65, 115, 119, 163–178
    bureaucracy in, 44–45
    concept of security, 9
    culture of defense, 131–147
    Islamic movement in, 175–178
    legal system, 114–116, 211
    politicization of society, 46
    religious-secular relations, 107–130
    rise of political extremism, 149–162
    see also specific political parties; Zionism
Israeli Arabs, 65, 115, 119, 163–178
Israel Philharmonic Orchestra, 145–146

Jabotinsky, Vladimir-Zeev, 85–87
Jarjon, Safia Saliman, 194
JDL *see* Jewish Defense League
Jebusites, 23
Jericho, 70
Jerusalem, 23, 56, 70, 71, 128, 214
    see also East Jerusalem
Jewish Defense League (JDL), 159–160
The Jewish State: An Attempt at a Modern Solution of the Jewish Question see Der Judenstat (Herzl)
Jordan, 59, 62, 65, 67, 68, 87
Jordan River, 48
Judaism, 24–25, 98–99, 106, 107–130
    see also Israel; Zionism; specific sects

Kabbalah, 98
Kach movement, 160–161
Kahane, Meir, 159–161
Kalkiliya, 70
Khader, Majid, 173
Kibbutzim, 112, 125–126, 197–206
Kibiyah (Jordan), 94
Kickbacks, 218
Kinship, 169–170
Kirya, 145, 146

Kissinger, Henry, 40, 83, 121
Kook, Yehuda Zvi, 120
Koran, 176
Kurds, 3

Labor
  Israeli, 45–48, 76
  Palestinian, 182–183, 209
  see also Unemployment
Labor (political party), 46, 48, 52, 54,
  56, 66, 73, 75–76, 84–85, 88, 95,
  105, 108, 123, 156, 158, 199, 210,
  231, 233
Lahat, Shlomo, 5
Lamdan, Ya'acov, 134
Land, 43
Landlords, 172
Language manipulation, 193–194
Law of Return, 16, 115, 119, 170, 226
League of Nations, 33
Lebanon, 65, 144, 153
Legal system, 114–116, 211
Legislation, religious, 126
Lehi, 150–151
Leibovitz, Yeshayahu, 72–73
Leisure time, 213
Levies, 208
Levy, David, 156
Liaison Bureau, 224
Life expectancy, 167
Likud, 1, 54, 75–76, 84, 88–89, 93,
  95, 97, 105–106, 108, 121, 122,
  123, 149, 154–156, 210, 225, 230,
  231, 233
Loan guarantees, 220, 227
Lovers of Zion see Hovevey Tsion
Luxury articles, 208

Ma'abara, 19
Madrid peace conference, 233
Maimonides see Ben Maimon, Moses
Malnutrition, 217
Management, 205
Manasra, Abd a-Salam, 163–166, 168,
  174
Mandate enclave, 56
Marriage, 119, 214
Marxism, 52
Marxist Zionism, 50
Masada, 133–134, 143

Massacres, 61–62
Mea Shearim, 111
Media, 139–140
Medical insurance, 218
Mehta, Zubin, 146
Meir, Golda, 76–79, 82–84
Menuhin, Yehudi, 40
Meridor, Dan, 154
Messianism, 42, 109–110
Middle class, 209–210
Military service, 113, 123, 136–137,
  166, 173–174
Mizrahi, 111–112, 119
Modernization, 168, 169
Moledot movement, 161
Morocco, 17
Mortgages, 171
Mossad, 17, 89, 137, 147, 152, 224
Mosse, George, 133, 143–145
Music, 51–52
Mussolini, Benito, 151
Mysticism, 98–101

Namir, Ora, 127
Nationalism, 36, 48, 54, 233
National Military Organization see
  Irgun
Nazareth, 56, 164
Nechamkin, Arik, 61
Neot Mordechai, 204
Netanyahu, Benjamin, 154
Netivot, 100
Neturei Karta, 111
Neue Freie Presse (newspaper), 27
New York City, 30
Nigeria, 32–33
1948 war see War of Independence
Nuclear weapons, 80–82

Occupied territories, 73–74, 93,
  180–196, 208
Olmert, Dan, 154
"Operation Moses," 230
"Operation Solomon," 230
Oriental Jews, 19
  see also Sephardis
Orthodox Jews, 122–124, 127–128,
  171, 175, 231
Oved, Yaacov, 205
Oz, Amos, 105

Palestine, 16, 37, 89
Palestine Liberation Organization
(PLO), 55, 92, 153, 181–182, 190
Palestinians, 59–66, 70–71, 92–93,
164, 180–196, 228, 233
Partition, 56–57
Paternalism, 193
Patriotism, 135
Patriot missiles, 7–8
Patronage, political, 46, 155
"Peace for Galilee," 144, 153
Peel, Robert, 56
Peretz, Yitzhak, 123–126
Persian Gulf War *see* Gulf War
Philistines, 24
PLO *see* Palestine Liberation
Organization
Pogroms, 26
Political patronage, 46, 155
Pollution, 48
Poverty, 216–217
Prejudice, 102–105, 168
Prisons, 29
Propaganda, 60
Prostitution, 29, 228
Proteksia, 46
Psychological warfare, 61
Purim, 179

Rabin, Yitzhak, 1, 84–85
Racism, 102–105, 160–162, 196, 231
Radio, 140
Ramat Aviv, 5, 64
Rappoport, Gabriel, 200–201
Ratosh, Jonathan, 117–118
Reagan, Ronald, 219
Reform congregation, 128
Refrigerators, 207–208
Refugee camps, 188
Refugees, 59–60, 63–64, 70
Religion *see* Christianity; Islam;
Judaism
Religious-secular relations, 107–130
Remembrance Day, 133
Renaissance (political party), 93
Renaming, 41–42
Restraint, policy of, 9
Return *see* Law of Return
Revisionist movement, 86–88
Rioting, 54

Roman Empire, 24, 157
Royal Commission of Inquiry, 56
Russia, 26, 45
see also Soviet Union
Russian Jews, 223–229

Sabra, 20
Sadat, Anwar, 78–80, 83, 89–92
Safed, 97–98
Sali, Baba, 100
Sawad, Khaled Nimer, 172
Schulte, Eduard, 14
Scud missiles, 1–9
Sea of Galilee, 63, 64
Second Aliyah, 41, 43, 197
Second Temple, 157–158
Segal, George, 131
Segregation, 115, 172
Sephardis, 13, 17, 20–22, 78, 97–106,
119, 123, 124, 155, 228–229
Service sector, 203
Settlements, 71–72, 89, 93, 95, 150,
157, 219–220
see also specific locations
Sex education, 51
Shabak, 88, 181, 183–184, 188–189
Shabat, 112–113
Shaked, Gershon, 6
Shamir, Yitzhak, 7, 86, 149–152, 154,
156–158, 233
Shareholding companies, 205
Sharon, Ariel, 93–95, 154, 157
Shas (political party), 123–127, 175
Shaul Hamelekh Boulevard, 145–147
Sheikh Munes, 64
Shitrit, Meir, 155
Shomrim *see* Hashomir Hatzair
Shopping malls, 213
Shtetls, 25
Sinai Campaign, 81, 138
Sinai Desert, 81
Sinai peninsula, 67, 68, 78, 81, 83, 91
Sivan, Emanuel, 126, 130
Six-Day War, 67–69
Socialism, 35–36, 42, 44, 45, 48–52,
198
Soldiers, 40
Solomon (Biblical king), 24
Soviet Union, 67, 224–225
see also Russia

Special units, 199
Spengler, Oswald, 24
Spiegel family, 144–145
Sport clubs, 46
Sports, 213
Stern, Avraham, 150–151
Stern Gang see Lehi
Subaru, 207, 210–211
Sudan, 230
Suez Canal, 68, 80, 81
Suez Crisis see Sinai Campaign
Suicide, 137, 231
Swindlers, 100–101
Syria, 40, 63, 65, 67, 68, 83

Taxes, 208
Tel Aviv, 1, 4–5, 8, 57, 135–136,
    145–146, 214–215
Tel-Aviv (Herzl), 29
Tel Aviv Museum, 145
Television, 124, 139–140, 212–213, 214
Temple Mount, 121–122
Terrorism, 87, 121–122, 182, 192
There Is No Other Place (Shaked), 6
Third Temple, 121–122
Tolstoy, Lev, 198
Torture, 184
Tourism, 134
Toynbee, Arnold, 24
Trade unions, 45
    see also Histadrut
Transfer, 161–162
Transit camps, 230–231
Transjordan, 87
    see also Jordan
Travel, 141–142
Trumpeldor, Yosef, 135, 143
Tsadik, 98
Turk, Rifat, 168–169

Unemployment, 166–167, 187, 227,
    230
Unions see Histadrut; Trade unions
United Nations, 33, 44, 57
United States, 7, 15, 30, 83, 150–151,
    156–157, 215–217, 219–220

Universities, 167
Urbanization, 169

Wages, 204–205
Wailing Wall, 69
War memorials, 143–145
War of Independence, 58–59, 163–164
Weizmann, Ezer, 158
West Bank (Jordan River), 43, 62, 68,
    69, 71, 89, 92, 93, 95, 180, 220
Women, 170, 176
World War II, 14–15, 57

Yad Vashem, 134
Yafo, 54
Yarkoni, Amos see Khader, Majid
Yarkon River, 48
Yediot Aharonot (newspaper), 150
Yemen, 17
Yemenis, 104
Yerida, 14
Yiddish, 25, 30
"Yom Kippur Bicycle Syndrome, The,"
    129
Yom Kippur War, 40, 79–80, 82–83
Young Watchman see Hashomir
    Hatzair
Youth movements, 48–52, 141,
    198–199
Yuppies, 215

Zaim, Colonel, 63
Zealots, 157
Zeevi, Rehavem, 161
Zion, 23–24
Zionism, 4–10, 20, 23–34, 39–40,
    42–44, 74, 86, 191, 232
    and immigration, 15–17
    Marxist, 50
    Orthodox views of, 109–112, 118
    and youth movements, 49
Zionist Federation, 28
Zipker family, 144–143
Zvi, Shabtai, 109–110
Zweig, Stefan, 26

Histadrut

Zion - city of Jerusalem

Sephardis - Spaniard Jew

~~Sephred~~

oleh: new immigrant

Falashas - black Jew from Ethiopia

Mossad - Secret Services

ashkenaz - Jewish name for Germa

Sabra - nickname for native Israeli

~~Pogram~~

Pogrom - antisemitic riots
       to destroy
From the ashes of the pogroms arose
the political movement of Zionia

Gush Emunim: Hard core force
   religious militant settlers of Palasti

Halacha - Jewish legal codex - code u
    for identifying those con
     verted by an Orthodox Rabb